Starting with Foucault

An Introduction to Genealogy

C. G. Prado

Westview Press

Boulder • San Francisco • Oxford

All rights reserved. No part of this publication may be reproduced or transmitted in any form or by any means, electronic or mechanical, including photocopy, recording, or any information storage and retrieval system, without permission in writing from the publisher.

Copyright © 1995 by Westview Press, Inc.

Published in 1995 in the United States of America by Westview Press, Inc., 5500 Central Avenue, Boulder, Colorado 80301-2877, and in the United Kingdom by Westview Press, 12 Hid's Copse Road, Cumnor Hill, Oxford OX2 9JJ

Library of Congress Cataloging-in-Publication Data
Prado, C. G.
  Starting with Foucault : an introduction to genealogy / C.G. Prado
    p.   cm.
  Includes bibliographical references and index.
  ISBN 0-8133-1790-8. — ISBN 0-8133-1791-6 (pbk.)
  1. Foucault, Michel. 2. Genealogy (Philosophy) I. Title.
B2430.F724P73   1995
194—dc20   95-2425
                                                              CIP ·

Printed and bound in the United States of America

The paper used in this publication meets the requirements
of the American National Standard for Permanence of Paper
for Printed Library Materials Z39.48-1984.

10   9   8   7   6   5   4   3   2   1

175478

BELMONT UNIVERSITY LIBRARY

Starting with Foucault

B
2430
. F724
P73
1995

AAZ-0390

For Catherine

Contents

Acknowledgments

My thanks go to Spencer Carr for his patience and to Westview Press's readers for their help. My thanks also go to Scott Horst and Jon Taylor Howard and to three students who made the project worthwhile: Nathan Brown, Melissa Watson, and Jason Gorber.

C. G. Prado

1 The Challenge of Foucault

"At the time of his death ... Michel Foucault was perhaps the single most famous intellectual in the world" (Miller 1993:13). So opens James Miller's biography of Foucault. Alan Ryan is even more positive, asserting that when Foucault died "he was the most famous intellectual figure in the world" (Ryan 1993:12). David Macey's biography makes the more modest claim that when Foucault died "he was without doubt France's most prominent philosopher," but Macey adds that Foucault's "international reputation has almost eclipsed his reputation in France" (Macey 1993:xi). Miller goes on to say that across the academic spectrum "scholars were grappling with the implications of [Foucault's] empirical research and pondering the abstract questions [he] raised" (Miller 1993:13). Jonathan Arac goes further, saying that "Foucault's work ... changed the basis for the work of all scholars" (Arac 1991:vii).

This estimation of Foucault is shared by many North Americans in disciplines ranging from political science through sociology and literary criticism to film studies, and it is, if anything, even more enthusiastically held by students who consider Foucault a champion in the struggle against what they regard as a stultifying academic establishment. But there is another side, one hinted at by Macey's speaking of Foucault as a philosopher while Miller and Ryan call him an intellectual. Speaking of visits by Foucault, in the early 1980s, to the University of California at Berkeley and at Los Angeles and to the University of Vermont, Didier Eribon observes in his biography of Foucault that though by then Foucault "drew huge crowds," he was "completely ignored by most [North] American philosophers" (Eribon 1991:313). Foucault's earlier visits to Berkeley, beginning in 1975, were at the invitation of departments other than philosophy; the philosophers did not consider Foucault to be doing anything relevant to their interests and areas of expertise (Miller 1993). However, the indifference of the philosophers was not quite that; Foucault was not only ignored, he was also disparaged in a rather hostile manner. According to Richard Rorty, "a distinguished analytic philosopher" (who I believe on good authority was D. M. Armstrong), "urged that 'intellectual hygiene' requires one not to read ... Foucault" (Rorty 1982:224). Foucault was aware of this hostility, and he seemed to relish it, claiming he was "very proud" that some thought him dangerous for

1

being, in their view, "an irrationalist, a nihilist" (Martin et al. 1988:13; compare Allen 1993:181).

Foucault had a huge influence on the humanities and social sciences in one way or another, having raised questions about "the reach of power and the limits of knowledge, ... the origins of moral responsibility and the foundations of modern government, ... the character of historical inquiry and the nature of personal identity" (Miller 1993:13). But despite some of these questions being philosophical by nearly anyone's standards, Foucault does not figure in the bulk of the writing and teaching of professional North American analytic philosophers. When they acknowledge Foucault's work, it is more often alluded to than discussed; when read, it is in snippets and more from curiosity than real interest; if read more comprehensively and carefully, his work is more often criticized than utilized. Whether for hygienic reasons or not, philosophers in the "analytic" tradition, that is, philosophers owing more to Gottlob Frege and G. E. Moore than to Maurice Merleau-Ponty and Ferdinand de Saussure, pointedly ignored Foucault when he began to achieve global notice, and most continue to ignore his work. Although some of their number have taken a belated interest in that work, if only because of its current prominence and its having defied predictions of modish transiency, the majority remain indifferent to it. When Foucault's work is considered by analytic philosophers, treatment of it often runs more to invective than to sympathetic investigation or exposition. A paper typifying this treatment describes Foucault as not only wrong about nearly everything he did say, but as ultimately having "nothing to say" with respect to "philosophical theories of truth and knowledge" (Nola 1994:3).

Foucault remains intellectually distant to most analytic philosophers, not only because he is outside their tradition but because they tend to believe his writings belong to a tradition the standards and methods of which fall short of their own. Foucault thought and wrote in the so-called "Continental" tradition, a tradition perceived by analytic philosophers as vaguely more literary than rigorous and technical. Speaking of Foucault's work, Eribon remarks that North American philosophers "saw no need of this 'literature,' which they ranked in the ... French tradition of [Henri] Bergson and [Jean-Paul] Sartre" (Eribon 1991:313; compare Rorty 1982:223–27; see also Ricoeur 1992:16–17). Perception and characterization by philosophers of Foucault as too literary and unrigorous ensures that many North Americans who are interested in learning about him but are trained in or influenced by analytic philosophy approach Foucault as someone outside the pale of technical (read "tough-minded") philosophy—and so as someone whose work neither can contribute importantly to their debates nor merits the close study they give to more familiar writings. Alternatively, some North Americans may approach Foucault as an iconoclastic champion opposed to technical (read "sterile") philosophy, claiming to find in his work all sorts of ideas supportive of their favorite rival to the philosophical or other disciplinary establishment. Perception and characterization of Foucault's work by analytic philosophers, as too problematic in conception and development to be seriously pursued, elicits two opposed but equally unproductive responses to Foucault among those whom analytic philosophers directly or indirectly influence. Aspirants to orthodoxy ignorantly dismiss Foucault as too literary on the implicit or explicit say-so of the professionals; would-be radicals fervently but equally ignorantly embrace various more-or-less popularized versions of Foucault's views. In numerous seminars on Foucault, I have had to work as hard to disabuse his fans of basic misconceptions as to engage those who dismiss him.

Foucault's writings are not difficult in the way that Immanuel Kant's are, but his mode of expression and his style are unfamiliar enough to North American readers to mislead and even to irritate them, thereby making what is not inherently difficult nonetheless inaccessible (Bernauer, J. 1993:2–3). But aside from style, the focused nature or topical specificity of Foucault's work, its cardinal marginality, a measure of intellectual craftiness, and some important shifts in his thinking conspire to invite misinterpretation. There is no single work that adequately represents the complex, variegated, and evolutionary totality of his philosophical vision. In fact, it is problematic whether there is a single vision. Foucault resists holistic interpretation (Gutting 1994:3–4). In spite of his own avowals about the unity of his project, his books "hardly ever refer back to his previous works" (Gutting 1994:3). This is why those who read only spottily in his work, basing their impressions on one or two books or articles, invariably form distorted and often astonishingly different ideas of his views (compare O'Hara 1986). This is common when some-one reads *The History of Sexuality* because of its popularity and then, because impressed or baffled, reads the quite differently conceived *The Order of Things* or *Madness and Civilization* seeking more of the same or clarification. Unfortunately, even systematic reading of several works does not ensure understanding of Foucault by those who approach his work from outside his intellectual tradition. This is in part because of differences in idiom and tradition, in part because of internal development in his thought, and in part because Foucault always addresses circumscribed issues and always in opposition to established philosophical and historical scholarship.

It is a basic premise of this book that a special strategy is necessary in approaching Foucault's work. Not only is it insufficient to read only one or two books or articles to get the gist of his thought, but unlike with most philosophers, one should not begin at the beginning in reading Foucault. To start with *Madness and Civilization* is to risk an erroneous initial impression that Foucault's work is not philosophical enough; to start with the much discussed and in some ways most imposing "archaeological" works, *The Birth of the Clinic, The Order of Things,* and *The Archaeology of Knowledge,* is to risk misconstruing his middle and last books as less philosophical than they actually are because in spite of their originality, these earlier works are methodologically and even thematically closer to traditional philosophy than are those that follow them. Of greatest importance in Foucault are his challenges to traditional philosophical methods and assumptions and to established conceptions of truth and knowledge. Those challenges are raised most clearly and definitively in his "genealogical" works, so it is counterproductive to approach his work in a manner that in any way erodes the philosophical force of those works.

To get a good understanding of Foucault, one must begin in the middle, with the major genealogical works: *Discipline and Punish* and *The History of Sexuality, Volume I.* That is where we find the most pointed indictments of traditionally conceived truth, knowledge, and rationality. That is where we find the sharpest articulations of ideas such as that truth and knowledge are products of power and that the rationality traditional philosophy takes as legitimizing its activities is itself an historical product. Once the nature and scope of these challenging ideas is appreciated, it is possible to go back to *Madness and Civilization* or *The Order of Things,* and forward to *The Use of Pleasure* or *The Care of the Self,* and productively understand the progression of Foucault's thought. Alternatively, the major genealogical works suffice to convey what is most philosophically significant in Foucault. As Foucault contends, what is of greatest moment "is not error, illusion, alienated consciousness, or ideology; it is truth itself" (Foucault 1980b:133; compare Allen 1993:149–76).

The aim of this book is to provide those who have not read or have only dipped into Foucault's writings with an accessible introduction to his genealogy. Once a reader grasps Foucault's radical ideas concerning truth, knowledge, and rationality and understands how truth, knowledge, and rationality may be products of power-relations, he or she will have what is most important in Foucault and be able to approach the earlier and last writings in the most rewarding way. The book also has a therapeutic aim. Whether or not because of their philosophical significance, though one would hope because of it, *Discipline and Punish* and *The History of Sexuality* are probably Foucault's most widely read books. Unfortunately, these are probably also the most often misinterpreted and misused of his works. Because it is in these books that we find Foucault's most revolutionary insights, and so what is most intellectually exciting in his work, the ideas presented are prone to distortion and hasty appropriation. My intent, then, is to provide a clear and accessible account of what Foucault is doing in *Discipline and Punish* and *The History of Sexuality* in order both to provide an introduction to his genealogy and to dispel some misconceptions and misinterpretations.

It merits noting that many consider *The Order of Things* Foucault's most important work. Philosophers in particular see *The Order of Things*, with its emphasis on linguistic and epistemological topics, as the most properly "philosophical" and therefore significant of Foucault's books. As suggested, that perception is largely correct. But it is precisely because it is correct that one should focus elsewhere to discern the deeper import of the work of this most anti-philosophical philosopher. Giles Deleuze observes that Foucault offers "counterphilosophy" and that his work is most productively read as a counterpoint to established philosophical assumptions and practices, especially analytic ones (Deleuze 1984:149). There is less to be gained by concentrating on those of Foucault's books that better meet one's disciplinary expectations and standards than on those that seem to flout good philosophical sense. As will be considered later, Foucault most values mind-stretching alternity in conception and perception. To achieve alternity of thought, particularly in his genealogical period, he concentrates on the unfamiliar, the enigmatic, the shunned, the obscure, the neglected, the suppressed. In the spirit of his work, then, if the philosophical tradition values *The Order of Things* over *Discipline and Punish* and *The History of Sexuality,* it is the latter that most deserve our attention.

Making a Start

To better situate Foucault with respect to a North American reader's background and likely expectations, I need to clarify the reasons for the largely negative view that analytic philosophers have of his work. Foucault not only worked in the "Continental" or European philosophical tradition, he was much influenced by Friedrich Nietzsche and especially Martin Heidegger: "I am simply a Nietzschean"; "Heidegger has always been for me the essential philosopher" (Foucault 1989:327, 326). Miller quotes Foucault as saying that his "entire philosophical development was determined by [the] reading of Heidegger" (Miller 1993:46). And Heidegger's influence on Foucault was more than narrowly philosophical, for he was deeply affected by Heidegger's interest in pressing beyond the limits of conventional intellectual inquiry. But as Miller notes, someone prepared to "descend into what Heidegger called the 'unthought'" must be prepared to probe "beyond the limits of reason," and so to think "without statute or rule, structure or order" (Miller 1993:49–50). To Heidegger, and to Foucault, this is an intellectual challenge, but to analytic philosophers it is rejection of reasoned inquiry in favor of undisciplined speculation.

Whereas Nietzsche has often served as a model of intellectual excess for many analytic philosophers, they have perceived Heidegger as the paradigm of pretentious obscurity from the time of his initial prominence and consequently ignored and disparaged him even more than they did Nietzsche (Ryle 1929; Carnap 1931). Three histories of philosophy, which were important in the training of many of the analytic philosophers who are now senior university professors and have educated several academic generations, illustrate the antipathy to Nietzsche and Heidegger and, by extension, to those who follow either or both. Though all three histories give Nietzsche some coverage, Bertrand Russell's much-read history of philosophy offers a typical assessment: "Nietzsche ... was a literary rather than academic philosopher. He invented no new technical theories in ontology or epistemology" (Russell 1945:760). This assessment not only typifies the attitude toward Nietzsche, it also highlights what Russell and those he influenced thought most important in philosophy. As for Heidegger, he does not even warrant an entry in the index to Russell's history. W. T. Jones's much-used history also ignores Heidegger, leaving a yawning intellectual gap between the two twentieth-century European figures it does discuss, Edmund Husserl and Jean-Paul Sartre. W. I. Matson's popular history of philosophy, which runs to nearly five hundred pages in its revised edition, allots a mere sixteen lines of remarkably uninformative text to Heidegger (Russell 1945; Jones 1969; Matson 1987:468).

Of course European philosophy is not limited to Nietzsche and Heidegger and their followers. Some European philosophers, like Husserl, Merleau-Ponty, and especially Jürgen Habermas, have been widely read by analytic philosophers. There have also been efforts to link the work of leading analytic philosophers to that of equally prominent European philosophers, as in the case of connecting Donald Davidson's more recent views on language to the hermeneutics of Hans-Georg Gadamer (Ramberg 1989; see also Malpas 1992; compare Staten 1984). It is notable, though, that Habermas is as critical of Foucault as are his own North American admirers. In spite of some cross-pollination, then, it is not philosophers but political scientists, sociologists, literary critics, more specialized academics like film theorists and organizational behaviorists, and, most recently and surprisingly, professors of accounting, who read and use Foucault extensively in North America (Burrell 1988; Hooper and Pratt 1993).

There are more specific reasons, other than mere disparity of traditions or antipathy to influential predecessors, for the neglect of Foucault by analytic philosophers and also for the often overly enthusiastic acceptance of his work by their opponents. One reason is that Foucault is considered a founder-member of postmodernism, which analytic philosophers view with suspicion, if not disdain, and which their opponents usually see as the onset of the millennium. Branding him a postmodern, analytic philosophers too often and rather ignorantly lump Foucault with Jacques Derrida and characterize both as offering only a modish and sterile travesty of learned polemics and critical inquiry.

Derrida, who in the eyes of many analytic philosophers inherited the mantle of undisciplined reflection and arrogant impenetrability from Nietzsche and Heidegger, was simply written off a decade ago by John Searle, acting more or less as a spokesperson for analytic philosophers, as not being a serious philosopher (Searle 1983). That dismissal was reiterated in 1992 when Cambridge University awarded Derrida an honorary degree. Nineteen academics, including philosophers like Armstrong and W.V.O. Quine, wrote to the *Times* in an unsuccessful attempt to block the granting of the degree, contending that philosophers "working in leading departments throughout the world" judged that Derrida's work "does not meet accepted standards of clarity and rigor" (Rée 1992:61). The irony was that those objecting to Derrida's honorary degree "made themselves ... absurd because the authority to which they were appealing was none other than themselves" (Rée 1992:61). Foucault, though usually taken somewhat more seriously than Derrida, is nonetheless seen by analytic philosophers (and some in other disciplines) as like Derrida in embodying the intellectual, normative, and political fragmentation and bankruptcy that supposedly characterize the last decades of the twentieth century (Bell 1992).

A second specific reason for the dismissal of Foucault, supposedly on methodological grounds, is recognition that like many European philosophers of our time, such as Sartre and Habermas, Foucault's philosophizing is significantly motivated and shaped by political considerations, in particular the need to come to terms with the ideological failures that led to World War II and the recent disillusionment with Marxism (Miller 1993:17). In addition to these abstract political considerations, the developments that culminated in World War II ensured that Foucault grew to adulthood with "a particular sense of menace" that heightened his political awareness (Bernauer, J. 1993:7). But whereas political motivation and coloration in philosophical thought is perceived by most Europeans as legitimate, admirable, and even necessary, it is perceived by analytic philosophers as violating what they understand to be the sacrosanct objectivity of philosophy. Foucault's views are therefore seen not as informed by political considerations but as tainted by nonphilosophical motives and interests.

A third specific reason for the neglect of Foucault is the perception that he opted out of serious philosophy by adopting a wholesale relativism diametrically opposed to the Enlightenment values, presuppositions, methods, and goals that still constitute bedrock for analytic philosophical thought. The question of Foucault's relativism is labyrinthine in complexity, as we will see, but the important point here is that he is wrongly thought to have wholly relativized truth to socio-political contexts. This is a common misinterpretation that I hope to dispel and about which Foucault remarked, "Those who say that for me the truth doesn't exist are simple-minded" (Foucault 1989:295).

As indicated, there undeniably has been some interest in Foucault on the part of analytic philosophers or philosophers with analytic backgrounds (Dreyfus and Rabinow 1983; Bernauer, S. 1987; Flynn 1989; Schurmann 1989; Seigel 1990; Shumway 1992; May 1993; Gutting 1994). But the perception of Foucault's work as unrigorous, as philosophically compromised by political considerations, and as vitiated by relativism means that even those analytic philosophers who might be most disposed to pursue Foucault's work do not do so. A case in point is Charles Taylor, who is analytically trained but comfortable with and even proselytic about Foucault's intellectual tradition, yet who portrays Foucault's work as bad philosophy and discusses it primarily as a focus for criticisms of postmodernist ideas. Taylor casts Foucault as a disciple of Nietzsche's, having inherited most of Nietzsche's confusions and his reliance on rhetoric, and charges that Foucault's conception of power is incoherent because it lacks contrast (Taylor 1984, 1987; compare Allen 1991; Bové 1988). This view of Foucault in particular and postmodernists in general as doing bad philosophy is perhaps best exemplified in Searle's reading of Derrida, about which Rorty comments: The "weakness of Searle's treatment of Derrida is that he thinks of him as doing amateurish philosophy of language rather than as asking metaphilosophical questions about the value of such philosophy" (Rorty 1991b:94n).

Even more striking than Taylor is the case of Rorty himself. In spite of being perhaps the North American philosopher having the most in common with Foucault and the one who has done most to focus North American philosophical attention on contemporary European thought, Rorty has not made as much use of Foucault as one might expect and invokes his name surprisingly little. Unlike Taylor, Rorty does not think Foucault philosophizes badly, but he is distrustful of what he feels are traditional metaphysical and epistemological implications in Foucault's work. Rorty claims that John Dewey awaits at the end of the road Foucault travels and that Deweyan pragmatism is capable of yielding "all that is politically useful in the Nietzsche-Heidegger-Derrida-Foucault tradition" (Rorty 1982:xviii; 1991c:3, 1991b). Rorty also seems to share the view of Foucault held by some North American philosophers: that Foucault offers too bleak a vision of political reality and possibility. Rorty claims that Foucault had a "dangerous" influence on the American political left, prompting "disengagement," and that his lack of a political program produced "profound resentment" (Borradori 1994:111).

Despite Rorty's benign neglect of Foucault, there are important similarities between them, and it will prove useful to note those similarities as we proceed. This is the case even if some readers are as unfamiliar with Rorty's work as with Foucault's, because Rorty's idiom is more immediately accessible to North American readers. Where there is congruence of ideas, use of Rorty's versions often facilitates understanding of Foucault's.

Among philosophers in the broadly analytic tradition, feminists have been the ones to most directly engage Foucault (Diamond and Quinby 1988; Bartky 1990; Hartsock 1990; Code 1991; Sawicki 1991; Ramazanoglu 1993). However, feminists have tended to concentrate on the political implications of Foucault's work or to relate his ideas on power and the body directly to their own projects. They have rightly focused on those parts of Foucault's work that most directly interest them or affect their own positions. This sort of response to and use of a philosopher outside one's own tradition is just what is expected in regard to the integration of a body of important but unfamiliar ideas into a given tradition. Yet even though feminists have shown openness to ideas developed outside their own tradition, feminist criticism and sympathetic development of Foucauldian ideas have not gained for his work anything near the recognition it deserves among North American philosophers.

For the most part, then, Foucault's work is regarded by analytic philosophers as largely external or even inimical to their philosophical projects. This is the case even with respect to his views on the most fundamental philosophical issues. For instance, Foucault said a lot about truth, but to cite him in a discussion of truth conducted by typical North American philosophers would most often be seen as facetious. I have observed a great deal of joking dismissal of Foucault. Such dismissal is not acknowledged as such, but one need only look at one or another feminist work on the negative roles of humor to appreciate how real it is (Mackie 1990). Foucault's views on truth should be considered relevant to most discussions of the topic, if only because his pluralistic view of truth challenges the traditional unitary conception and may get us past the impasses the latter generates. For example, a pluralistic understanding of truth may resolve our apparent inability to jettison the notion of truth as correspondence in spite of not being able to give it viable articulation. This is why an introduction to Foucault, aimed at a reader influenced by or trained in analytic philosophy, should not be only an attempt to win respect for a body of work that is acknowledged to be intellectually distant and likely to remain of merely peripheral interest. The point of this introduction is not only to familiarize the reader with a methodologically foreign body of work; the point is to make some of Foucault's most provocative ideas usefully accessible.

Foucault offers historicist views of truth, of knowledge, and of rationality; he thinks that the most important philosophical projects have to do with understanding how and why we hold some things true, how and why we deem some things knowledge, and how and why we consider some procedures rational and others not. These views look to many traditional analytic philosophers as if Foucault could only be doing sociology of knowledge or expounding relativism. But that perception presupposes just the methodological assumptions and particular conceptions of the nature of truth, knowledge, and rationality that Foucault challenges. If Foucault argues, against the tradition, that there is no Truth but various truths, he may have something more useful in mind than a simple relativism. If, as Todd May puts it, Foucault argues against the tradition that "[t]here is no Knowledge; there are knowledges" and that "[t]here is no Reason; there are rationalities," then Foucault may be contending more than that inquiry and its standards are contextual. If he insists that "it is meaningless to speak in the name of—or against—Reason, Truth, or Knowledge," he may be teaching us a valuable lesson about justification rather than denying its possibility (May 1993:2).

As to what Foucault does contend, analytically trained or influenced readers will expect exposition of theories and arguments in what follows. However, Foucault mainly offers not so much theories and supporting arguments as persuasive and sometimes compelling characterizations and "pictures." In this he can be compared to the later Ludwig Wittgenstein. Still, many readers will be impatient with claims about the value of views not consisting of theoretical claims and supporting arguments. But tolerance of the lack of familiar presentation is the price that must be paid to appreciate Foucault's radical thought. Moreover, that tolerance is rewarded when Foucault's views emerge in spite of the paucity of detailed arguments and the often indirect elucidation of what are theories only in the broad sense of being ways of looking at things.

Although Foucault does not proceed as some would expect (making theoretical claims and offering detailed arguments for or against them), that should not obscure ideas that are initially startling but ultimately equally productive and provocative: his Nietzschean misgivings about the absolute value of truth; his historicist view of knowledge; his distrust of the evident, of what manifests itself as obvious; his view of truth and knowledge as functions of how we make ourselves certain kinds of subjects to whom the world is then a certain way; his querying of how we came to regard ourselves as objects of disciplined knowledge; his insightful conception of disciplines as both fields of study and systems of control; and his "decentralization" of the subject or his vision of the self, and hence the knower, as emergent from social and discursive relations and practices. All are decidedly postmodern ideas in the sense of being opposed to conception of truth as of ultimate worth, to conception of some truths as evident to reasoned inquiry, to conception of truth as objective, to conception of knowledge as possession of truth, and to conception of the self as a unitary subject which is the condition of cognition. Thus, we cannot reasonably expect or demand that these ideas be packaged in the theories and arguments that are the staples of traditional philosophy.

Having said that, I should add that this introduction to Foucault's genealogy is not an ecumenical exercise in reconciling diverse traditions (compare Rorty 1982:225–26). Neither is this introduction a misguided attempt to present the "real" Foucault—an effort Foucault would have despised (Eribon 1991:xi). I have no intention of trying to offer either a new interpretation or a comprehensive outline of a body of work that ranges from the brilliant to the possibly incoherent (compare Gutting 1994:3–4). There are some excellent comprehensive treatments of Foucault's work (Dreyfus and Rabinow 1983; Bernauer, J. 1993). As indicated, my objective is to introduce the reader to what I judge to be the most central and productive of Foucault's ideas, ideas that are most fully developed in the middle part of his career. What I offer is an introduction that concentrates on Foucault's genealogical analytics, that is, his investigations concerned with how the development of discursive practices and interactive conventions produce truth and knowledge and so shape and define subjects and subjectivity. These are the Foucauldian ideas with the greatest epistemological import; these are also the ideas most perplexing to those trained in or influenced by analytic philosophy.

Foucault represents an extreme point of contrast to the basically Cartesian assumptions and methods that still dominate epistemology, especially with respect to the natures of truth and the subject (Prado 1992). In particular, Foucault does not offer only a constructivist alternative to the Cartesian subject as George Herbert Mead did, for example. Constructivists like Mead regard the subject as a product of cognition rather than a condition of cognition, but that is basically an ontological thesis, albeit a radical one, about the origin and nature of the subject. The most significant difference between constructivist views, like Mead's, and Foucault's conception of subjectivity is captured by Taylor, who observes that Mead "is still too close to a behaviourist view, and doesn't seem to take account of the constitutive role of language in the definition of self" (Taylor 1989:525, n12). Because of the constitutive role of discourse and the possibilities thus afforded, Foucault goes farther, maintaining that "the subject ... is obviously only one of the ... possibilities of organizing a consciousness of self" (Dreyfus and Rabinow 1983:175). He also asks whether "the subject is the only form of existence possible," whether there might not be "experiences in which the subject ... isn't given any more?" (Foucault 1991:49). It is to mark this more extreme and language-based version of constructivism that I describe Foucault's vision of the subject or self as "emergent."

But the radicalness of Foucault's ideas should not lead to counterproductive exaggeration of the difference between his thought and more familiar philosophy. I disagree with those who anguish over "the demise of the tradition" and construe Foucault's work as part of some alleged holistic displacement of modernism by postmodernism (Nielsen 1989; Nielsen and Hart 1990; compare Latour 1993). Foucault explicitly dismisses the idea that postmodernism constitutes some sort of wholesale intellectual reorientation: "There is no sense at all to the proposition that reason is a long narrative which is now finished, and that another narrative is underway" (Foucault 1988b:35; compare Bernstein 1992). Rorty admits similarities between his own views and Foucault's and even tolerates the label "postmodern" as applied to himself, but he is "not fond of the term" precisely because he also rejects the idea that it designates a new and systematically different way of thinking (Rorty 1991c:n18). Rorty thinks postmodernism, indeed any "post" position, is simply "the gradual encapsulation and forgetting of a certain philosophical tradition" (Rorty 1992:71). Rather than misguidedly exaggerating the differences between traditions or the magnitude and totality of presuppositional and methodological changes and innovations, we should try to make productive use of Foucault's ideas, some of which pose the most pointed challenges to traditional conceptions of truth and knowledge in the 350 years since *Meditations on First Philosophy* and the two and a half millennia since *Theaetetus*.

As acknowledged earlier, these challenging ideas are not as accessible as they might be because of idiomatic and background differences, but regretfully they are made even less accessible by Foucault's own interpretive efforts. Foucault was a highly regarded French intellectual, which means he was a public figure in a manner academics rarely are in North America. As a consequence, not only must his readers and interpreters contend with his substantial and diversely oriented primary writings, they must also deal with a profusion of interviews, many an-thologized, in which Foucault has too much to say about his own work (Foucault 1980b, 1988b, 1989). Foucault had a "revisionist" view of his own work and tended to retrospectively see more coherence and pro-gressive development in it than it exhibits—and this despite his some-times speaking of having changed his mind and of later works supersed-ing earlier ones: "To write a book is ... to abolish the preceding one" (Foucault 1989:303; compare Foucault 1991a:27; Gutting 1994:1–27). Foucault was also impatient with others' misunderstanding and misin-terpretation of his work and especially with what he deemed ignorant or ill-conceived criticism. So in addition to his revisionary statements, there are many corrective pronouncements in various secondary writ-ings—commentaries, forewords, afterwords, and annotations that were solicited or volunteered and published in anthologies on his work. There are similar contentions in transcribed lectures that have been published in various collections. A good deal of what Foucault says in these "clarifications" of his work clarifies only from his perspective of the moment, and a fair bit is ironic, provocative, and, on occasion, has all the earmarks of lack of due consideration.

The upshot is that, aside from the complexity of his primary writings and whatever problems they may raise, Foucault's secondary writings and interviews, taken together with his primary writings, support too many diverse interpretations. (For a unified and somewhat metaphysi-cal reading of Foucault, see Deleuze 1988; for a decidedly political read-ing, see Fink-Eitel 1992; for a more literary reading, see Mahon 1992; for an epistemologically and psychologically oriented reading, see May 1993; for a somewhat ethically oriented reading, see Bernauer, J. 1993; for a more historiographical reading, see Gutting 1994; see also O'Hara 1986 and Polan 1982.) It is possible to find passages at odds with some supposedly central contention and also to come across comments sug-gestive of alternative readings of substantial tracts. The breadth of inter-pretive possibility would be troublesome enough if inadvertent or only a consequence of continuous revision, but a great deal of it must be taken as quite deliberate. We will see that providing this sort of interpretive possibility is integral to Foucault's conception of philosophizing. Eribon quotes Georges Dumézil, "who knew [Foucault] better than almost any-one else," as saying that Foucault "wore masks, and he was always changing them." Eribon adds that "there are several Foucaults—a thou-sand Foucaults" (Eribon 1991:xi; compare Macey 1993; see also Foucault 1989:193–202).

There is some difference, though, between providing interpretive breadth and how Foucault often speaks of his work as of a piece. The in-tegration he sees in his work is problematic. Even a cursory reading of his claims to unity, found mostly in interviews and pieces like his "Two Lectures" and "The Subject and Power," makes it clear that the integration he speaks of has more to do with the topics that interest him than with what he has to say about those topics (Foucault 1989, 1976, 1983a). This is evident in the emphasis put on the nature and formation of the subject, the topic that does afford the greatest measure of continuity and consistency to his investigations but that he may nonetheless overestimate. Foucault insists that the goal of his work "during the last 20 years" was not to analyze the phenomenon of power but rather "to create a history of the different modes by which ... human beings are made subjects" (Foucault 1983a:208). He lists as one of the most basic questions he considers, how "the human subject took itself as the object of possible knowledge?" (Foucault 1988b:29).

The question illustrates how many of Foucault's most intriguing ideas are often articulated in uncharacteristically compact ways and serves as a cautionary case in point to those tempted by his style to read his work too perfunctorily. The question is: How did we come to take ourselves to be the sorts of things that can be studied and known and understood as subjects of broadly scientific or disciplinary investigation, as opposed to known and understood only as friends or adversaries, cooperators or competitors, teachers or students, lovers or enemies? The question is about how we objectified ourselves as the subject matter of various disciplines, and it is perhaps Foucault's most perceptive impulse to wonder about "the objectivizing of the subject" (Foucault 1983a:208).

To proceed, I devote Chapter 2 to situating genealogy, which is the focus of subsequent chapters, both in relation to my intended readers' philosophical framework and Foucault's own earlier work. With respect to the former, I try to say just enough to heighten the contrast with Foucault's most challenging ideas to avert misunderstandings; with respect to the latter, I try to say just enough about Foucault's mainly archaeological work to give the reader a working idea of its character. Chapter 3 is devoted to a single article, the importance of which some think "cannot be exaggerated" with respect to "understanding Foucault's objectives" (Bouchard 1977:139n). In chapters 4 and 5 I consider the two Foucauldian texts that embody the most thorough application of his genealogical analytics and that are, in my estimation, the most central to Foucault's thought (compare May 1993). These are *Discipline and Punish*, where Foucault first explicitly addresses the matter of power and its role in the formation of subjects, and *The History of Sexuality, Volume I: An Introduction*, where he considers how formation of subjects is effected in the area he deemed most central to the formation and development of identity (Miller 1993:15–16). In Chapter 6 I offer what I believe to be a novel way of sorting out Foucault's views on truth. In Chapter 7 I discuss how genealogy relates to archaeology and Foucauldian ethics and say a little about what will emerge as a major issue, namely, the question about why Foucault's philosophical claims are cogent or intellectually compelling.

2 The Domains of Analysis

Understanding Foucault requires heightened awareness of some important presuppositional and methodological differences between his thought and the more familiar philosophical methods and ideas that form the background to, if not always the content of, intellectual inquiry in North America. Deleuze is quite right in saying that what Foucault offers runs counter to established philosophical methods and objectives (Deleuze 1984:149). But the very thing that is countered may not always be obvious. One's own philosophical presuppositions are rarely self-evident, perhaps especially when they most should be, as in the process of trying to understand and assess novel and unfamiliar ideas. A necessary prelude to consideration of Foucault is a brief outline of what Foucault's genealogical views most sharply counter.

In the introduction I contrasted the "analytic" tradition with the "Continental" or European tradition and clearly implied that the bulk of North American philosophers are analytic philosophers. The people I have in mind share presuppositions, priorities, techniques, methodologies, interests, and goals that have defined philosophy in the United States, Great Britain, Australia, and Scandinavia for much of this century. The sort of philosophy these people do is analytic, not in the pejorative sense now used by some postmodern critics to describe all philosophizing that is not postmodern, but in the sense of being a generally dissective or taking-apart style of intellectual inquiry as opposed to a more synthesizing or putting-together sort of inquiry. This contrast is often drawn in histories of philosophy, as in comparing philosophers like Hume and Russell on the one hand and G. W. Leibniz and Henri Bergson on the other. The former are described as analytic because they try "to understand complexes by reducing them to their ... parts and to the relations in which these parts stand"; the latter are then described as "integrative" because they believe the things we try to understand "are parts of larger unities" and can be fully understood only when fitted into those unities (Matson 1987:403).

The analytic approach to intellectual inquiry began in earnest with Plato's *Theaetetus* and *Sophist* and Aristotle's *Prior Analytics,* was paradigmatically illustrated in René Descartes's *Discourse on Method* and *Meditations* and Hume's *Treatise on Human Nature,* and became the definitive methodology for Anglo-American philosophers after Russell and Moore. The Logical Positivists gave "analytic" a technical sense in redefining philosophy as concerned with the analysis of meaning and hence as prior to science's assessment of empirical claims. This technical sense still has a good deal of currency, but more important is how it is characteristic of mainstream analytic philosophy. Searle's ridicule of Derrida reveals this defining element in analytic philosophy's self-image as rigorous and objective in contrast to literary and politically colored philosophizing. This, not relativism, is the nub of the analytic philosopher's dismissal of Foucault in particular and postmodernism in general. Relativism is unpopular with analytic philosophers, but relativistic positions are assorted and are not all disdained in the way Foucault and postmodernism are disdained (Krausz 1989). Foucault and postmodernism are seen as somehow not serious, as Rorty sums up in his remark about Searle's assessment of Derrida as "doing amateurish philosophy of language" (Rorty 1991b:94n). The old contrast between dissective analysis and integrative speculation has in effect metamorphosed into one between "real" philosophy, conceived as rigorous and ahistorical because of the ultimacy of its subject matter, and a kind of philosophy *manqué* deemed to be only frivolous historicist reflection deeply embedded in its time and culture and characterized more by modishness than real significance.

The Hegelian idea that philosophy is its time held in thought, which is the wellhead of postmodern historicism, is turned on its head by analytic philosophers who see postmodern thought as our time imprinted on philosophy. What they most reject in Foucault and postmodernism is not so much relativism as historicism, for subordination of truth and knowledge to history is seen as the abandonment of governing standards for intellectual inquiry.

In order to delineate the undeniable differences between Foucault and analytic philosophers, then, one must understand the thoroughly and deeply historicist nature of his views, especially his conception of rationality itself as historical. Foucault maintains that "forms of rationality are created endlessly" and rejects as fundamentally misconceived the conception of any form of intellectual inquiry as having access to objective external correctness-criteria (Foucault 1988b:35). This is perhaps the closest similarity between Foucault and Rorty, who puts the point succinctly in saying there is "no criterion that we have not created in the course of creating a practice," and hence that there is no rationality "that is not obedience to our own conventions" (Rorty 1982:xlii).

Analytic philosophy is characterized by a conception of rationality as necessarily prior to all intellectual inquiry and as transcending historical, disciplinary, and cultural contexts. Against this, it is part of Foucault's project to "isolat[e] the form of rationality presented as dominant, and endowed with the status of the one-and-only reason ... to show that it is only one possible form among others" (Foucault 1988b:27). As for the tradition he opposes, he charges that it "operates as though a rational critique of rationality were impossible, or as though ... a contingent history of reason were impossible" (Foucault 1988b:27). The furor over Derrida's honorary Cambridge degree provides an example of what Foucault has in mind: David-Hillel Ruben claimed that although "philosophers love a good argument about anything," Derrida disqualified himself from participation in such arguments by questioning philosophers' rules of "clear, rigorous, rational discussion" (Rée 1992:61). Apparently "anything" does not include the rules by which argument is conducted, so if one questions established rules for rational discussion, one can only be embracing irrationalism.

The contrast between analytic philosophers and Foucault can be summed up as one between philosophers committed to real progress in intellectual inquiry governed by ahistoric rationality versus someone who sees such notions of progress and rationality as themselves subjects for historical explication. The contrast, therefore, is less one between representatives of distinct traditions; it is more between those who conceive of themselves as employing a methodology governed by objective standards and a thinker who considered every appeal to an objective standard to be a constitutive move in the production of a set of norm-setting practices.

Foucault's rejection of the idea that objective standards govern intellectual inquiry and enable us to attain perspective-neutral knowledge poses what has been characterized as the paradox of reflexivity, or what Hilary Lawson describes as the inescapable "turning back" on ourselves—on our beliefs, language, and practices—in the conduct of intellectual inquiry (Lawson 1985). The acknowledgment of reflexivity, perhaps postmodernism's defining feature and biggest problem, is basically a reconception of inquiry as only a highly complex form of self-awareness. A remark Rorty makes primarily about the unviability of the correspondence theory of truth can be generalized to make the point: We are unable "to step outside of our current theory of the world" in order to evaluate whether it fits the world, so we have no standard to appeal to in checking the soundness of our methods of inquiry (Rorty 1979b:85). Two other celebrated North American philosophers who concur with Foucault regarding the internality of standards, though presumably unknowingly, are Thomas Kuhn and Paul Feyerabend (Kuhn 1970; Feyerabend 1978). But Foucault's rejection of objective standards for inquiry is unique because of his conception of power-relations. His is not only a critique of philosophical inquiry, conceived as governed by ahistorical standards and capable of discerning "conceptual" truths, and/or of scientific inquiry conceived as capable of limning empirical truths. In his genealogical analytics Foucault offers detailed historical accounts of how such conceptions themselves have their genesis and come to achieve regulatory dominance. He tries to "make visible" the interrelatedness of power and knowledge, especially their mutually determining and enabling roles; he tries to show that rather than knowledge yielding power, through accurate description and hence the enabling of manipulative control, "power perpetually creates knowledge and, conversely, knowledge constantly induces ... power" (Foucault 1980b:51).

The philosophers to whom Foucault is most opposed see themselves as having advanced on their predecessors, as being at a contemporary intellectual pinnacle that they have hopes of raising higher. They attribute progress already made, and that to be made, to adherence to ahistoric inquiry-governing rationality. For Foucault, when we look back on what has ensued in the claimed achievement of knowledge, or look ahead to what might be achieved, power-relations dictate what we see. As for inquiry-governing rationality, he contends that "reason is self-created" and that rather than rationality being unitary and ahistoric, "rationalities engender one another, oppose and pursue one another" (Foucault 1988b:28–29). For Foucault, not only do disciplines not progress by cumulative discernment of objective truths, but the histories of philosophy, science, and other disciplines are interpretive constructs imposed on a number of events selectively identified and described. Such histories are not chronicles of events that are independent of construal and that constitute an objectively progressive sequence irrespective of our historical stories. Rorty makes the point in saying that it is only after a given vocabulary has become established, or "normal" in the Kuhnian sense of being generally accepted by the community of inquirers, that we "can tell a story of progress" (Rorty 1989:55).

Foucault's denial that the historical accounts we give of disciplinary knowledge do or could capture objective progress is fundamental to his genealogical analytics. There is no story-independent progress that history discerns and describes because history records sequences of occurrences that power-relations determine to be significant events. This denial of an independent subject matter for history, a subject matter that historians might or might not correctly trace and record, perplexes many, often forcing them to adopt dubious interpretations of Foucault's genealogical work to make it more manageable and to mold it to their own expectations. But this denial, together with the mechanisms he describes to account for why we have the histories we do have, is why Foucault's work poses so great a challenge to disciplinary scholarship and inquiry that, now, "to defend a subject against Foucault requires redefining the subject" (Arac 1991:vii).

The Three Domains

The dominant elements in Foucault's intellectual milieu were phenomenology, originating with Husserl and developed by Merleau-Ponty; hermeneutics, as reconceived by Heidegger and developed by Gadamer; and structuralism, arising from Saussure's semiotics and developed in diverse ways by Claude Lévi-Strauss and others such as Louis Althusser and Roland Barthes. Marxism was a broader background factor and colored phenomenological, hermeneutic, and structuralist positions. Hubert Dreyfus and Paul Rabinow believe that in order to understand Foucault one must triangulate him among phenomenology, hermeneutics, and structuralism. But they correctly contend that Foucault's "interpretive analytics" (their term) goes beyond all three to constitute a novel way of grasping "how in our culture human beings have become the sort of objects and subjects structuralism and hermeneutics discover and analyze" (Dreyfus and Rabinow 1983:xii; also xi–xxvii; but see Gutting 1994:3–5). Miller paints a more adversarial picture in which existentialism, personified in Sartre, had a stranglehold on philosophy in France; structuralism was an oppositional movement that attracted Foucault and provided the springboard for the phenomenal success of *The Order of Things* and Foucault's sudden advancement to the front ranks of the academic community (Miller 1993:123–64, esp. 147–51).

In spite of Foucault's denials that he was ever a structuralist, his early work was quasi-structuralist in character (Hoy 1986:4). In his "Foreword to the English Edition" of *The Order of Things*, Foucault remarks that "half-witted" commentators labeled him a structuralist, adding that he has been "unable to get it into their tiny minds" that he used "none of the methods, concepts, or key terms that characterize structural analysis" (Foucault 1973:xiv). However, these remarks are at odds with Foucault's own statement of purpose in *The Order of Things* (Foucault 1973:xx–xxii). Miller, speaking of the reception of *The Order of Things*, says that the reviewer for *L'Express* "never used the magic word 'structuralism' because she did not need to," since Foucault's "structuralist sympathies" were evident in his talk of "system" and his references to Lévi-Strauss (Miller 1993:148). *The Order of Things* and *The Archaeology of Knowledge* do seem to aspire to be contributions to a successor discipline to epistemology as structuralism aspired to be (Hoy 1986; Dreyfus and Rabinow 1983). In those works Foucault does seem to think that though philosophical inquiry cannot justify knowledge claims, as the tradition would have it do, philosophical inquiry can successfully investigate the role of "discourse" conceived of as an autonomous determinant of cognitive and social practices.

However, in the late 1960s Foucault effectively abandons the sort of theorizing that aims at discerning underlying epistemological or metaphysical determinants, mainly through a change of emphasis. Dreyfus and Rabinow tell us that early in his career Foucault "used variants of a strict analysis of discourse," but that particularly after 1968 "Foucault's interests began to shift away from discourse" (Dreyfus and Rabinow 1983:104). Foucault begins to focus on power-relations, which in 1968 "had not been previously thematized" (Dreyfus and Rabinow 1983:104). Foucault admits that his work lacked "the problem of 'discursive regime,' the effects of power" (Foucault 1980b:105). In focusing on power Foucault discards his inclination "to treat language as autonomous and as constitutive of reality," and so rids himself of the traces of idealism that "lurk in the structuralist suggestion that discourse organizes ... all social practices and historical epochs" (Hoy 1986:4).

Because of the move away from conception of discourse as an autonomous determinant of cognitive and social practices, Foucault is thought of as a poststructuralist by most of his European peers, whereas in North America he is more commonly thought a postmodern "deconstructionist," like Derrida. And despite his denials, the poststructuralist characterization seems justified to a point. Where the structuralists see cultural phenomena as determined by underlying structures best understood on the model of rule-bound systematic interrelations of signs, Foucault sees cultural phenomena as the results of power-relations. And where structuralists see the individual subject as a product of constitutive logical relations, Foucault sees the subject as emerging from cognitive and behavioral practices and from interactions with others equally so emergent. But Dreyfus and Rabinow are quite right to stress that Foucault is a truly innovative philosopher ill-served by familiar intellectual labels. Certainly facile characterization of Foucault as a postmodern and/or deconstructivist, where those terms connote intellectual superficiality, is quite mistaken.

With respect to his originality, the tendency to see Foucault as a disciple of Nietzsche is much too simple if not altogether wrongheaded; it is also prejudicial if used to dismiss Foucault on moralistic grounds or as too unrigorous to be taken seriously. Later we will consider Foucault's most concentrated discussion of Nietzsche, but not with a view to portraying Foucault as owing most of his ideas to Nietzsche. It is with regard to truth that Foucault owes the most to Nietzsche. I do not believe, as many do, that Foucault owes his notion of power to Nietzsche's "will to power." Nietzsche's sister compiled a book on the will to power from a mass of notes of dubious importance and intent and very likely did

Nietzsche a disservice. But it is decidedly a disservice to trace Foucault's notion of power-relations to that book. Foucault himself tells us that his debt to Nietzsche had to do with the question of the value of truth: "What I owe Nietzsche, derives mostly from the texts of around 1880, where the question of truth, the history of truth and the will to truth were central to his work" (Foucault 1988b:32; Allen 1991).

Whatever intellectual debts he may owe to Nietzsche, Heidegger, and others, Foucault is an innovative thinker whose stock-in-trade is the overturning of established "knowledges." In his first major work, *Madness and Civilization*, his doctoral dissertation, he shows himself possessed of a disturbing originality by articulating his initial "central intuition" that madness is an *invention*. He portrays psychiatric reforms, such as those of Samuel Tuke and Philippe Pinel, as an "insidious new form of social control" that created a class of malady and then assigned it a negative moral status (Miller 1993:103, 113; note that Miller erroneously gives Tuke's name as William). As we will see in subsequent chapters, in *Discipline and Punish* Foucault recasts penal reform as the imposition of equally insidious control, and in *The History of Sexuality* he rethinks sexuality as a deployed subject-defining and regulating "regime."

Foucault's originality was wrapped up with his Heideggerian ambition to think the "unthought" and a Nietzschean interest in the *daimonic*. His goal was to come to terms with the Nietzschean question: "How did I become what I am and why do I suffer from being what I am?" (Miller 1993:109). Foucault's efforts in this direction go well beyond academic philosophy to interests in death and sadomasochism, which appear to many as pathological. But it is precisely one of Foucault's aims "to disarm this reflexive response" to what is deemed unnatural and to have us rethink the limits of reason (Miller 1993:112). In my view, Foucault's genealogical analytics offer an intellectually challenging rethinking, not only of penality and sexuality, but of truth, knowledge, and rationality, which demands consideration whether it is ultimately endorsed or rejected.

Foucault's intellectual career includes fairly distinct stages characterized more by different emphases on topics of interest and diverse approaches to them rather than the radical shifts that marked careers such as Wittgenstein's. Hinrich Fink-Eitel paints a reasonably accurate picture of these stages, describing Foucault's career as divisible into four stages that correspond very roughly to the 1950s, 1960s, 1970s, and 1980s. In the first stage Foucault "was especially oriented to Heidegger's philosophy"; in the second stage Foucault "became an archaeologist of knowledge and wrote a 'theoretical' philosophy of objective, autonomous ... discourse and knowledge formation"; in the third stage he "became an archaeologist for the genealogy of power"; and in the fourth stage Foucault "became an ethical writer" (Fink-Eitel 1992:72). So long as we are careful not to take useful distinctions too rigidly, we can set aside the first stage, during which Foucault was still forging his philosophical identity, and work with the three remaining more-or-less standard divisions of Foucault's work; we'll dub them "domains of analysis," as does Arnold Davidson (Miller 1993:37–65; Davidson, A. 1986:221). The first domain of analysis is *archaeology*, which most characterizes Foucault's earlier books, published from 1961 to 1969; the second is *genealogy*, which most characterizes the books published from 1971 to 1976; the third domain of analysis is *ethics*, which most characterizes Foucault's last two books, both published in 1984, the year of his death. But as Dreyfus and Rabinow correctly and emphatically insist, these domains should not be thought of as separate or as superseding one another: *"There is no pre- and post-archaeology or genealogy in Foucault"* (Dreyfus and Rabinow 1983:104).

As I indicated in Chapter 1, it is not my intention to try for comprehensiveness in this introduction to Foucault. Therefore, I do not consider the domain of ethics, except briefly in Chapter 7. What I can say is that, for Foucault, ethics was self-directed rather than other-directed: Davidson describes Foucault's ethics as analysis "of the self's relationship to itself" (Davidson, A. 1986:221). Thus, in his approach to ethics, Foucault was closer to the Greeks and Romans he discusses in the second and third volumes of his history of sexuality (and from whom he also sought inspiration) than to his recent predecessors and contemporaries. Nonetheless, his ethical investigations do bear a family-resemblance to those of Paul Ricoeur, whose recent work has concentrated on determining the precise nature of the ethical subject (Ricoeur 1992).

With respect to the domain of archaeology, my interest is limited to providing a backdrop to discuss genealogy. I can situate genealogy relative to archaeology by citing Davidson's succinct descriptions of these two domains of analysis. Davidson describes archaeology as "analysis of systems of knowledge" and genealogy as analysis "of modalities of power" (Davidson, A. 1986:221). Foucault himself offered something akin to Davidson's tripartite characterization with specific reference to the social sciences, saying that his work included investigation of the sorts of forms of inquiry "which try to give themselves the status of sciences," investigation of "the objectivizing of the subject," and investigation of "the way a human being turns him- or herself into a subject" (Foucault 1983a:208–09). Of primary concern for us is the shift from archaeological analysis, in which discourse is deemed to shape practice, to genealogical analysis, in which discourse and practice are deemed to shape one another.

Archaeology

We can characterize archaeology as a form of inquiry primarily focused on the human sciences as systems of knowledge. Archaeology is a critical investigation of disciplinary systems of knowledge with the goal of understanding the discursive practices that produced those systems of knowledge. The archaeologist's interest, therefore, is in disciplinary discourse, in expert pronouncements and idioms. But it must be kept in mind that, as noted earlier, for Foucault a "discipline" is both a field of study and a system of control. The concern with expert pronouncements and idioms, then, involves both understanding how they constitute a learned practice and how that practice shapes behavior. What needs to be stressed is that archaeological investigation proceeds without concern as to whether what its target systems "say is true, or even … make[s] sense." Archaeology "must remain neutral as to the truth and meaning of the discursive systems it studies." Archaeology is concerned with mapping "all disciplines with their accepted concepts, legitimized subjects, taken-for-granted objects, and preferred strategies, which yield justified truth claims" (Dreyfus and Rabinow 1983:xxiv). The aim is not to assess the truth of a knowledge-system's claims, but to understand how those claims come to be claims, how they are then deemed justified or otherwise within the targeted knowledge-system, and how some of them come to constitute knowledge within that system.

As to how archaeology actually proceeds, Foucault makes a crucial point when he says that "[a]rchaeological comparison does not have a unifying but a diversifying effect" (Foucault 1972:159–60). Though archaeology also unearths hidden similarities, it is of paramount importance—with respect to archaeology itself and perhaps more so with respect to genealogy—that it undermines accepted continuities even while establishing connections between practices previously thought disparate. Archaeology is always diversifying in the sense that even in establishing surprising similarities it disrupts conventional views. Archaeology is comparative, but in the sense that its focus is not the accepted similarities but the neglected or suppressed similarities and differences between an established system of knowledge and superseded or suppressed ones. Archaeology has a diversifying effect in that its objective is to fracture the smooth totality of a disciplinary tradition's picture of itself or of one of its constitutive elements. The objective is to unearth, to excavate factors and events, overlooked likenesses, discontinuities and disruptions, anomalies and suppressed items, which yield a new picture of whatever has previously gone unquestioned and has been taken as definitive knowledge and truth with respect to a particular subject matter and more generally of how the world is. Foucault is everywhere concerned with exhuming the hidden, the obscure, the marginal, the accidental, the forgotten, the overlooked, the covered-up, the displaced. His subjects for investigation are whatever is taken as most natural, obvious, evident, undeniable, manifest, prominent, and indisputable.

Shored up by meticulous empirical research, Foucault's basic strategy in both archaeology and genealogy is to retell the history of a discipline or institution or practice by highlighting and connecting previously marginal and obscured elements and events, thereby presenting a very different picture of that discipline, institution, or practice. In archaeology, Foucault's targets are disciplines or sciences, but his method is not to engage in abstract debate about operant theories. Instead he probes the subject matters of disciplines or sciences as delineated and treated in institutional establishments. Cases in point are madness, the subject matter of psychiatry as dealt with in the asylum, and illness, the subject-matter of medicine as dealt with in the clinic.

The diversifying effect of archaeological investigation is not limited to particular disciplinary practices; it is also operant on a grander scale, namely, that having to do with what Foucault calls *epistemes.* These are essentially conceptual frameworks, distinguished from what readers with an analytic background would take to be conceptual schemes of the sort rejected as incoherent by Donald Davidson (Davidson, D. 1973/1974). The point of the distinction is to not preclude that *epistemes,* as conceptual frameworks, may be mutually translatable or "commensurable" whereas conceptual schemes, assuming their possibility, are not mutually translatable or "incommensurable." *Epistemes* are holistic frameworks that define problematics and their potential resolutions and constitute views of the world comprising the most fundamental of identificatory and explanatory notions, such as the nature of causality in a given range of phenomena. Whether Foucault conceived of these frameworks as incommensurable in a way making them vulnerable to Davidson's arguments is an interesting question, but of immediate concern is that much of Foucault's effort was directed at understanding the shifts between these frameworks.

An example of different *epistemes,* and of the shift from one to another, comes early in *The Order of Things* and is Foucault's discussion of the difference between the "Renaissance" and "Classical" conceptions of language, specifically the difference between "trinary" and "binary" conceptions of the relation of signs to what they signify. In making out the nature of the shift at issue, Foucault provides a good instance of his ability to occasionally season his often prodigal prose with beautifully compact statements the length of which are disproportionately short compared to their importance. Speaking of the shift to the "Classical" or modern *episteme* and the reconception of language, Foucault remarks that "knowledge that divined, at random, signs that were absolute" came to be replaced by "a network of signs" that was developed "in accordance with a knowledge of what is probable." The superbly tight addendum is: "Hume has become possible" (Foucault 1973:60).

Foucault's point is that in the *episteme* in place prior to Descartes, the conception of the relation between signs and what they signify was trinary in the sense that it comprised the sign, the thing signified, and an essential resemblance between the two. This was a conception of language as naturally, as opposed to conventionally, connected to its referents and that also distinguished among "that which was marked, that which did the marking, and that which made it possible to see in the first the mark of the second" (Foucault 1973:64). This last is what makes (Renaissance) language inherently *resemble* the world, as opposed to *representing* the world; resemblance is a matter of signs being natural correlates of things rather than arbitrarily assigned labels. For Descartes, words and things "were separated from one another," and though discourse "was still to have the task of speaking that which *is,* [it] was no longer to be anything more than what it *said*" (Foucault 1973:43). For Descartes, the conception of signification became binary and comprised only the sign and the thing signified. When Descartes recast consciousness as awareness of internal ideas, he detached language from the world. But in doing that, he did not only construe language more or less as Aristotle did in *Posterior Analytics*—as so many signs the assignation of which is essentially arbitrary and is regulated by convention—he made the assignation of signs contingent on an epistemologically problematic relation between ideas and their putative causes, thus enabling Humean skepticism.

But the enabling of Humean skepticism, as well as the recasting of truth as something about the content of utterances rather than about utterings, are philosophical points that, even though illustrating radical conceptual changes, fall short of conveying the scope of a shift from one *episteme* to another. Foucault's notion of this epochal change is more evident in less philosophically significant passages, such as one where Foucault quotes Claude Duret. Writing in 1613, Duret describes how various people write from right to left (Hebrews and Arabs), from left to right (Europeans), from top to bottom (Chinese and Japanese), and from bottom to top or in "spiral lines" (surprisingly, Mexicans—but it is noteworthy that the Aztec calendar is indeed a spiral). The right-to-left movement follows "the course ... of the first heaven"; the left-to-right movement follows "the course ... of the second heaven, home of the seven planets"; the top-to-bottom movement conforms to "the order of nature" evident in how people have "heads at the tops of their bodies";

and the bottom-to-top or spiral movement conforms to the sun's "annual journey through the Zodiac." For Duret, these five diverse manners of writing reveal not only "the world's frame" but also "the form of the cross" (Foucault 1973:37). What is important here is not the particulars of the example, but how language was seen as related to the world, not as a mere convention-governed invention, but as something the nature and use of which constituted a natural reflection of what there is and the structure of reality. It is only when there is appreciation of how language was seen as intrinsically mirroring reality, when the apparent absurdity of the example is dispelled by comprehension of language conceived as analogically resembling the world, that the magnitude of the change to language conceived as conventional can be fully understood.

Archaeology, then, is investigation of the discontinuities and newly established similarities that reveal abandonment of one conceptual framework and adoption of another, and in the process enable us to understand both. Archaeology is the unearthing of abandoned frameworks and the comparing of them with presently dominant ones; it is the meticulous mapping of established and excavated frameworks with a view to understanding the means of their production and their operation. But perhaps as illuminating as any positive characterization of archaeology is a negative one that says what happens when archaeology goes wrong.

Archaeology goes wrong when it turns into a theory about how things are and pretends to transcend its historical situatedness and discover hidden determinants underlying phenomena. These pretensions are just what Foucault rejects in structuralism and the vestiges of which he disavows in his own work. When archaeology takes a structuralist turn its focus is "deflected from an interest in the social practices that [form] both institutions and discourse to an almost exclusive emphasis on linguistic practices." The consequences are ill-conceived objectivization of discourse as a holistic determinator of cognitive and social practices and an ultimately ruinous "neglect of the way discursive practices are themselves affected by the social practices in which they and the investigator are embedded" (Dreyfus and Rabinow 1983:xii).

When archaeology claims objectivity for itself, it not only wrongly casts itself as capable of discerning underlying objective realities, it wrongly casts discursive practices as autonomous, as unilaterally determining the character and direction of social and institutional behavior while themselves somehow remaining unaffected by that behavior. Archaeology then becomes a form of bad idealist metaphysics. Properly done, archaeology is "an inquiry whose aim is to rediscover on what basis knowledge and theory became possible" (Foucault 1973:xxi–ii). The intent is to unearth the contexts in which truth and knowledge are produced, the activities and practices that manufacture and develop the methods we dub scientific and that fabricate the bodies of judgments and beliefs we dub sciences—and which we take as providing expert intelligence on whatever interests us. Because archaeology is the mapping of the enabling conditions for the production of truth and knowledge, it cannot be a method for discerning objective determinants, such as practice-determining discursive structures, lurking behind the appearances they supposedly produce. To do archaeology is precisely to understand how something like a discursive structure comes to be considered an underlying reality.

Nonetheless, for a time Foucault did seem to take archaeology as capable of discerning underlying appearance-determining realities, or at least his interest was deflected onto discourse in a way that gave to discourse the status of an autonomous determinant of practices. Even more problematic than this misconceived focus on discourse is Foucault's erstwhile ambition to get beyond practices and construals to something primitive that underlies even discourse. In 1961 Foucault wrote that we "must try to return to that zero point ... at which madness is an undifferentiated experience" before it is shaped and categorized by discourse and practices (Foucault 1965:ix). Though made at the very start of his archaeological period, this sort of remark causes Rorty to think Foucault was mistakenly trying "to make archaeology the successor subject to epistemology" (Hoy 1986:3). But no trace of archaeology so conceived is found in *Discipline and Punish* and *The History of Sexuality*. Even as early as *The Archaeology of Knowledge* Foucault warns that archaeology does not attempt to return to some zero point, that it "does not imply the search for a beginning" (Foucault 1972:131). By 1977 Foucault is openly scornful of vestigial epistemological ambitions to "rediscover the things themselves in their primitive vivacity" (Foucault 1988b:119).

To reiterate, archaeology is supposed to be detailed, descriptive, assessment-neutral investigation of disciplines, of expert idioms, of truth- and knowledge-determining systems. But it cannot claim to get behind appearances to ahistoric determinants. It aims to exhaustively track down and disinterestedly describe factors and events that enabled the emergence of the discipline or institution that is the subject of its inquiry. Archaeology begins by discounting received opinion, by rendering problematic what is least questioned, by reconstruing the apparently obvious and natural as suspect. It then searches out the discontinuities that mark shifts between conceptual frameworks. It searches out the disparate and accidental factors that result in the formation of such frameworks and the acceptance of something as knowledge.

The heart of Foucault's archaeological and genealogical investigations is what Ian Hacking describes as an effort "to rethink the subject matter." In archaeological investigation this means beginning "from the ground up, at the level of tiny local events where battles are unwittingly enacted by players who don't know what they are doing" (Hacking 1981:29). Although people "know what they do" and may even "know why they do what they do," Foucault maintains that "what they don't know is what what they do does" (Dreyfus and Rabinow 1983:187). In other words, they do not know the consequences of their actions. The archaeologist, then, looks beyond the holistic image of a discipline or science or institution projected by its practitioners and adherents into the component practices. The archaeologist recounts a restructured history of the targeted discipline, science, or institution by taking these tiny local events and interpreting them in light of data that "hardly anyone else ... noticed" (Hacking 1981:28). The result is "a reordering of events ... not perceived before" (Hacking 1981:29). The aim of the reordering is to understand "the empirical conditions under which [expert] statements come to be counted as ... true" by providing an alternative account in which the accepted truth of those expert statements is revealed as one possible set of construals and not unique and hard-won objective correctness (Hoy 1986:3).

Given the foregoing, it may seem that archaeology would be the Foucauldian domain of analysis most pertinent to epistemology, since it deals, if not with the justification of knowledge, then with the origins of what is deemed knowledge (Machado 1992). This introduction to Foucault, intended as it is for readers in a philosophical tradition dominated by epistemology, might seem better focused on archaeology than on genealogy, regardless of how much these domains of analysis overlap. But as indicated, genealogy is most central to Foucault's views, because it is in his genealogical analytics that we find the most direct challenges to traditional philosophical assumptions and methodology in the reconception of truth, knowledge, and rationality as products of power. It is also in genealogy that Foucault develops what he describes as his greatest debt to Nietzsche, namely, the question about the value of truth (Foucault 1988b:32; but see Mahon 1992).

In regard to the priority of genealogy over archaeology for the current project, keep in mind that the importance of genealogy is clearer than why and how Foucault himself makes the shift from archaeology to genealogy—always remembering that we are dealing here with matters of emphasis rather than disparate methods. Though not of immediate concern, one possible explanation is that over time Foucault becomes more concerned about the problem regarding the status of archaeological claims. Some see the problem as fatal to Foucault's position, though it does not, as some might expect, have to do with an inconsistently implied existence of underlying realities that all the talk about "unearthing" suggests. The problem instead has to do with the paradox of reflexivity, the fact that all possibility of methodological objectivity evaporates with the realization that everything theories postulate as external to themselves can be redescribed as internal by providing a suitable originative story. David Couzens Hoy notes that, on the one hand, Foucault's archaeology "makes truth relative to an *episteme*, that is, to what in Anglo-American philosophical vocabulary could be called a ... paradigm or conceptual framework" (Hoy 1986:5). But on the other hand, it looks as if in spite of abandoning attempts to unearth realities, the archaeologist inescapably exempts her or his own pronouncements from the relativization of truth and knowledge. In tracing what generates a discipline, expert perspective, or a knowledge, the archaeologist offers an account of the conditions within which one set of judgments and statements is deemed true. But then it looks as if archaeology must be done outside such conditions or be merely more of the same sort of knowledge produced within another set of conditions. As we will see in the following chapters, this problem about the point from where the archaeologist speaks plagues genealogical analysis as well.

I turn now to genealogy, which Dreyfus and Rabinow define as Foucault's investigation of "that which conditions, limits, and institutionalizes discursive formations" (Dreyfus and Rabinow 1983:104).

3 Genealogical Analytics

Like Kant's inversion of the priority of the objective over the subjective, Nietzsche's inversion of the Platonic universal over the particular also constituted a philosophical Copernican revolution. Foucault emulates Nietzsche's inversion in his own transpositions of the interpretive significance of the central and the marginal, of the priority of the supposedly natural and the constructed, and of the originative importance of the allegedly inevitable and the accidental. In his exposition of Nietzschean genealogy in "Nietzsche, Genealogy, History," Foucault acknowledges his intellectual debt to Nietzsche. In acknowledging that debt, Foucault effectively articulates the basic conception of his own genealogy. However, our interest in "Nietzsche, Genealogy, History" is less in Foucault's debt to Nietzsche than in grasping the broad outline and thrust of Foucault's genealogy in order to better understand its implementation in *Discipline and Punish* and *The History of Sexuality*. Though the article is, strictly speaking, exegetical and should not be taken as simply laying out Foucault's own position, it serves as an excellent guide to his position. This is why Donald Bouchard and others think it so important (Bouchard 1977:139n).

Foucault develops Nietzsche's idea that history is misconceived as "an attempt to capture the exact essence of things," that history is inherently flawed if conducted as a search for origins in the sense of essential beginnings (Foucault 1971:78). The proffered alternative to history so conceived is genealogy, which "opposes itself to the search for origins" (Foucault 1971:77). The heart of the concept is that there are no essences to be discerned behind historical developments and none that explain why things are as they are. To highlight a limiting example of what genealogy opposes, we might use the Augustinian view of history as a divinely scripted cosmic drama. Augustine's linear conception of history was of a consolidated, teleological sequence of events set in motion and supervised by God; for Augustine, history is an unfolding story with a beginning (the Creation), a middle (the Incarnation) and an eventual end (the Last Judgment) (Matson 1987:200). Under this conception the historian's task is to integrate what are apparently unconnected events and discern, behind the resulting integration, the hand of God. This is precisely what genealogy repudiates: the idea that behind events is a guiding hand or set of regulating principles that are the grand determinants of the present. Genealogy "does not pretend to go back in time to restore an unbroken continuity" and so to discern in past events a harmony that reveals the hidden forces that "animate the present, having imposed a predetermined form [on] all its vicissitudes" (Foucault 1971:81).

Foucault insists with Nietzsche that "if the genealogist refuses to [do] metaphysics" what he finds underlying historical events is "not a timeless and essential secret, but ... that they [events] have no essence or that their essence was fabricated" (Foucault 1971:78; allusion is to Nietzsche's *Dawn*, #123). Later, Foucault speaks of "eventalization" in describing a "breach of self-evidence." What he has in mind is focusing on particulars, as opposed to glossing over them, in order to make "visible a *singularity* ... where there is a temptation to invoke ... an obviousness that imposes itself uniformly" (Baynes *et al.* 1987:104).

Genealogy does not operate on a murky field of elusive but objective events, trying to sift out the continuities that reveal the causes of the present. Genealogy does not claim to mine a continuous vein in which determinants of later events can be found if only our research is good enough. Instead genealogy "operates on a field of entangled and confused parchments, on documents that have been scratched over and recopied many times" (Foucault 1971:76). What genealogy finds is the antithesis of essences; it finds happy and unhappy accidents and coincidences united by interpretation. As Rorty might put it, genealogy maps the "reinterpretation[s] of our predecessors' reinterpretation[s] of their predecessors' reinterpretations," which themselves were scratched over and recopied as often as needs and priorities changed (Rorty 1982:xlii).

The core of the genealogical inversion is that rather than providing synthesis and discernment of unity, history is only the painstaking tracking of complexity and disparity; rather than searching through the myriad details of the past for future-determining continuities, history is only a tireless sifting out therefrom of the disparate components that our interests then turn into notable episodes in some imposed progression. But the contrast here is not simply one between attention to universal categories and teleologies, on the one hand, and attention to micro-particulars on the other. Universalist accounts may well demand attention to particulars, and some anti-universalist accounts may not. The contrast is between conceiving of micro-particulars as components of some broader process and seeing them as exhaustive of the subject matter of history.

Before looking more closely at "Nietzsche, Genealogy, History," it is worth stressing the broader implications of Foucault's endorsement of

Nietzsche's rejection of the quest for origins. It is not just history that is here under consideration, but also reason or what might be better described as the nature and development of reasoned inquiry. Foucault contends that an examination of reason's own history reveals that it "was born ... from chance." He denies that reasoned inquiry developed progressively through the honing of increasingly successful investigative principles; he maintains that it was the haphazard compilation of complex practices and maneuvers that "slowly forged the weapons of reason" (Foucault 1971:78; allusions are to *Dawn*, #123, and *Human, All Too Human*, #34). The discussion that follows is not just about history as a discipline; it is about history as a case in point of intellectual inquiry.

Foucault begins "Nietzsche, Genealogy, History" by considering Nietzsche's use of a number of terms denoting origin, emergence, beginning, and descent-from. (*Ursprung*/origin; *Herkunft*/origin, descent; *Entstehung*/emergence; *Abkunft*/descent; *Geburt*/birth.) His point is to show how Nietzsche introduced a contrast between a search for origins, in the humdrum sense of causes and sources, and a quest for Capital-O Origins as "an attempt to capture the exact essence of things" (Foucault 1971:78). But the contrast is not merely one between two aims or methods; the contrast is reductive. Nietzsche and Foucault want to show that the quest for essences is wholly misconceived and that what "is found at the historical beginning of things ... is disparity." Foucault describes historical beginnings as "lowly: not in the sense of modest ... but derisive and ironic, capable of undoing every infatuation." He adds that it is a "cruelty of history that compels ... abandonment of 'adolescent' quests: behind the always recent ... truth, it posits the ancient proliferation of errors" (Foucault 1971:79). To illustrate his point Foucault quotes a biting remark from Nietzsche that captures the irony: "We wished to awaken the feeling of man's sovereignty by showing his divine birth: this path is now forbidden, since a monkey stands at the entrance" (Foucault 1971:79, quoting *Dawn*, #49).

In clarifying the distinction between the search for origins and genealogy, Foucault considers Nietzsche's attempt to make the notion of descent (*Herkunft*) normally used to speak of extraction or lineage, capture not only likenesses, such as familial traits, but differences within general likeness. Foucault notes that "analysis of descent permits ... dissociation" and that by unearthing lost details it enables "recognition and displacement [of] empty synthesis" (Foucault 1971:81). It is through analysis of descent that genealogy reveals the miscellaneous and discontinuous nature of beginnings. In contrast to readings of historical data that search for grand designs, genealogy attempts to "identify the accidents, the minute deviations ... the reversals ... the errors, the false appraisals, and the faulty calculations that gave birth to those things that ... have value for us" (Foucault 1971:81). The more discontinuous or disassociated details are excavated, the less possible it is to impose some grand synthesis or design on the past.

In discussing descent Foucault makes a point important to understanding both the role of and the emphasis on the body in *Discipline and Punish* and *The History of Sexuality*. He asserts that analysis of descent applies also to the body, that the body "and everything that touches it ... is the domain of *Herkunft*." This is because the body "is the inscribed surface of events (traced by language)." It is the body that bears and manifests the effects of regulating discourses in its habits and gestures, in its postures, in its speech. It is therefore genealogy's task "to expose a body totally imprinted by history" (Foucault 1971:82; allusion is to *Gay Science*, #348–9). It is also genealogy's task to show how the body is "the locus of a dissociated self (adopting the illusion of a substantial unity)" (Foucault 1971:83). The body supports a self, a subject, which does not recognize itself as emergent but takes itself as prior to the effects of discourse. Genealogy, as the analysis of descent, painstakingly exposes the tiny influences on a body that, over time, not only produce a subject of a certain sort, a subject defined by what it takes to be knowledge about itself and its world, but a subject under the illusion that it is a substantial, autonomous unity.

Here we have yet another compact passage in which Foucault articulates fundamental philosophical points. Referring to the body as the "inscribed surface of events" and as supporting an emergent self that believes itself to be a "substantial unity" encapsulates much of what is central to *Discipline and Punish* and *The History of Sexuality*. Additionally, the parenthetical amplification "traced by language" alludes to what was mentioned in connection with archaeology and is evident in *Discipline and Punish* and *The History of Sexuality*—that it is expert discourse, disciplinary discourse, that shapes subjectivity and establishes regimes of truth. Foucault is not concerned with ordinary talk; he is concerned with expert or learned talk, with the idioms of science, of the academy, of authority. But in contrast to any earlier inclination to construe discourse as autonomous and as a unidirectional determinant of practice, in genealogy Foucault gives full weight to practice's reciprocal enabling and shaping of discourse.

However, it is not enough to trace descent, to mark likenesses and differences within likeness; the analysis of descent is incomplete without the complementary analysis of emergence (*Entstehung*) in the complex sense of both initial appearance and of achieved dominance. In the analysis of descent the aim is to understand the miscellany of beginnings; in the analysis of emergence the aim is to understand catalytic coming-to-be. But as in the analysis of descent, the point is to produce accounts that, by showing the variety of generative factors, belie the idea that history traces underlying determinative continuities. The point of analyzing emergence is to produce accounts of whatever comes-to-be as not "the final term of a historical development" (Foucault 1971:83). The analysis of emergence denies historical progressive evolution by showing that what comes-to-be is not a result of teleological processes but "is always produced through a particular stage of forces." What emerges or comes-to-be does so because of a compilation of disparate factors; what emerges is not the culmination of anything but is a consequence of an accumulation of factors with no inherent interrelatedness. If those factors appear to be more than coincidentally related, it is only because of the retrospective imposition of some historical interpretation. We misconceive history if we think of it as discerning continuities; we misconceive history if we think of it as discerning goal-directed processes. The analysis of emergence traces the unknowingly combative campaigns that accidentally constituted forces "wage against each other" and shows how something comes-to-be as a product of blind conflict instead of an "obscure purpose that seeks its realization at the moment it arises" (Foucault 1971:83).

At this point we approach the notion of power. In describing the interplay of forces that result in emergence, Foucault speaks of it as "the endlessly repeated play of dominations" (Foucault 1971:83). Also at this point we see the divergence between the Nietzschean and Foucauldian views. Alluding again to Nietzsche, Foucault offers, as examples of the play of dominations, the domination of some individuals by others, which "leads to the differentiation of values," and the domination of one class by another, which "generates the idea of liberty" (Foucault 1971:85; allusions are to *Beyond Good and Evil*, #260, and *Wanderer*, #9). But the remarks about differentiation of values and generation of ideas are Foucault's glosses. As will become clear, unlike Nietzsche, Foucault does not think of domination only in terms of the control of one class or individual over another. Power-relations, which encompass domination and are not exhausted by it, may differentiate values and generate the idea of liberty, but not simply as coercion of groups or individuals. As we will see in Chapter 4, power-relations are not just the various dominations of individuals or classes by other individuals or classes; the dominations are power-relations not only in being the control of individuals or classes, but also in being the generation of values that allow and support the establishment of hierarchies and of notions like that of liberation from subjugation. Power or power-relations enable both the domination of individuals or classes and the values and ideas employed in effecting and justifying that domination as well as in resisting it.

Emergence is appearance or advent enabled by clashes of forces, some of which enhance one another, some of which nullify others, some of which redirect one another, and some of which form force-vectors constituting new forces. As to what it is that emerges, the list is diverse and includes value-sets, institutions such as representative government or human sexuality, and concepts such as that of inalienable rights or, for that matter, of historical inevitability. What emerges and gains dominance is everything that orders our lives and which appears natural to us in those lives. What emerges and gains dominance not only looks to be predetermined, it is legitimized in terms of its apparent inevitability. Whether it be an idea or value, a discipline or an institution, the first task of its adherents is to establish it and its supporting principles as natural, as inevitable, as truths that have been discerned. It is the task of genealogy to counter the view of the emergent as inevitable by recording its lowly beginnings, by tracing "the history of morals, ideals, and metaphysical concepts, the history of the concept of liberty or of the ascetic life" (Foucault 1971:86). Genealogy must analyze the descent and emergence of morals, ideals, and metaphysical concepts in order to show them and their like to be neither discovered truths nor preordained developments, but rather the products of conglomerations of blind forces.

With respect to exposing the lowly beginnings of morals, ideals, and metaphysical concepts by tracing their descent and emergence, Foucault describes genealogy as "gray, meticulous, and patiently documentary" in method and application (Foucault 1977:76). But the putative meticulously documentary nature of genealogy poses a problem we encountered earlier. Some interpreters of Foucault are not prepared to accept his insistence on the exhaustiveness of genealogy, on the impossibility of discerning event-determining essences, and still acknowledge that he is doing philosophy or history (O'Farrell 1989). The issue is what the allegedly documentary nature of genealogy can amount to if genealogy is not to violate its historicist conception. The problem is the same as that noted in connection with archaeology. Foucault can be read as implicitly but perhaps inconsistently contending—or as committed to contending—that genealogy can get things *right*, that it can yield objective knowledge of events. As we shall see later, there is an ambiguity or complexity in Foucault's conception of truth that may limit his skepticism about objective knowledge. Nonetheless, it seems insufficient to deny essences to remain historicist, if the method by which essences are exposed as constructed and banished is to document objective sequences of events that have been somehow distorted. That is, the claim that those sequences have been misinterpreted, if made to look integrated and teleological, seems to entail that the genealogical account of those events is the correct one. The alternative, as we saw with archaeology, is to accept that genealogical accounts are so many more stories on an equal footing with the stories genealogy opposes.

At this point one feels the bite of the Nietzschean nihilism that haunts Foucault's work. This is the core of what Rorty sees as bleak in Foucault, and it is this possible nihilism that is so regularly softened or denied in North American interpretations of his thought, leading Rorty to claim that it is the French Foucault that "is the fully Nietzschean one," whereas the Americanized Foucault has most of the threatening nihilistic tendencies "drained away" (Rorty 1991b:193). There is a reason for this transatlantic interpretive difference: When North Americans turn to European thinkers, they often do so looking for productive ideas to revitalize their own philosophical projects. They are then sometimes unprepared to accept the bleakness of what they find. North American philosophers who take an interest in Foucault's work tend to assume that his eminence is due to his success in proffering positive theories and are therefore reluctant to acknowledge Foucault's thoroughgoing critical historicization of philosophical methods and assumptions. These philosophers try to see the Nietzschean element in Foucault as only provocative, as only challenging hyperbole. But this is to distort Foucault in order to avoid the nihilism. In his most critical phase Foucault did not seek absolutes of any sort; he was not trying to overcome what Richard Bernstein calls Cartesian anxiety by seeking certainty in power-relations rather than in epistemological arguments (Bernstein 1983). The nihilism, or at least the threat of nihilism, is real.

The nihilist threat is that questions about the historicist nature of genealogy and archaeology suggest that critical assessments, of how power produces truth and knowledge and criterial concepts like rationality, can only be more products of power. It seems that genealogy can be fully historicist only if, as just noted, its meticulously documentary accounts are acknowledged to be only so many more productions of power. We seem, then, adrift among accounts revealed as only interest-determined interpretations that we have no effective way of distinguishing as better or worse and some of which we prefer only because of whatever shapes our propensities and inclinations. Crippling doubts can be raised about any one interpretive account, to the extent that alternatives attract us. Beyond the strictly theoretical sphere, in the political arena, it seems as if struggle against oppression is pointless, as it can result only in obtaining different forms of oppression. Foucault's political activism was often challenged or impugned on just this basis, so it seems no political alternative can be endorsed as inherently better than another.

Rorty deals with the threat of nihilism through irony. He advocates admitting that we have "radical and continuing doubts" about our vocabulary—our established discourse—because we are "impressed by other vocabularies" (Rorty 1989:73). Rorty advocates the additional admission "that argument phrased in [our] present vocabulary can neither under-write nor dissolve those doubts" (Rorty 1989:73). Rortyan ironists understand that "there is nothing beyond vocabularies which serves as a criterion of choice between them" (Rorty 1989:80). This solution will not satisfy many and is not Foucault's, who puts his faith in novelty of thought as we will see later. Fortunately, an introduction to Foucault's genealogy is not the place to attempt to deal with the question of nihilism, though I will return more than once to the question of the historicist status of genealogy.

Once he has characterized genealogy, Foucault addresses the question of how to best understand the relation between genealogy and traditional history. The denial of origins, of course, is not a rejection of history as such. Genealogy is opposed to history only as a quest for origins, because it requires history in the mundane sense of annals of the past. The genealogist "needs history to dispel the chimeras of the origin" (Foucault 1971:80,77). If we think of history as neutrally as possible, as just so many extant chronicles and records of past times, we realize that it is the only raw material available to both genealogists and origin-seeking historians. Genealogy, if anything, is more deeply concerned with historical data than is the quest for origins, which takes a broad view of historical data in trying to discern large-scale patterns supposedly revelatory of great forces at work. Genealogy can only focus on minutia, so it "depends on a vast accumulation of source material" and "demands relentless erudition" (Foucault 1971:76–77). Genealogy needs the archives, chronicles, diaries, journals, logbooks, memoirs, official records, and registries that are the historian's raw material. Without that material to work with, neither genealogy nor essence-seeking history could be attempted.

Genealogy even needs the historians' grand narratives, because without them it would have no counterpoint. Without those epics claiming to depict underlying continuities, geneology would have no marginal and neglected items to notice and use in building alternative accounts. It is this contrast with traditional grand-narrative history, then, that needs to be fleshed out. In order to do so Foucault continues his consideration of Nietzschean genealogy by setting Nietzsche's notion of *wirkliche Historie* or "effective history" against history that claims "a suprahistorical perspective" and takes its main task to be fashioning the "diversity of time into a totality" (Foucault 1971:86; allusions are to *Genealogy*, preface, sec. 7, and chap. I, sec. 2, and *Beyond Good and Evil*, #224).

Totalizing history is possible only given belief in ahistorical absolutes, because it requires something that is able to unify disparate historical events, something that molds those events into coherent progressions from outside those progressions. Nietzsche understood that Origin-seeking historians assumed such things—that "words kept their meaning, that desires still pointed in a single direction, and that ideas retained their logic" (Foucault 1971:76). Against this, Nietzsche's effective history eschews metaphysical absolutes. Instead of attempting to unify on the basis of assumed ahistorical principles, effective history "distinguishes, separates, and disperses" and focuses on "divergence and marginal elements" (Foucault 1971:87). Effective history "differs from traditional history in being without constants"; it discards traditional concepts and methods designed to achieve comprehensiveness and that attempt to retrace "the past as a patient and continuous development" (Foucault 1971:87–88).

The contrast between traditional and effective history, then, turns on totalizing history's requirement of absolutes that it uses in assimilating or "dissolving the singular event into an ideal continuity." Effective history "deals with events in terms of their most unique characteristics" (Foucault 1971:88). For the genealogist, the events that make up history are not, as they are for the traditional historian, so many determinate assassinations, battles, coronations, decisions, elections, revolutions, and treaties. Instead the events that make up history for the genealogist are changes in force-relationships; they are such things as "the reversal of a relationship of forces, the usurpation of power, the appropriation of a vocabulary turned against those who had once used it" (Foucault 1971:88). These events are not so much delineated occurrences as they are relational changes. Their particularity is crucial, for each relational change must be understood, not against overriding generalities, but in terms of specific, detailed accounts of as many as possible of the factors that contribute to its coming about. Effective history "shortens its vision to those things nearest to it"; effective history reverses historians' "pretension to examine things furthest from themselves" (Foucault 1971:89).

Foucault turns to consideration of perspectivism in ending his discussion of how effective history relates to traditional history: the "final trait of effective history is its affirmation of knowledge as perspective" (Foucault 1971:90). In contrast to traditional history's conception of its inquiries as at least ideally objective, effective history is avowedly perspectival. Effective history never forgets or obscures its own temporal and cultural situatedness, as well as the cultural and temporal contexts of its subjects, and it rejects as absurd the idea that history can be done objectively, that it can be done from no particular point of view. But effective history goes further than rejection by casting traditional history's invocation of "objectivity, of the accuracy of facts, and of the permanence of the past" as a mask for vested interests operant in the production of its narratives (Foucault 1971:91).

Near the end of "Nietzsche, Genealogy, History" Foucault pursues the contrast between effective and traditional history with a discussion of how history must be mastered "so as to turn it to genealogical uses, that is, strictly anti-Platonic purposes" (Foucault 1977:93). He offers a three-way characterization of uses of history that correspond to but oppose Platonic "modalities." These uses are the parodic, dissociative, and sacrificial. The first use of history is parodic in being "directed against reality, and [opposed to] the theme of history as reminiscence or recognition"; the second is dissociative in being "directed against identity, and [opposed to] history given as continuity or representative of a tradition"; and the third is sacrificial in being "directed against truth, and [opposed to] history as knowledge" (Foucault 1971:93; allusion is to *Beyond Good and Evil*, #223).

The parodic use of history opposes the traditional historian's imposition of singular, integrated identities and offers "alternative identities" to defeat essentialist notions of all sorts, such as attempts to show our origin as the embodiment of rationality or as an act of divine creation. The point of the parodic use is to impugn preferred images by providing alternatives that serve their purpose all the better if tinged with absurdity. The passage cited earlier, in which Foucault quotes from Nietzsche, provides a pithy example of the parodic use: Our self-description as the children of God is challenged by evolutionary theory's replacement of our communal father, the God-created Adam, with "a monkey" (Foucault 1971:79).

The dissociative use of history differs from the parodic in that instead of only furnishing challenging possible alternatives to imposed identities, it systematically impugns imposed identities from within those identities. The dissociative use proceeds by discovering and highlighting discontinuities and inconsistencies. The dissociative use is directed against traditional history's imposition of images—of human beings as the children of God or as the embodiment of rationality—as much as is the parodic. But the dissociative use seeks to demonstrate that history does not "discover a forgotten identity" but instead unearths "a complex system of distinct and multiple elements" that defy synthesis (Foucault 1971:94; allusion is to *Human, All Too Human*, #274).

The sacrificial use of history counters traditional history's pretensions to neutrality and objectivity by forcing the forfeiture of invented subjects of knowledge (Foucault 1977:95–96). This use exposes traditional history's claimed discernment of a delineable subject—an institution, a discipline, an archetype, an era—as only the manufactured product of "the will to knowledge," the contrived focus of the quest for essential natures and absolute truth. Additionally, the sacrificial use reveals how the quest for truth, rather than preserving the complexity of its subjects, strips away every aspect of a subject's temporal, historical, and cultural situatedness as supposedly only incidental to its imagined essence. This is why Nietzsche "reproached critical history for ... sacrificing the very movement of life to the exclusive concern for truth" (Foucault 1971:96–97).

The parodic, dissociative, and sacrificial uses of history are designed to prevent Platonistic reification or what Foucault speaks of as consecration of the past. The uses in question foil claimed discernment of teleological development; they thwart "Whiggish" interpretation that reads prior events as culminating in the present state of affairs. History is no longer allowed to pretend that it is an exercise in recollection, that it goes back in time to recover something determinate and objective. In this way genealogy achieves nothing less than "a transformation of history into a totally different form of time" (Foucault 1971:93). That is, the past ceases to be a sort of frozen sequence of integrated, determinate events, and our historical narratives cease to be reports on such events made possible by the communal memory of written and oral records. Instead history becomes a present-tense exercise: Doing genealogy "means that I begin my analysis from a question posed in the present" (Foucault 1988b:262).

It is important to understand that the foregoing has less to do with history than with a picture of intellectual inquiry as essentially practices, the governing standards of which are thoroughly historical and the actual workings of which are masked from their participants. Those participants see their activities as regulated by ahistorical precepts and as ongoing discernment of truth and therefore as the acquisition of knowledge. Nor is that acquisition of knowledge deemed mere fact-gathering; instead it is seen as gradual augmentation of a growing and increasingly integrated accumulation of ultimately related discoveries. These discoveries are then seen as falling into various categories that correspond to and delineate proper subjects of inquiry and that are associated with appropriate disciplinary methods and standards. Against this backdrop of intellectual inquiry, genealogists try to show that the practices in question—history in particular and intellectual inquiry in general—discern nothing, discover nothing. Instead these practices manufacture their own subjects, their own content, and entrench themselves as self-serving traditions with no greater objective than survival. These practices achieve no egress beyond their own idioms and self-made subjects. Genealogists show that rather than ways of limning the world, these practices are woven-together and refined agglomerations of a myriad of repeated individual maneuvers that had their beginnings in widely varying responses to hugely diverse incidents and situations. Weaving these numerous maneuvers together into established practices is expert discourse. Discourse provides the context in which these maneuvers congeal into learned dialects and procedures; discourse then facilitates extension of the ranges of those dialects and of the jurisdictions of those procedures.

In the picture that emerges, truth is not how things are and knowledge is not achieved perception of how things are; rather, truth and knowledge are the highest-order value and the most elevated category in an established but transient practice or set of practices. In like manner, reason, or rationality, is not an extrahistorical absolute that defines a nature that can be instantiated and determines the essences of coherency and cogency. Instead reason and rationality are terms or notions that function as accolades and shibboleths in a practice or set of practices. As in the case of all other derisive and ironic historical beginnings, the generative sources of truth, knowledge, reason, and rationality are lowly (Foucault 1971:79).

Chapters 4 and 5 discuss what makes Foucault's vision—of truth, knowledge, and rationality as the contingent results of unrelated events—something other than an immediately dismissible academic lunacy. But at this point a methodological or strategic point should be clear: Foucault does not add arguments to his exegesis of "Nietzsche, Genealogy, History." He presents the picture Nietzsche painted; rather than working through point-by-point rebuttals of traditional history's claims, we can discern a holistic impeachment of traditional history's synthesizing priorities, its attempts to assimilate individual events into progressions, and its preparedness to count as significant only those events that can be so assimilated. The article's indictment of traditional, synthesizing, essentialist history is achieved by instantiating a serious alternative to the traditional conception of history. The strategy or method in "Nietzsche, Genealogy, History" is typical of Foucault. His strategy of providing alternatives is perhaps most briefly captured in "Two Lectures," where he focuses less on redescribing history itself and more on unearthing "popular knowledges" that traditional history has "disqualified" and placed "beneath the required level of cognition or scientificity" (Foucault 1980b:82). Disqualified or suppressed knowledges constitute particular alternatives to what is accepted as properly intellectual and truly scientific, so their notice is disruptive of disciplinary history. By calling attention to suppressed knowledges, Foucault demonstrates that synthesizing history continually obscures lores and practices to maintain and enhance continuity, again indicting by example rather than with detailed arguments, in the process supplying a plausible alternative to traditional historical accounts.

In posing a philosophical challenge simply by providing an alternative construal of history, "Nietzsche, Genealogy, History" is what Rorty calls redescription in a new vocabulary, rather than provision of a new theory competing on issues of truth with what it seeks to supplant. Such redescription highlights the difficulties in what it challenges, presents itself as a productive construal, and invites uptake and development. Foucault's redescription of history renders the claimed status of traditional synthesizing history problematic, by highlighting the discontinuities that that history tries to gloss, and provides an alternative account of the unstable syntheses traditional history offers. But we are not dealing only with mere possibility of uptake and development. There are those who argue that history has become widely genealogical in practice, if not in name (Szeman 1993).

A New Analytic or an Old Relativism?

Given my intended readers' philosophical framework, some may already be disaffected by what has been said about Foucault and genealogy. This section, therefore, is devoted to some metaphilosophical points by which I hope to convince even the most resistant readers to accept, at least provisionally, that genealogy is neither surreptitious nor disingenuous ahistorical theorizing nor hopeless one-view-is-as-good-as-another relativism.

Foucauldian genealogical analysis usually frustrates its opponents because it seems to violate all philosophical rules of engagement by daring to target reason and truth and thus what supports those rules. However, it is not violation; it is usurpation. The point of genealogical analyses is not to engage but to displace what they oppose through redescription. When the objective is to rethink something in its entirety, there can be no advantage gained in piecemeal polemical engagement that tacitly sanctions what is to be rethought. Failure to appreciate this strategic fact leads to the sort of misunderstanding that we saw in the condemnation of Derrida's tactics. The most common negative response to genealogical analysis is to claim that redescription of fundamental ideas and methods ignores, contravenes, and/or flouts the standards of reasoned inquiry itself. Nor is this response surprising. Those who find their disciplines and canons redescribed out from under them, and who in addition find themselves being admonished not to apply their methods and standards to the undermining redescriptions, seem to have no option but to cry foul.

As a holistic critic, Foucault has no option but redescription, for his goal is not to modify but to displace the views and traditions he opposes. The trick is to offer redescriptions that are recognized as challenges to the views and traditions he critiques. As Rorty notes in connection with his own critical work, the role of holistic critics of the philosophical tradition is a difficult one, for they must try "to find ways of making antiphilosophical points in nonphilosophical language." The reason is that they "face a dilemma: if their language is too unphilosophical, too 'literary,' they will be accused of changing the subject"; if their language "is too philosophical it will embody Platonic assumptions" (Rorty 1982:xiv). Holistic critics must balance on a knife-edge in order to articulate their critiques in a recognizably relevant manner without adopting the language, and hence too much of the doctrines and conventions, of the opposition. Holistic critics gain nothing if they engage in polemics that grant the traditions they oppose legitimacy by conducting debate in the idioms of those traditions.

But therein lies a potentially paralyzing impasse, because those whose traditions are criticized and redescribed may fail or refuse to recognize the critique and redescription as cogent if not assessable by what they consider universal established standards. Philosophers are particularly prone to reach this impasse because they consider their disciplinary standards to be the embodiment of a rationality that allows no alternatives. For instance, Hilary Putnam argues against historicizing reason by claiming that historical standards "cannot define what reason is" because historical standards "presuppose reason ... for their interpretation" (Putnam 1987:227). Philosophers consider rationality to be "a regulative idea" that governs all inquiry and so enables us "to criticize the conduct of all activities and institutions" (Putnam 1987:228). Foucault charges those who take this position with "blackmail" and with reacting to "every critique of reason or every critical inquiry into the history of rationality" with imposition of a falsely exclusive dichotomy by arguing that "either you accept rationality or you fall prey to the irrational" (Foucault 1988b:27). But Foucault's charge does not resolve the impasse; it only intensifies it. The impasse, then, again raises the question about the status of genealogy and the cogency of its accounts and analyses.

Foucault rethinks not only history but also reason, rationality, truth, and knowledge, denying that they are anything other than historical, practice-generated standards and procedures. What does Foucault see that makes him think he can offer historicizing but still cogent critiques of reason, rationality, truth, and knowledge? How can his inevitably reflexive analysis of reasoning conclude that reasoning's regulative principles are historical products yet claim compelling intellectual import for that conclusion? Rorty, like Habermas and Hoy, doubts that Foucault managed to keep his analytics wholly historicist. We saw that Rorty re-gards Foucault's archaeology, conceived of as an essence-unearthing ac-tivity, as no more than a replacement for epistemology. As for genealogy, Rorty is concerned that it, along with all postmodernist critiques, may be vitiated by an inability to expose false appearances while disavowing commitment to hidden realities (Rorty 1986; 1991c). As archaeology generates a dilemma by seeming to require exemption from historicism, the genealogical historicization of reason, rationality, truth, and knowl-edge seems to generate the same dilemma because of the apparent im-possibility of conforming to the historicist conception of genealogy without demoting its analyses to just so many more historically contin-gent accounts on a par with those they oppose.

In our brief consideration of Rortyan ironism a serious question emerged: why an account or assessment's being historically contingent should mean that the account or assessment is somehow inherently less worthy than if it were ahistorical. If we cannot have recourse to external standards to choose among contingent accounts, we have no alternative but to be ironists. But there is a way of dealing with the question that precedes the embracing of ironism, and it is a maneuver both Foucault and Rorty implement. Rorty construes historicist critiques not as offer-ing replacement theories but instead as obstructing synthetic theoriz-ing. The point is to reverse priorities, to reject ahistorical theories as the idealized objectives of reasoned inquiry, and accept contingent ac-counts as the norm. If contingent accounts are the norm, then they will not appear to be less worthy than ahistoric theories. The main task, therefore, is to impugn the possibility of ahistoric theories.

This is precisely what Foucauldian genealogy tries to do. As we have seen, Foucault contends that all we can do in intellectual inquiry is to trace the descent and emergence of both what we theorize about and what we use to theorize. Whatever we might conclude about his archae-ology, this theory-blocking reading of Foucault's genealogy is the most productive one. We see that the "demotion" of genealogical analyses to historically contingent accounts is not a demotion at all; it is instead ac-knowledgment of the impossibility of discernment of ahistoric truth.

Neither Foucault nor Rorty can allow their theory-obstructing conten-tions and redescriptions to be taken as so many moves in the theorizing game, as provision of alternative theories. That would be to illegiti-mately exempt themselves from historicity. Rorty maintains that, when pragmatists propose "we not ask questions about ... truth" they are not offering some " 'relativistic' or 'subjectivist' theory of Truth"; rather prag-matists "would simply like to change the subject" (Rorty 1982:xliii). Fou-cault's genealogical analyses are changes of subjects from theoretical proposals about underlying continuities to descriptions of putatively exhaustive surface discontinuities. Foucault does not offer competing theories; he offers redescription that reveals the pointlessness of theorizing. He is not, therefore, surreptitiously exempting himself from historicity. Foucault offers a new perspective that, by showing theories to be historical products, shows their inability to achieve the objectivity that is their main reason for being. If we take holistic critics like Foucault or Dewey as offering competing theories about truth or knowledge, about reason or rationality, "we shall get them wrong. We shall ignore their criticisms of the assumption that there ought to be theories about such matters" (Rorty 1982:161).

We can now see how Foucault thinks himself able to step back from reason, rationality, truth, and knowledge and still offer cogent redescriptions of them. Recognizing that he does not offer competing theories helps us to understand how Foucault thinks "a rational critique of rationality" and a "contingent history of reason" are possible (Foucault 1988b:27). What enables Foucault's historicization of reason, rationality, truth, and knowledge is profound appreciation of what was "glimpsed at the end of the eighteenth century," which was "that anything could be made to look good or bad, important or unimportant, useful or useless, by being redescribed" (Rorty 1989:7).

What started as a glimpse of the potency of redescription developed until it "became possible, toward the end of the nineteenth century, to ... juggle several descriptions ... without asking which one was right." It became possible "to see redescription as a tool rather than a claim to have discovered essence" (Rorty 1989:39). Redescriptions came to be not exclusively competing accounts but inclusively alternative ones that, instead of vying with one another for unique correctness, came to be assessed relative to particular purposes. Redescription escaped the boundaries set by the bivalent logic that is the judicial branch of the regime of traditional rationality. Encountering two descriptions ceased to be a matter of having to choose between them. At the heart of redescriptions ceasing to be mutually exclusive competitors was the legacy of Kant's abandonment of the Platonic/Cartesian idea that description is always of something autonomous that remains unaffected by how it is described. Rorty contends that once we move from Plato to Kant, once "the realist conception of objects waiting around to be accurately represented goes, then nothing is left save utility" (Rorty 1984).

Once the objectivity of representation was abandoned, doubts soon arose about the objectivity of reason and rationality. It then became possible to speculate about how reason and rationality might be differently described with respect to different sets of interests and purposes. It is the possibility of juggling redescriptions without obligation to decisively choose among them, or the hard idea that alternative descriptions might not be necessarily mutually exclusive, that make Foucault's vision possible. But this idea looks to many observers like relativism, and so as ultimately irrealist or idealist denial of an objective world.

Foucault is not an idealist or irrealist. Put at its crudest, when he denies that history chronicles objective events or, as we shall see, denies that we have an objective sexual nature, what he denies is not the world, but that the world plays an epistemic role in the justification of what we say about it. Brute reality is not at issue; it cannot be at issue if we reject Cartesian epistemology's conception of reality as mediated by always problematic representational ideas. At issue is what determines the correctness of what we say, and it is not the world, as the sum of objective essences, that determines the correctness of what we say. Foucault maintains that we must "substitute for ... 'things' anterior to discourse, the regular formation of objects that emerge only in discourse" (Foucault 1972:47). Justificatory factors are always internal to discourse, are always intralinguistic, and here Foucault concurs with an unlikely ally, Davidson, who insists that "[n]othing ... no *thing*, makes sentences and theories true: not experience, ... not the world, can make a sentence true" (Davidson, D. 1984:194).

What, then, becomes of philosophical debate? In offering philosophical redescriptions Foucault aspires to be what Harold Bloom calls a strong poet—a thinker who redefines himself or herself in new terms, who invents new metaphors, and so provides a new vocabulary for the rest of us. Strong poets are the creators of new logical spaces wherein fresh thoughts can be thought and familiar things redescribed (Rorty 1991c). They are the innovators who enable us to accomplish things not previously imaginable in our old vocabularies (Bloom 1973:80). Plato and Descartes were successful strong poets; they invented vocabularies that made possible traditional metaphysics and epistemology, which are still largely in use. Isaac Newton, Albert Einstein, and Sigmund Freud were equally successful strong poets. Karl Marx was also a strong poet, though his new vocabulary proved shorter-lived than its initial success promised. Each of these thinkers provided a vision that initiated the sort of radically new holistic perspective that, in science, Kuhn calls a new paradigm. And as with scientific paradigms, the core of each proffered vision was not assessable by the methods and criteria integral to the vision it replaced.

Though philosophical argumentation proceeds according to normal practices within a given paradigm, when philosophizing is a matter of offering a new vision, of proposing a novel holistic perspective of the sort Wilfrid Sellars describes as saying, in the most general way, how things hang together, in the most general way, then overcoming resistance to a proposal cannot be a matter of marshaling decisive arguments. Instead, "rebutting objections to one's redescriptions of some things will be largely a matter of redescribing other things." The strategy must be "to try to make the vocabulary in which these objections are phrased look bad, ... rather than granting the objector his choice of weapons and terrain by meeting his criticisms head-on" (Rorty 1989:44). Philosophical debate, then, becomes what Foucault offers in the two books we will consider in chapters to follow and in the article just discussed. That is, philosophical debate becomes detailed presentation of a perspective or redescription in the expectation that it will prove more useful to us than those it is intended to replace.

Of course all of this looks hopelessly untenable to analytic philosophers and many others; it looks like reduction of intellectual disputation to no more than a swapping of stories or what John Caputo calls "just talk" (Caputo 1983). Additionally, I am compounding the problem by closely relating Foucault and Rorty, in using the latter to clarify the ideas of the former. Many of my readers are likely to be even more negatively disposed to Rorty than to the less familiar Foucault. But in spite of contrary views, I think the assimilation justified and enlightening (compare Norris 1994). However distasteful to some, the point is well put by Rorty, who observes: Once we understand "that there is no standpoint outside [a] particular historically conditioned and temporary vocabulary ... from which to judge this vocabulary," we have to give up "the idea that intellectual ... progress is rational, in any sense of 'rational' which is neutral between vocabularies" (Rorty 1989:48). The hard fact is that philosophy has no way of evading the paradox of reflexivity, no ground on which to stand while it assesses the rationality of its own history or standards or of new visions or redescriptions. Philosophy is simply no longer capable of maintaining itself as self-appointed adjudicator of reason, because we have finally understood that it does not have recourse to objective correctness-criteria. This is why Foucault finds that there is now "something ludicrous" about philosophy when it tries "to dictate to others, to tell them where their truth is and how to find it" (Foucault 1986:8–9). Rorty agrees wholeheartedly, saying that "philosophy makes itself ridiculous" when fundamental interpretive issues arise and "it steps forward ... to adjudicate" (Rorty 1989:51).

There has been no demise of modernity, assuming there is a holistic way of thinking so describable (Latour 1993). Nonetheless, we can no longer do philosophy on the assumption that at least some of our standards are ahistorical. Foucault saw this decades ago, and he saw his only viable intellectual option to be genealogical analysis and redescription of disciplines, institutions, methodologies, and reasoned inquiry's most sacrosanct principles.

4 The Formation of the Subject

The briefest thing to be said about *Discipline and Punish* is that it is about how certain people who were subjects of a sovereign became subjects of a new kind. The people in question were lawbreakers, malefactors, criminals—those who were apprehended and punished for contravening the sovereign's laws. They became and continue to be individuals who, having contravened the laws of societies having modern legal structures, undergo complex processing in institutionalized judicial and penal systems that center on the incarceration of offenders. *Discipline and Punish* is ostensibly about the change from lawful punishment as brutal monarchical vengeance to lawful punishment as humanized deterrence and rehabilitation. What the book is really about is the production of subjects through the imposition of disciplines; it is about how the process of constant observation, assessment, and control of inmates in the modern penitentiary manufactures new subjects through the employment of management techniques that intrude into and govern every aspect of life. But what makes *Discipline and Punish* more than a study of penality is its portrayal of techniques employed in the manufacture of these new subjects as those more widely used in the production of the contemporary norm-governed social individual.

As stressed earlier, Foucault's point of departure in rethinking a subject-matter is to impugn the commonplace, to query accepted knowledge. In applying genealogy to penality, Foucault impugns the commonplace view that our present penitentiary-centered penal system is the result of the progressive humanization of earlier, more ruthless methods of retributive punishment. Foucault begins by discussing how spectacular public punishments and executions constituted standard procedure for dealing with lawbreakers in the European monarchical order to roughly the mid-eighteenth century. He then considers two notable changes that took place: punishment and execution came to be conducted within official enclosures, and incarceration in penitentiaries emerged as the chief means of punishment and deterrence. Foucault challenges the accepted view that these changes were due to an increasingly humane attitude toward criminals. He offers an alternative account of how and why treatment of criminals ceased to be public, and of how and why the penitentiary, an establishment without strong precedents at the time, emerged as the favored institutional device for dealing with lawbreakers.

At the heart of Foucault's alternative account is characterization of what he calls "disciplines" or what can be glossed as techniques for managing people. His point is that disciplinary or managerial techniques were initiated and developed into a technology for the control of individuals. The new techniques continued to operate on the body, as had monarchical torture, but they did so by imposing schedules, restrictions, obligatory comportment, and examinations. In contrast to their brutal predecessors, the new techniques did not inflict violence on the body. Instead of inflicting pain, the new techniques instilled controlling habits and value-sustaining self-images. But keep in mind that though these techniques developed in the context of penality, the intent actually was less redress or rehabilitation than the increase of universalizable, efficient subjugation and control. And instead of remaining unique to the burgeoning penal system, the disciplinary techniques in question proliferated in all institutions involving the management of large numbers of people: the convent, the school, the barracks, the hospital, the factory (Foucault 1979:135–228).

Foucault considers the exclusionary institutional treatment of the newly defined insane in *Madness and Civilization* and the exclusionary institutional treatment of the variously afflicted in *The Birth of the Clinic* (Foucault 1965, 1975). But in *Discipline and Punish* Foucault's real focus in considering exclusionary institutions emerges most clearly. That focus is a putative knowledge of the body that is not limited to "the science of its functioning." The knowledge in question goes beyond investigation and even control of the body as an organism to "what might be called the political technology of the body" (Foucault 1979:26). The aim of this technology is not mere control, as in the effective imposition of restrictions and prohibitions, but rather pervasive management gained through enabling as well as restrictive conceptions, definitions, and descriptions that generate and support behavior-governing norms. This kind and degree of management requires the complicity of those managed in a way not imagined in the era of monarchical dominion, because it demands not only obedience to laws and commandments, but what is more clearly thematized in *The History of Sexuality*—the deep internalization of a carefully orchestrated value-laden understanding of the self.

Development of the Political Technology

Discipline and Punish begins with a horrendous account of the drawing-and-quartering of a regicide, an account made even more ghastly because the victim was fully conscious and had to have some sinews and tendons partially severed before the horses could tear his body apart. Foucault spares no detail and recounts the execution in a detached academic manner that makes his description all the more gruesome. The point of the story is to show how the person was a juridical subject on whom monarchical power was brought to bear in a hideous but legal exercise of restitution and reestablishment of authority.

Public punishment, consisting of torture and maiming (mutilation, branding, and cutting off of the hands), and public execution (hanging, beheading, and drawing-and-quartering) were routine in the exercise of monarchical power, serving both to punish transgressions against the sovereign's laws and, even more important, to "reconstitute" the defied sovereign's power. But public retributive punishment of those who defied the sovereign's laws was not a customary, though lamentable, abuse of monarchical power; it was quite legal. The carrying out of retribution on a given transgressor was a fearsome but legitimate display of total domination. The transgressor was broken or killed as a subject of the offended sovereign or, in effect, as the property of the sovereign. The display thus served to warn others that they were vulnerable to the same retributive treatment and reminded them that they were vulnerable because they too were subjects.

Sometime during the mid- to late seventeenth century the practice of public torture and execution began to decline. The common view is that the changes were due to an increasingly enlightened and humane perception of lawbreakers. Foucault's central claim is that the changes had nothing to do with growing enlightenment and humanization, but rather with a basic reconception of the lawbreaker, which was part of the growth of a new management-oriented conception of human beings. This conception centered on exercising control not through violence and the threat of violence, but through reconfiguration of the subject or redefinition of subjectivity.

The new conception of the subject involves two separate aspects. The first aspect is the status of the subject, as subjugated by or dependent on another or others (Foucault 1983a:212). The second aspect is the experience of subjectivity, not in the sense of sheer sentience, but in the sense of being defined as an intentional being by one's self-knowledge, by one's awareness or image of who and what one is (Foucault 1983a:212). Throughout Foucault's discussions of "subjectivity," particularly in his genealogical works, the notion is at once inclusive of and deliberately ambiguous between how one is a subject as a member of a governed society and how one is a subject in being an entity with a specific belief-defined identity.

Foucault provides a welter of factual material in tracing the change from harshly retributive to subject-defining punishment. This material is the substance of the genealogical account of the development of the prison and the reconception of those imprisoned. Unfortunately, it also may limit productive interpretation of *Discipline and Punish* by making it appear only as a kind of contrary socio-historical account of the development of the contemporary penal system. Foucault can be plausibly read as offering an account that challenges the established account that attributes the development of the penitentiary-based penal system to reform due to a change in the perception of criminals from being the property of the sovereign to being subjects owed a measure of humane consideration. But if read in this way, Foucault is taken as arguing only that penality changed not because of a genuine humane regard for the criminals it processes but because of vested interests operating covertly behind a mask of humaneness. As will become clear, this possible but limited interpretation seriously distorts Foucault's notion of power by attributing the changes in penality to concealed or conspiratorial agency.

Foucault contends that a "soul" was introduced into legal and penal proceedings as an integral part of the reconception of subjectivity (Foucault 1979:29). The claim is that a whole new dimension of personhood is invented in making possible new kinds of control not previously envisaged. The soul, then, is not a recognized basic humanity or new or revitalized ontological notion, but something "born ... out of methods of punishment, supervision and constraint" (Foucault 1979:29). The production of the soul in the context of the development of penality is not recognition of anything; it is a shift from a premodern to a modern conception of the self. The manufacture of the soul constitutes a conceptual shift from a self defined by familial, social, and political roles and possessed of the identity-determining immortal soul of religion, to a self defined by Cartesian autonomy and inwardness and one that is wholly self-determining. The modern self is one that contains the ground of intentional consciousness as an inherent property; it is a self that is "self-constituting" in being itself "the source or agent of all meaning" (Marshall 1992:82). The result is that the modern self is an irreducible node to which beliefs and affective states are ascribed; it is the ultimate source of action. Given this conception, it then becomes possible and necessary to shape the self through discipline in a way that it will regularly initiate the right sorts of actions. The way to achieve this end is to imbue the self with the right sorts of beliefs and affective states. *Discipline and Punish* portrays how disciplines developed to imbue selves with the right beliefs and affective states.

Foucault's focus on the introduction of the soul is an attempt to show that the self is not a singularity, a self-sufficient Cartesian ego overlaid with beliefs and intentions and located at the heart of action. Foucault wants to show that the modern self is a construct, a product of precisely those techniques that supposedly only shape it. In *The Archaeology of Knowledge* Foucault speaks of wanting to "cleanse" history of "transcendental narcissism" (Foucault 1972:203). In *Power/Knowledge,* he maintains that "the individual is not a pre-given entity" and that "we must rid ourselves of the constituting subject, rid ourselves of the subject itself." He contends that we must produce "an analysis which can account for the subject itself within an historical account" (Foucault 1980b:73,117).

For Foucault, the subject is something to be understood as an historical product, as emergent. There could not be, then, discernment or acknowledgment of the soul in the process of humanizing penality. Instead, the process of changing penality contributed to the creation of the modern self in that "the subject" is a product of discourse. Rather than the subject being prior to discourse, the subject emerges in discourse. Rather than being "the majestically unfolding manifestation of a thinking, knowing, speaking subject," discourse is the generative context in which the subject arises. Once this is understood, discourse is seen as "a totality, in which the dispersion of the subject and his discontinuity from himself may be determined" (Foucault 1972:55). When we understand what we are actually doing in speaking as we do about people, by attending to the discontinuities genealogy uncovers, we appreciate that "the subject" is what we say it is. This is clearly a philosophical view of the self; it is not a socio-historical account of the recognition of some basic humanity.

It is crucial for readers with an analytic background, and hence certain philosophical expectations, to appreciate that Foucault is not doing metaphysics or philosophy of mind in focusing on subjectivity, at least not in any straightforward sense of contributing to ongoing debates. If he is doing metaphysics or philosophy of mind, it is in a "deflationary" way, because he wants to block ontological theorizing and deal with questions about the self in genealogical terms. His interest in the historicity of the subject is not an interest in familiar ontological issues about the self or self-identity. The decentralizing of the subject and dissipation of apparent unity and totality has to do with the locus of power and with denial of traditional philosophy's monolithic subject as the bearer of cognitive and affective attributes and as the initiator of action. For Foucault, subjectivity is not, as it is for Descartes and Kant, a "given" that is the condition of everything cognitive, affective, and behavioral. That is why Foucault insists that it is the body that bears subjectivity or is the "locus of a dissociated self" that adopts or comes under "the illusion of [being] a substantial unity" (Foucault 1971:82). It is the body, in its habits and gestures, in its postures, in its speech, in how it is dealt with, that bears the emergent subjectivity that is the multifaceted total effect of regulating discourses. The disciplined body is logically prior to subjectivity. The task, therefore, is not to establish the nature of the self and to articulate that nature in a philosophical theory, but rather "to expose a body totally imprinted by history" (Foucault 1971:83).

As noted earlier, Foucault's concern with the subject is such that in his revisionary retrospectives of his own work, articulated largely in explanatory asides and self-commentary in interviews, he claims that his goal over two decades was not to "analyze the phenomena of power," but rather to "create a history of the different modes by which, in our culture, human beings are made subjects" (Foucault 1983a:208–09). Foucault's efforts to present his work as more homogeneous, coherent, and focused than it was should be judiciously assessed, but the subject or subjectivity is unquestionably a focal point of the texts we are considering. This caution must be taken seriously: "the subject" here is not the entity figuring in debates in the philosophy of mind or ontology; it is something that is at once what is produced in and borne by a disciplined body and something held in the sway of institutionalized authority. Keeping this in mind, we can now look at *Discipline and Punish* in more detail.

Unlike "Nietzsche, Genealogy, History" and *The History of Sexuality*, *Discipline and Punish* does not lend itself to systematic exposition because of the detail it contains. Miller says of *Madness and Civilization* that "the author's own convictions are insinuated more than argued, ... leaving an impression that outweighs page after page of detailed, often intricate historical documentation" (Miller 1993:98). This is even more true of *Discipline and Punish* than of *Madness and Civilization*. In both books Foucault's philosophical points are embedded in massively detailed historical discussion. *Discipline and Punish* is full of often wearisome discussion of legal procedures, the efforts of particular penal reformers, the French, English, and American penal systems, and even of architectural plans for the construction of schools, prisons, and other institutions. Foucault even provides illustrations of discipline-enhancing features of schools and prisons and of disciplinary devices such as spanking machines (Foucault 1979: ten "figures" inserted between pages 169–170). My strategy here will be to discuss the text only in general terms, stressing what is of greatest relevance to understanding Foucault's project and devoting a full section to consideration of what permeates *Discipline and Punish:* Foucauldian power.

The Birth of the Prison

Discipline and Punish is in three parts, the first two concerned with torture and punishment, the third with discipline. To cite an example of how philosophical points are buried in detailed discussions, in a passage that looks like a prelude to a socio-historical treatise, Foucault claims that during the time the penal system established "by the great codes of the eighteenth and nineteenth centuries" has been in operation, "a general process has led judges to judge something other than crimes" (Foucault 1979:22). At first glance this may look like an observation that judges increasingly considered social factors involved in the commission of crimes. But the point is considerably more important than it appears. In fact, it is central to the book.

Discipline and Punish is about changes in penality that led to "a whole new system of truth." The book, in describing the development of that new system of truth, is a "history of the modern soul and of a new power to judge" (Foucault 1979:23). The claim about the changed nature of judgment does not have to do with criminal acts coming to be judged in more socially responsible ways. The claim is that the focus of judgments became "souls" rather than acts. Foucault describes the notion of a soul as "the correlative of a technique of power" (Foucault 1979:101). The soul is a manipulable representation that facilitates control well beyond physical domination. The soul is the mind conceived or reconceived "as a surface of inscription for power, with semiology as its tool." The notion of the soul facilitates "the submission of bodies through the control of ideas" (Foucault 1979:102). Judges came to assess not particular crimes but the perpetrators of those crimes. Souls were judged not just by the severity of their crimes, but in how they were to be managed, manipulated, and controlled to contain and eradicate desires and behavior deemed unacceptable in comparison to the behavior of the privileged model, the "normal" person.

The changes in penality also included reconception of the lawbreaker, from someone who defied the authority of a sovereign to someone who defied the authority of society. Punishment accordingly underwent reconception from "the vengeance of the sovereign" to "the defence of society" (Foucault 1979:90). Most important about this latter reconception is that punishment came to be less a retributive practice than "a procedure for requalifying individuals as subjects." Unlike retributive monarchical punishment, disciplinary punishment is "essentially *corrective*" (Foucault 1979:130,179). Modern punishment "*normalizes*" (Foucault 1979:183). When the lawbreaker is perceived as threatening society, as opposed to defying a sovereign, correction and deterrence come to be seen as less a matter of inflicting compensatory and authority-reconstituting suffering than of rehabilitating the lawbreaker and thereby better serving society. This is how normalizing judgment is not limited to court-presiding judicial agents of society; the "judges of normality are present everywhere." Our society includes "the teacher-judge, the doctor-judge, the educator-judge, the 'social worker'-judge," and it is on all of these agents of society "that the universal reign of the normative is based" (Foucault 1979:304).

It is with mention of a privileged paradigm, the normal person, that we encounter a characteristic Foucauldian methodological ploy, namely, his calling attention to the important role of exclusionary "binary division" in the conceptions operant in the changes he chronicles. Foucault contends that "all the authorities exercising individual control function according to ... binary division and branding" (Foucault 1979:199). In *Madness and Civilization* the division and branding is between the sane and insane; in *The Birth of the Clinic* it is between the healthy and unhealthy; in *Discipline and Punish*, and even more clearly in *The History of Sexuality*, it is between the normal and abnormal.

Given the binary division among normal and abnormal, how is the "universal reign of the normative" implemented? How does it mold the disciplined subject? How is the self imbued with the right beliefs and affective states? The basic idea presented in *Discipline and Punish* of how the subject is shaped is surprisingly simple, and it can be literally made concrete through construction of Jeremy Bentham's ideal prison or "Panopticon."

The idea embodied in the panopticon is that "the fact of being constantly seen, of being able always to be seen ... maintains the disciplined individual in his subjugation" (Foucault 1979:187). In Bentham's ideal prison, inmates are always observable to watchers who are not visible to the inmates. Though inmates know that they cannot be constantly watched, they also know that they may be under observation anytime. Therefore, because they do not know when they are in fact being watched, they can only behave as if watched constantly. The practical effect is the same as constant surveillance. Therefore the panopticon embodies the realization that the only prudent course of action in the face of possible ever-present observation is behaving as if in fact always observed.

Foucault's embellishment of Bentham's idea is that surveillance can turn submission to directives into conformity with norms. That is, panopticism can transmute calculated obedience of regulations into a habitual compliance with norms that comes to constitute adoption of those norms. This embellishment is an excellent example of Foucault's ability to see and show how physical, regulatory, and/or judicial confinement becomes the confinement of values, beliefs, and self-identity. It is part of Foucault's genius "to discover and describe the confinements that imprison human life and thought" (Bernauer, J. 1993:6).

Compliance with and adoption of norms concern us most, because the disciplinary techniques described in *Discipline and Punish* constitute the model for methods of control that came to be operant well beyond the penitentiary's walls. Yet widespread use of disciplinary techniques should not be thought of as merely an expansion of the use of those techniques, in the sense that procedures found to work well in the penitentiary were applied elsewhere. Rather, it results from the invention of the (modern) soul, of the reconception of the subject. And it is precisely that, not success in the penal system, that causes the disciplinary techniques Foucault describes to work in the school, the hospital, the factory, and society at large.

To understand this, one must discern that the disciplined penitentiary inmate is not only made and kept obedient by being overseen, but is made a specific sort of person by being imbued with certain beliefs and habits that define a new subjectivity. Recall the dual-aspect nature and deliberate ambiguity of Foucault's notion of the subject: To be a subject is to be subjugated, to be "subject to someone else by control and dependence"; to be a subject is also to have one's identity defined "by a conscience or self-knowledge" (Foucault 1983a:212). The immediately relevant connection is that the subject, in its subjugation, is made to adopt a certain construal of his or her thoughts and actions and so of his or her very self. The subject's "conscience or self-knowledge" is an imposed one, but it is a construal that the individual experiences as what he or she *is*. Adoption of that construal is definition or redefinition of one's subjectivity. In the particular case of penality, an inmate, aware of having been judged, sentenced, and incarcerated, is also aware of being the object of legitimate categorization, study, and assessment. The inmate becomes a person on whom there is a definitive dossier, a person about whom certain experts know a great deal more than he or she does, a person who is a particular sort of felon, a person who is abnormal— and so a person who requires retributive and rehabilatory treatment.

The identity-defining role of disciplinary techniques clarifies how the soul as discussed in *Discipline and Punish* is not some basic humanity, recognition of which drove the development of modern penality. The soul upon which judgment bears is something new: "unlike the soul represented by Christian theology," the soul in question is "not born in sin and subject to punishment, but is born rather out of methods of punishment, supervision and constraint" (Foucault 1979:29). The very methods for supposedly treating criminals more humanely create a soul that, as a manipulable representation or "correlative of power," can then be assessed and managed beyond the mere imposition of physical con-straints on the body. It is through management of souls that "discipline produces subjected and practised bodies, 'docile' bodies" (Foucault 1979:138).

With respect to specifics regarding how souls are managed and docile bodies produced, Foucault describes interwoven developments during the early evolution of the modern penitentiary-centered penal system. He offers reasons why public torture and execution began to decline and why punitive measures were concealed behind the walls of official buildings, which then symbolized the threat and power of the processes they sheltered. Foucault notes that public punishment could be a risky occasion; spectacles like that detailed in the opening to *Discipline and Punish* could precipitate a conflict of wills between the sovereign and the people if the person being punished was popular or represented what was perceived as merited opposition to the sovereign (Foucault 1979:73). Additionally, there were genuine efforts made by humanitarian reformers. It is not Foucault's intent to deny that these occurred; his concern is to show what these efforts actually achieved, regardless of the intentions that drove them. There were also economic reasons for the development of the penitentiary, such as the increasing reliance on pris-ons for cheap labor. And there were changes of administrative and pro-cedural sorts, such as the nature and importance of evidence, the man-ner of eliciting and treating confessions, and the invention of the police as a force separate from the sovereign's armed retinues. The last change marked a critical shift of emphasis from enforcement of laws to surveil-lance.

Foucault offers a list of five devices, used during the development of the prison and other institutions, that dealt with significant populations gathered into a compact space. They are hierarchical observation, nor-malizing judgment, the examination, panopticism, and surveillance. These devices can only function in the context of an institution, such as a school, industrial plant, prison, or asylum. To be effective, discipline "requires *enclosure*, ... a place heterogeneous to all others and closed in upon itself" (Foucault 1979:141). Whether the place be a monastery, cor-poration, hospital, factory, school, or prison, observation and discipline of large groups require that they be gathered and restricted to a given place for significant periods of time. They must also be constantly aware of a localized seat of authority—the principal's or warden's office, "up-stairs," the administration wing, the executive suite.

Hierarchical observation means physically structuring institutions to maximize visual and/or auditory access by those with greater authority and responsibility over those with less authority. An example is tiered work-areas, where increased height affords oversight from a given level over echelons below. Normalizing judgment, the second device, is negative assessment of individuals or groups that turns not on outright criticism or condemnation, but on invidious comparisons with a favored paradigm real or imagined. An example is the glorification of a work-team or other cohort as a model of high morale and productivity. The third device, examination, is the requirement and application of all manner of tests, usually presented as ways of enabling those tested to achieve their full potential and of enabling the managing authorities to treat those tested in the most appropriate and supposedly beneficial manner.

Panopticism, as sketched previously, is implementation of the idea embodied in Bentham's Panopticon, which is an ideally efficient prison designed as a hollow cylinder with an observation tower at its center. The cells are located in stories in the hollow cylinder; the inside and outside walls of each cell are made transparent, using glass or bars; the walls between cells as well as the floors and ceilings are opaque. Prisoners are thus isolated from each other while their every move is visible to guards in the central tower. The central tower has smoked windows or narrow observation slits, so prisoners in their cells never know when they are being observed. In this way a few guards can maintain surveillance over many prisoners. The device of surveillance is, of course, actual observation. But Foucault has in mind something more extensive, which includes the compiling of detailed reports and dossiers that track patterns of behavior and incorporate expert assessments, thereby providing bases for prediction of behavior and preemptive action.

Central to the foregoing devices is the idea best captured by panopticism—"being able always to be seen" keeps the disciplined individual subjugated (Foucault 1979:187). Initially observation is thought of in terms of agents of the relevant authority being empowered to conduct surveillance of those to be watched. But once the effectiveness of panopticism is appreciated, once it is seen that the ever-present possibility of observation works as well as constant surveillance to keep individuals subjugated because of what those under surveillance believe, it is a small step to realize that if the subject can be made complicitous in the surveillance through adoption of certain additional beliefs, that is, through the internalization of norms, then control may approach near-perfect completeness and efficiency. What follows is a shift in emphasis from the enforcement of rules and regulations to the inculcation of norms through disciplinary techniques. The objective then is to normalize individuals, to rehabilitate wrongdoers, to train productive members of society. What actually occurs is that new subjects are manufactured through disciplinary techniques.

Foucault maintains that the development and use of the disciplinary techniques caused the penal system to become more a place for "administering illegalities" than of attempting to eliminate them (Foucault 1979:89). This was not a matter of the authorities despairing of eliminating crime, or being overcome by cynicism, or using crime to serve their own purposes. Though all of these were to some extent true, the main point is that as penality developed into the imposition of increasingly elaborate administrative and management techniques, the techniques grew in complexity and sophistication and acquired a self-sustaining importance. The penal system came to be perceived as the institution best able to deal with what was in turn perceived as a deplorable but ineradicable subclass of individuals whose offending but ineliminable actions necessitated an effective means of control and containment.

In Part Three of *Discipline and Punish* Foucault considers models of disciplinary institutions to show how managerial practices contributed to make the prison the establishment it is today. One model (the Flemish) allowed the length of incarceration to be determined by administrators in light of inmate conduct, involved obligatory but remunerated labor, and relied on continual supervision and strict timetabling to instill good habits to aid rehabilitation. Another model (the English) also involved remunerated labor, supervision, and scheduling, but added isolation to offer the opportunity for reflection that was provided by the Christian monastic cell. A third model (the Philadelphian) again allowed administrative moderation of sentences, involved supervision, scheduling, and compulsory, individually rewarded labor, but used isolation for punishment and added a measure of confidentiality in that the judicial penalty was known only to the administration and the prisoner.

All were products of reform, and those who sought to reform penality were generally future-oriented in seeking controlled deterrence of recidivism and transformation of the criminal. There was, then, great emphasis on habit development and compulsory but remunerated labor. For reformers, punishment was not to be backward-looking and retributive, but productive and open to individual variables, such as inmate conduct, in order to better transform the criminal into a normal citizen by rewarding progress. But Foucault stresses that though reformers thought mainly in terms of abstractions of crime and of the criminal, corrective penality acted directly on the bodies of criminals; the model policies and methods were implemented as directives bearing on incarcerated bodies. Penality is thoroughly corporeal, using rigorous physical repetition of disciplinary routines and constraint to modify conduct. Whatever the abstract constructions and goals of the reformers, Foucault maintains that penality's objective is not the reformation of minds, but the production of "docile," obedient bodies (Foucault 1979:138).

The results of the development and implementation of the model policies and methods Foucault reviews round out a picture of a massive system for managing people excluded from society. But it is a system the reasons for which seem unrelated to their collective effect. Perhaps most notably, attempts to judge the conduct of persons, as opposed to only narrowly delineated illegal acts, led not to wiser and more productive assessment and treatment of lawbreakers, but to vastly more intrusive and extensive control of people than under the most powerful sovereigns. It appears that any development in the penal system bore little likeness to the design envisaged. Take the reform efforts just considered: the implementation of supposedly enlightened policies and methods did not result in inmates and parolees with more socially responsible attitudes and more productive habits, but merely docile bodies. Moreover, instead of the penal system correcting a societal problem, it provided the elements of all-pervasive societal control.

Foucault contrasts the "juridical" and "carceral" systems by cataloging devices central to each. The juridical system centered on the law, the courts, a juridical subject, definite offenses, and express juridical penalties articulated in sentences detailed as to punishment and duration. The key to the nature of the juridical system is the specificity of its elements. The law is, mainly, a series of prohibitions of carefully delineated acts; the courts operate under strictly defined procedures; the subject is presented to the court as an offender charged with a specified act or responsibility; offenses are circumscribed and defined and are articulated as unequivocal charges; penalties are specified or stipulated within fairly narrow ranges; and sentencing consists of exacting specific demands for specified periods of time. Most important, once an individual is sentenced and imprisoned, exacting demands is a matter of meeting rather minimal requirements: keeping the individual jailed for the assigned term, administering the assigned punishment, collecting the determined fine, and so on. Beyond this, there is little concern with how the inmate responds to the process so long as he or she conforms adequately to prison and parole regulations.

The modern carceral system, centering on the penitentiary, relies on devices that have a far greater impact on the inmate. First, it relies on devices bearing on how inmates are handled: politico-moral isolation (the cell, strict supervision), compulsory labor (daily chores, the workshop), and techno-medical normalization (the infirmary, "corrective" counseling). Second, it relies on devices that presuppose a theoretical basis for treatment of inmates: "disciplinary rationality" or the transformation of the premodern juridical subject into the modern psychological subject. This constitutes transformation of the juridical subject guilty of specific offenses into a delinquent characterized by an abnormal case history.

Third, it relies on devices having to do with organization: inmate and parolee populations comprising different classes of offenders (juvenile, petty, serious) and being grouped together physically or by level of police supervision (prison guards, parole officers). Fourth, the carceral system relies on reform movements operating within the system. Finally, it relies on reconception of the police as less concerned with enforcement than with surveillance. All of these devices go well beyond simply restricting a person's freedom of movement and/or inflicting certain punishments, such as hard labor. By operating on the body and determining category inclusions and exclusions, they shape behavior and, in that way, shape selves.

The punitive or disciplinary mechanisms surveyed in *Discipline and Punish* changed institutionalized punishment, from specific retribution taken on monarchical subjects for specific offenses into the "requalification" of abnormal members of society. Crude punitive methods turned into political strategies (Foucault 1979:23). Momentous as all this may be, the deeper point has to do not with understanding the development of the penal system, but with grasping how Foucault reconceives power in the process of analyzing how disciplinary techniques manufacture subjects. The first step in doing so is "ceas[ing] once and for all to describe ... power in negative terms" as always prohibitive, repressive, coercive (Foucault 1979:194). *Discipline and Punish* tells a story of the development of awesomely effective techniques for controlling people, so it is a story about the manufacture and control of the soul by power. But *Discipline and Punish* is more than a story about institutionalized management and regulation because the techniques it details do not work only by compelling and forbidding. They work by enabling as much as by inhibiting. Nor do those techniques enable only acts; they enable the production of truth and knowledge, and so of reality.

Power is enabling in that "it produces reality; it produces domains of objects and rituals of truth" (Foucault 1979:194). The disciplinary techniques Foucault describes produce a reality in which normal society is pitted against a subclass of its members: the criminally abnormal. The enabling techniques, as institutionalized practices, also produce the means for society to conduct its struggle against crime and abnormality: the knowledges of the various scientific and administrative disciplines concerned with criminals and crime as well as the institutions and procedures developed to employ those knowledges. In structuring the struggle against crime, the techniques produce domains of objects: the criminal subclass, "first offenders," incorrigible recidivists, "white-collar" criminals. The techniques, in being implemented, produce the police, parole boards, prison guards, forensic psychologists, and pathologists. Additionally, the disciplinary techniques produce rituals of truth or procedures through which truths are established. These include indictments, trials, testimony by expert witnesses, compilation of definitive dossiers on defendants and convicted felons, categorization of convicted felons, parole hearings, and endless statistics-based generalizations about crimes and motives. Each of these rituals or procedures determines that something is the case; that something establishes something else; that someone is of a certain type; that something is or is not relevant to a case or judgment; that something does or does not merit consideration regarding a charge, a sentence, or parole; that something was or was not done and is or is not likely to be done again.

Throughout what Foucault calls the "penal ritual," beginning with "the preliminary investigation" and carrying on through "to the sentence and the final effects of the penalty," something is being created and sustained: a subject, both in the sense that an individual is subjugated and that an individual is manipulated to define herself or himself in terms of certain conceptions and descriptions. The penal system creates and sustains subjects "by solemnly inscribing offenses" on bodies it makes docile through enforcement of disciplinary routines. All of this is legitimated by treating the individuals dealt with as "susceptible of scientific knowledge," as amenable to effective theory-based study and consequent systematic control, and so manageable through the disciplinary techniques employed. In this way, the penal system imbues "the mechanisms of legal punishment with a justifiable hold not only on offenses, but on individuals; not only on what they do, but also on what they are, will be, may be" (Foucault 1979:18).

Though my aim here is expository rather than critical, one obvious objection needs to be noted, even if briefly, because it helps to clarify the foregoing discussion. It may be argued that rather than the carceral system constituting or producing anything, such as a criminal "type," it deals with ongoing realities and that the only novelty is better recognition and description of those realities. In other words, it may be claimed that the shift from the juridical to the carceral system was a progressive move to more effective treatment of what was already there, rather than a shift to greater control enabled by the creation of new subjects and categories. This is precisely the issue between totalizing and effective history, for the objection turns on postulating certain "essences," in this instance criminal types and corresponding categories, which the penal system, rather than creating, comes to deal with more effectively in virtue of greater sophistication, accumulated experience, and better theories. But this is not an objection to be resolved with more diligent argument or research because it simply articulates the fundamental disparity between genealogy and what it opposes. The real force of the objection has to do with the cogency of genealogical claims and why we should deem them somehow superior to what they oppose, a matter now emerging as central to consideration of Foucault's work. However, the cogency of Foucauldian redescriptions and philosophical contentions is an issue that must await further exposition.

The modern soul is "the present correlative of a certain technology of power over the body" in the sense that disciplinary control of the body both subjugates individuals and shapes their subjectivity. But it would be wrong to think Foucault is saying that the soul "is an illusion or an ideological effect," that it is a mere device used to effect greater control. On the contrary, the soul "exists, it has a reality, it is produced permanently around, on, within the body by the functioning of a power that is exercised on those punished." Nor is the production of souls in any way limited to the penal system. Beyond the penal system souls are produced in "those one supervises, trains and corrects" (Foucault 1979:29). The soul is not a preexistent essence; it is produced wherever there is supervision and constraint as well as punishment.

The production of the soul through management or disciplinary techniques means that individuals are not enslaved, as is often lamented, by our social and cultural orders. The view that somehow free spirits, perhaps "noble savages," are hamstrung by the strictures of civilization is a romantic fantasy. There are no preexistent individuals to be enslaved; instead "the individual is carefully fabricated" in our social and cultural orders (Foucault 1979:217). The subject-fabricating techniques do not enslave free spirits; they act always on the body: "It is always the body that is at issue—the body and its forces, their utility and their docility, their distribution and their submission." The body is all that is available to power, because the soul is a product of power. It is the body that "power relations have an immediate hold on ... they invest it, mark it, train it, torture it, force it to carry out tasks, to perform ceremonies, to emit signs" (Foucault 1979:25). It is power that produces subjects or subjectivities. Thus we come to the nub of the matter, for the various management or disciplinary techniques detailed in *Discipline and Punish* embody power or power-relations.

Power

Power, simply put, is the relational environment in which actions take place, and so is the sum of influences on actions or what Foucault calls comportments (Foucault 1983a:221). Though power is given its fullest articulation in *The History of Sexuality*, this is why its operation is more readily discerned in *Discipline and Punish*. There we see power working in a focused manner in the disciplining and regulating of inmates' behavior. The trouble begins when we try to say what power is in the sense of saying just what the disciplining and regulating influences on behavior are. The expectation is that these influences are what we normally think of when we speak of constraints on behavior, namely, degrees of intimidation and coercion exerted by a person or group on another person or group. However, as we have seen, Foucauldian power is not intimidation or coercion; power is not something that someone or some group has and exerts on another person or group.

Discussion of Foucauldian power must say as much about what power is not, and about how it is misconstrued, as about what it is. Most readers with a traditional philosophical background will be impatient with this, because they will expect the question "What is power?" to be answered in a definitive way, given the importance of the notion to Foucault's thought. The difficulty is that in a crucial sense Foucauldian power is not, in itself, anything at all. Power has the same ontological status as relations because power is wholly relational; Foucault insists on "the strictly relational character of power relationships" (Foucault 1980a:95). He insists that we must be "nominalistic" about power because "power is not an institution, and not a structure; neither is it a certain strength" (Foucault 1980a:93). A definition of power, then, cannot be precise in the sense of yielding or articulating an essence, so much so that definitions of power, or better, characterizations of power, look hopelessly permissive in the sense of being too inclusive. The matter of contrast, or lack thereof, is a contentious one in discussions of Foucault's notion of power, but the reason why power strictly speaking has no contrast will become clear as we proceed. We can do so by saying that power is relations among actions that, as individual components of those relations, are neither strong nor weak, enabling nor inhibiting in themselves, but only in relation to one another and to the extent to which they constrain one another.

To the extent that we can say what power is, it is the sum of sets of past and present comportments as they qualify sets of presently ensuing comportments. Power is the conditioning of ongoing actions by the totality of previous and concurrent actions. This is how power is a "set of actions upon other actions" and not actions bearing on agents (Foucault 1983a:219–20). But to say that the comportments that are the components of power-relations are actions bearing on actions, and neither strong or weak, enabling or inhibiting in themselves, is not to describe acts of intimidation, coercion, or domination in the ordinary sense of "power"; it is to describe such acts as elements of Foucauldian power or power-relations. This is a point often obscured in critical discussion of Foucauldian power. Individual acts of coercion, domination, and intimidation are, of course, strong or weak, enabling or inhibiting, and bear on agents not actions. It is as components of Foucauldian power or the web of power-relations that such acts are neither strong nor weak, enabling nor inhibiting, and bear on actions rather than agents.

The idea is an elusive one, but grasping it is fundamental to understanding both *Discipline and Punish* and *The History of Sexuality*. To begin to make out this difficult idea, we need to reiterate some of what was said about subjectivity, because it is in the shaping of subjectivity that power is most importantly operant.

Difficult as the idea of power as actions acting on actions may be, more difficult still is Foucault's claim that something as fundamental as our subjectivity, that which Descartes found most evident and unquestionable, is historical and is a result of discourse and practice. Though we can understand being a subject as historical, in the sense of being, say, a juridical subject, we tend to be baffled by the idea that the subject each of us experiences being could be an historical product. We can imagine not having certain beliefs or attitudes, or having different beliefs or attitudes, but it is much harder to imagine ourselves as fundamentally *other*, had our lives been different. Moreover, we have seen that Foucault goes beyond conceiving of the subject as a construct to the speculation that consciousness might not have been subject-centered. He thinks that the subject is "obviously only one of the … possibilities of organizing a consciousness of self" (Dreyfus and Rabinow 1983:175). We must, then, not only imagine ourselves as possibly having been other than the subjects we are, but as possibly having had our subjectivity organized, for example, as a multicentered consciousness in a manner presently deemed pathological (for example, schizophrenia).

The subject, then, is historical as a particular and as a kind. But because Foucault's discussion of subjectivity is not couched in the traditional language of metaphysics or the philosophy of mind, the full implications of his views may be missed. Foucault may be understood to be saying only that the subject, the self, is not a Cartesian ego, that it is historical in the sense of being a construct; that is, Foucault might be read as a constructivist in the tradition of Mead. As touched on earlier, Mead characterized what we experience as our self as a product of cognition rather than a unity that must precede cognition. However, like most constructivists, Mead offered his characterization of the self as an ontological alternative to the Cartesian or Kantian conception of the self as a preexistent ego. Writing of how postmoderns decenter the subject, Susan Hekman remarks that though they see the subject as "constituted within discursive formations," they do not merely "replace the constituting subject with the constituted subject." Instead they "advance a conception of the subject that explodes the polarity between constituted and constituting by displacing the opposition" (Hekman 1990:47). Foucault is decidedly postmodern in this respect, because unlike Mead he does not offer a competing ontological conception of the self. Brenda Marshall points out that the postmodern critique "is most consistently an impulse to look at the historical, philosophical, and cultural construction of the subject" (Marshall 1992:82). "Construction" here means investing a body with a pattern of beliefs and habits. Foucault's treatment of the self is not a matter of displacing one ontological theory with another; it is not a matter of replacing the Cartesian ego or the Kantian "I think" with something like Mead's "combination" of remembered selves and internal responses to actions (Thayer 1982:355).

What Foucault does is displace the theoretical opposition of a preexistent and a constructed self by repudiating the need or possibility of an ontological theory of the nature of the self. He does this by providing a genealogical account of what it is to become and be a subject through power's disciplining of the body. Foucault undercuts theorizing about the self by showing the subject to be historical, by showing how becoming and being a subject is a matter of being defined in discourse by coming to have certain beliefs and so thinking and acting in specific ways. He shows that the subject is the result of "a process of self-knowledge," that it is a consequence of an "obligation to seek and state the truth about oneself" (Foucault 1988b:240). To be a power-produced subject is to define one's subjectivity by "learning" what one is through internalization of the truths and knowledges power produces.

For Foucault, the issue of emergent subjectivity is not an abstract metaphysical one about the ultimate nature of the subject; it is instead one about what it is to hold certain things as true about oneself, to have a certain perspective on the world, and to speak certain things about oneself. As we have seen, one way of being a subject is as a constantly observed penitentiary inmate; as we will see in Chapter 5, another is as a norm-defined gendered being. In both cases bodies are made to bear particular subjectivities, to be or become specifically defined subjects. "[T]he individual is not a pre-given entity. ... The individual, with his identity and characteristics, is the product of ... power exercised over bodies" (Foucault 1980b:73–74). The power exercised over bodies includes the pronouncements of judges, doctors, and other experts; it includes routines imposed by prison guards and teachers; it includes the approbation and condemnation of peers.

Unfortunately, the negative things Foucault says about power—that it is not domination, that it is not anyone's power—seem inconsistent with power's subject-defining role. The inclination then is to think that if it can manufacture subjects, power must be something more than relations among actions. Power must be a determinant of some sort, and most likely hidden coercive persuasion, indoctrination, and/or domination. Foucault is aware of this inclination and interprets it as an inability on the part of some of his readers and critics to not construe power as determining and conspiratorial. He remarks that as many wrongly take history to be "the ruse of reason," many equally wrongly believe that "power is the ruse of history" (Foucault 1980a:95).

Distortion of Foucauldian power as a determinant of behavior and as conspiratorial, as covert domination, goes like this: power or power-relations are reified as Capital-P Power, the possession and use of which, whether knowing or otherwise, determines the behavior of those on whom it is exerted; Capital-P Power then replaces historical inevitability or class struggle or the hand of God as what explains why people think and behave as they do. Foucault's claim that power produces truth and knowledge then is read as meaning that what passes for truth and knowledge, as opposed to what is the case and might be known to be the case, are the products of Capital-P Power acting as a conditioning force, that is, as the ruse of history. Usually another and particularly un-Foucauldian idea is grafted onto this misconceived interpretation, namely, that if we get clear enough on the role of Capital-P Power and how it is exerted on us, we can liberate ourselves from it. If the interpretation is more sophisticated, it will include description of how Foucault's own intellectual history led him to develop the idea of Capital-P Power through adoption of Nietzsche's "will to power" and reinterpretation of Marxian deterministic economic forces. If the interpretation is still more sophisticated, Foucault's Capital-P Power-producing reinterpretation is taken to be not of Marxian but of structuralist underlying determinants.

Distortion of Foucauldian power as a kind of determinant is unfortunately supported by some of his own remarks and methods. Foucault handles power by cataloging the techniques by which behavior is conditioned by expert knowledges, and so how societies shape the subjectivity of their members. The books we consider here relate how this shaping occurs in the prison through the imposition of disciplines and in society at large through the deployment of sexuality. Thus it looks as if *Discipline and Punish* and *The History of Sexuality* are exposés that reveal large-scale and basically conspiratorial determination of behavior. The conspiratorial aspect of this impression can be shown to be wrongheaded by emphasizing that, though Foucault does portray power as "masked" and does present his treatments of penality and sexuality as showing what actually happened under the appearance of reform and repression, he is careful to maintain that power is impersonal. This is overlooked in interpreting power as conspiratorial, where imposition of constraints is reflectively or unreflectively conceived as deliberate or witting action on the part of someone or some group. Even Rorty seems to overlook the impersonal nature of power when he ambiguously describes "the most valuable part" of Foucault's work as that which shows "how the patterns of acculturation characteristic of liberal societies have imposed on their members ... constraints of which older, premodern societies had not dreamed" (Rorty 1989:63). But Foucault does not reveal these constraints by discerning and revealing hidden manipulative devices and exposing conspiracies; he reveals these constraints by describing the impersonal workings of power.

Foucault does not merely inventory subtle manipulative devices; if he did only that, his notion of power would be superfluous, for the manipulative devices he reveals, in being conspiratorial in nature, would be explicable in terms of the traditional conception of power as the ability to coerce, to prohibit, and to dominate. Foucault provides a novel discourse in which we can articulate something of the vast complexity of subject-shaping constraints by saying how behavior is impersonally regulated. What needs to be said about conspiracies and domination, whether covert or overt, is that we can abstract numerous particular instances of intimidation, coercion, prohibition, and domination from the hugely complex web of interrelated constraints that constitutes power-relations. But it is a mistake to see those instances as constitutive of power, to see particular instances of intimidation, coercion, prohibition, and domination as the elements of power, as if power simply were the inclusive whole of such instances.

A related distortion of Foucauldian power that merits mention is equation of power and knowledge (Nola 1994:21–24). This error occurs in spite of Foucault often describing knowledge as a product of power and his insisting that the two are reciprocally related, which entails that they are distinct: "The very fact that I pose the question of their relation proves clearly that I do not *identify* them" (Foucault 1988b:43). Foucault's use of the term "power/knowledge" does not imply the identity of what is on either side of the slash. Foucault's point is that "[i]t is not possible for power to be exercised without knowledge [and] it is impossible for knowledge not to engender power" (Foucault 1980b:52). When behavior is constrained by power, as in the implementation of the reform policies and methods discussed earlier, expert knowledge is what grounds and authorizes the constraining. But the constraining of behavior also generates or adds to knowledge by "confirming" what is claimed to be known when the results are as expected, and by prompting further theorizing and research when unexpected results occur. Power is not knowledge nor is knowledge power. Power and knowledge are the dual aspects of the comportment-conditioning environment within which individuals act, and so within which subjects are formed and have their being.

The impersonal nature of power, which Foucault describes as its "nonsubjective" character in the sense of not being what someone deliberately exercises with a particular aim in mind, clarifies how power constrains comportments rather than agents (Foucault 1980a:94). The traditional conception of power is as attributable to and exercised by agents ("subjective") and as exercised on agents. Agents possessed of power do the coercing or prohibiting, and what is coerced into acting or prohibited from acting are agents who lack power and must do something or not do something the empowered agents desire done or not done. The acts in question are secondary, for they are merely what ensues or is prevented from ensuing by the exercise of power. Foucauldian power, because of its wholly relational nature, is not a force exercised by empowered agents on disempowered agents. Foucauldian power is a constraint on action itself; power "is a way in which certain actions modify others." Power is not a coercive or prohibitive force bearing on agents, compelling them to behave or not behave in specific ways; power "is a mode of action which does not act directly and immediately on others. Instead it acts upon their actions." Power is a "set of actions upon other actions"; power is "a total structure of actions brought to bear upon possible actions" in the sense that power enables some actions and inhibits others (Foucault 1983a:219–20). As I said at the beginning of this section, this is how power is the sum of influences on actions or comportments.

How power acts on actions and not agents needs to be amplified by mentioning a likely objection. It could be pointed out that if the traditional ontological notion of the self is abandoned, and an agent is the sum of his or her actions, it appears pointless to contend that power operates on actions and not agents. But the contention that power acts on actions not only describes how power is the environment in which agents act, it is itself part of the rejection of the traditional ontological notion of the self. As ever, Foucault is consummately "political" in presenting his contentions in ways highly responsive to his intellectual context. Developing the notion of power has a positive aspect—the characterization of power as the constraining of comportments—and, by implication, a negative aspect, bearing on the established Cartesian/Kantian conception of the self.

The impersonal nature of power also clarifies why resistance is internal to power, why "resistance is never in a position of exteriority in relation to power," and how power incorporates and "depends on a multiplicity of points of resistance" (Foucault 1980a:95). Resistance is never to Foucauldian power as such; resistance is always to particular constraints that enable some comportments and inhibit others. Thus resistance, in balancing constraint, completes relations of power. Anything that counts as an action—for example, as an instance of domination or resistance to domination—occurs within power's dynamic environment. Thus the internality of resistance to power in turn shows how power is all-pervasive. Foucault contends that it is wrongheaded even to assert that we cannot escape power, because that would be to imagine power as delineable and thus distinct from the intricate web of constraining interrelationships that obtain the moment there is more than one agent. To imagine power as delineable and as possible to escape would be "to misunderstand the strictly relational character" of power and so to misunderstand the way in which power has no contrast (Foucault 1980a:95).

The impersonal nature of power may clarify how power constrains actions rather than agents and how power embraces or contains resistance, but these remain the most problematic aspects of Foucault's notion of power. These are aspects that both make power a novel and productive philosophical idea and prompt philosophers like Taylor to argue that Foucauldian power is incoherent. Of these, perhaps the most difficult aspect to grasp is the impersonal nature of power; the idea is basic to Foucault's thought and project. It is not that individuals have or fail to have power, it is that individuals are produced by and exist in power-relations. Foucault insists that rather than individuals possessing power or suffering power, "it is ... one of the prime effects of power that certain bodies, certain gestures, certain discourses, certain desires, come to be identified and constituted as individuals" (Foucault 1980b:98). Power is prior to particular individuals in that what counts as a dominating or dominated individual is a product of power-relations. The individual is not "a sort of elementary nucleus, a primitive atom ... on which power comes to fasten or against which it happens to strike" (Foucault 1980b:98). Individuals only are what they are in a web of power-relations.

That power is all-pervasive and is without contrast is only slightly less difficult an idea than that it is impersonal. There can be no liberation from power, because there cannot be interaction among individuals outside power. There can be no state of affairs in which we are both agents among other agents and do not constrain each other's actions. Being an individual and interacting with other individuals involves imposing constraints on actions, so all interactions occur within the environment of power. Power-relations "permeate, characterise and constitute the social body" (Foucault 1980b:93). A person outside power would be a solipsistic entity and only potentially a subject and an agent. Power "is not something that is acquired, seized, or shared," because it is the ever-present environment in which we are subjects and agents (Foucault 1980a:94,93).

Given that it is impersonal, is totally pervasive, and constrains actions rather than agents, power looks dubiously coherent as a philosophical notion. Any definition or account or characterization that makes something as abstract, inclusive, and wholly relational as the foregoing discussion makes power will look very dubious to most readers. Can the notion be made out more clearly? It may be worthwhile to briefly restate what I have said in somewhat different terms. We begin with Foucault's description of power as "a complex strategical situation in a particular society" (Foucault 1980a:93). The "strategical situation" is how innumerable relations of mutual constraint on actions stand at any given time in a given society. As I have stressed, it is only in the context of that distribution of relations, in the relational environment thus provided, that something is an instance of coercion or resistance. Power, then, is first of all the dynamic distribution of all interpersonal relations: "Relations of power are not in a position of exteriority with respect to other types of relationships" (Foucault 1980a:94).

The strategical situation or distribution of relations that is Foucauldian power "must be understood ... as the multiplicity of force relations immanent in the sphere in which they operate and which constitute their own organization" (Foucault 1980a:92). Power is not merely the total conglomeration of relations; it is a structured totality. This is how power is an environment and how it is the sum of past and present comportments as they bear on presently ensuing comportments. But power is dynamic; it is not a passive environment. Power is the totality of relations as well as "the process which, through ceaseless struggles and confrontations, transforms, strengthens, or reverses" the relations it comprises (Foucault 1980a:92). Power is a vibrant, fluid totality; the relations it comprises are constantly altering and shifting, so the totality is constantly changing. Each act performed within power affects the relations within which it occurs and so affects the totality to a greater or lesser extent. This continuous, mutually influencing interaction is how power is the totality of relations, "the support which these ... relations find in one another," as well as "the disjunctions and contradictions which isolate [relations] from one another" (Foucault 1980a:92). In being the totality of comportment-enabling and comportment-inhibiting relations, power comprises both the various constraints on action that augment one another in their influence and those other constraints on action that obstruct, nullify, and exclude one another as influences.

Once the identity of power with the totality of action-constraining relations is appreciated, one understands that our traditional paradigm of power—the state—cannot be the fundamental model for Foucauldian power. Power is neither paradigmed nor exhausted by the state; Foucauldian power is only "embodied in the state apparatus, in the formulation of the law." As the acts of individuals are instances of coercion or resistance only within the web of power, so too the state's acts are instances of domination and regulation within power. In like manner, social groups possessing the capacity to intimidate and coerce, such as ruling elites and the wealthy, are not models of power or its possession, for power is embodied "in the various social hegemonies" such as caste systems and economic classes. What we normally take as archetypes of power are only instances of power's "institutional crystallization," not of power itself (Foucault 1980a:92–93).

Clarifying the environment-nature of power as the dynamic sum of relations defines how power constrains actions as opposed to agents. Consider Foucault's initially surprising contention that power can be "exercised only over free subjects, and only insofar as they are free" (Foucault 1983a:221). In other words, when an individual has no options, when his or her actions are wholly dictated by another or others, there can only be domination. Foucauldian power requires that there be, for each individual in a power-relation, "a field of possibilities in which several ways of behaving, several reactions and diverse comportments may be realized" (Foucault 1983a:221). In total enslavement it is precisely the agent who is constrained, not actions, because the agent's every act is coerced. Enslavement dictates the specific behavior in which individuals engage and excludes everything else. As the state fails to be a proper paradigm of Foucauldian power, enslavement, another paradigm of power as traditionally conceived, fails to be even an instance of Foucauldian power. "Where the determining factors saturate the whole there is no relationship of power; slavery is not a power relationship"; in slavery there is only "a physical relationship of constraint" (Foucault 1983a:221).

When we see that coercive determination of behavior is not Foucauldian power, it emerges that power constrains actions by providing a "field of possibilities" regarding behavior. Power enables a range of behavioral options that constitute electable courses of action for a given agent. Conversely, power inhibits other ranges of behavioral options for that agent. But this does not mean that power provides substantive-self agents with free choices among a number of reflected-upon behavioral options. Power's enabling and inhibiting of behavior is, first of all, the enabling and inhibiting of acts constitutive of agents; and second, enabling and inhibiting is not only a matter of making some actions possible and others impossible. Ranges of behavioral options are enabled and inhibited because power is how relations are structured at a given point in time; that structure facilitates certain acts and hinders others. But power also prioritizes the behavioral options in having shaped the subjectivity of the agent in a certain way. Because of the agent's self-image, beliefs, and values, any set of behavioral options open to that agent is automatically ranked in terms of the attractiveness of individual options. The range of enabled behavioral options, the field of comportment possibilities, is presented by, or perhaps better "in" power, but always to a power-shaped subject.

In spite of the resistance it prompts, Foucault's conception of power as impersonal is not as implausible as it first appears. Foucault contends that if Machiavelli "conceived the power of the Prince in terms of force relationships, perhaps we need to go one step further," which is, as noted earlier, to do "without the persona of the Prince" (Foucault 1980a:97). Taking this additional step is to understand power as a "strategy that is immanent in force relationships" and to go beyond conceiving of power as always present in the will of an agent or the collective will of a group or the state (Foucault 1980a:97). But this is not to reify power or to make it mysterious. Imagine a number of small magnets spread out on a surface but not quite close enough to one another to clump together. We can easily imagine the magnetic force-vectors established among the magnets. Iron filings scattered over the magnets will trace those vectors by following the magnetic patterns. Theoretically, we could exhaustively describe those force-vectors mathematically. Now imagine shifting the magnets around. In doing so we change the force-vectors, and scattering more iron filings will trace a new set of force-vectors. In this analogy, power is the force-vectors and agents are the magnets. Each move of a magnet, or each act on the part of an agent, changes the "strategical situation" in its vicinity and so affects the whole. Each magnet contributes to the totality of force-vectors, by being where it is or by moving; in like manner, agents' actions contribute to the relational totality that is power, but that totality is not any one agent's nor any group's power anymore than the totality of force-vectors is any one magnet's magnetic field.

I hope this illustration clarifies how power is all-pervasive. Because it is impersonal, because it is no one's power but the dynamic environment for human action, there is "no escaping from power." Power "is always already present, constituting that very thing which one attempts to counter it with" (Foucault 1980a:82). To escape from power one would have to be utterly alone and somehow free of all the enculturation and conditioning that make us social beings. The equally unachievable limiting case at the other end of the scale is that of complete enslavement, of being only the extension of another's will. Without achieving complete solitude or total enslavement, we cannot escape power. When we resist coercion or domination, we remain defined by and immersed in power. "Where there is power, there is resistance, and yet ... this resistance is never in a position of exteriority in relation to power" (Foucault 1980a:94–95). With the exception of a slave, who is not a partner in a power-relation, even a wholly passive person in a power-relation offers resistance in the sense that he or she partly defines that power-relation and so inescapably constrains the behavior of even the most intimidating or coercive partner.

The impersonal nature and inescapability of Foucauldian power bring out why the distinction we usually draw between legitimate and illegitimate coercion is of no use to us in understanding or identifying Foucauldian power. We tend to think of power in terms of its proper use and, derivatively, of its improper abuse, which is why we readily take as our paradigm of power its legitimate embodiment in the state. But Foucault argues that "the new methods of power [are] not ensured by right but by technique, not by law but by normalization, not by punishment but by control" (Foucault 1980a:89). Power is greatly more extensive than lawful coercion and, again derivatively, unlawful compulsion, because it is exercised through management techniques and societal norms, and compliance is exacted not by force but by habit-inducing routines. This is what *Discipline and Punish* most clearly shows, and this is how the exercise of power has been extended far beyond punitive disciplining to "methods that are employed on all levels and in forms that go beyond the state and its apparatus" (Foucault 1980a:89).

Another question, similar to those surrounding the impersonal and pervasive nature of power, is whether power itself has a history. These questions are similar because they are prompted in part by the interpretive inclination to think that given what Foucault says about it, power ultimately must be *something,* something about which we cannot be wholly nominalistic, regardless of his exhortation (Foucault 1980a:93). In this case the inclination is to think that power is something that must have a history. A good deal of what is said in *Discipline and Punish* and *The History of Sexuality* does tend to sound as if power is something fairly new, and so had either a relatively late historical beginning or an escalation in degree tantamount to a beginning. I have described power as the dynamic environment for human action, so what power comprises, namely, comportment-constraining strategies, must be as old as we are. But it could be a misinterpretation of Foucault to understand power or those strategies as coextensive with human history since, for example, much of the importance of *Discipline and Punish* has to do with the historically circumscribed displacement of the juridico-discursive regime's rule of law by the rule of norm and constraint by technique. The account of that displacement makes it look as if the strategies responsible for effecting it were novel ones. Certainly the broad developments described in *Discipline and Punish,* as well as in *The History of Sexuality,* are presented as historically circumscribed. Moreover, Foucault tells us explicitly that "from the seventeenth and eighteenth centuries onward, there was a veritable technological take-off in the productivity of power," pointing out that not only did "the monarchies of the classical period develop great state apparatuses (the army, police and fiscal administration)," but more importantly, "there was established at this period … a new 'economy' of power" (Foucault 1980b:119).

As suggested, one can construe the apparent emergence of power as only a matter of degree, but this is somewhat at odds with how Foucauldian power-relations do seem to have been themselves enabled by such things as increases in population, greater complexity of social interaction, more complicated societal structuring, increasingly sophisticated manipulative techniques, and refinements in enculturation. It seems plausible, then, to take it that power, or again, the strategies it comprises, is relatively new in human history and so has a history itself. If this indeed is the case, then we must consider that at some point the number of people interacting and the complexity of their interactions reached a "critical mass," resulting in new kinds of comportment-constraining strategies. This idea is compatible with Foucault's conception of power, except in that it suggests the notion of power is a theoretical one needed and produced to deal with a new phenomenon and that is incompatible with the character of genealogy—a point that I will return to.

Power's putative historical novelty is best construed in terms of comportment-constraining strategies that only become significant when there are large numbers of people being managed with techniques that are employed effectively only when applied to substantial populations. The deployment of penality requires large numbers of lawbreakers who pose a considerable collective problem regarding how they are to be dealt with; the deployment of sexuality requires whole populations to include the normal, the deviant, and the experts who distinguish among them. Until the totality of action-constraining relations among a relatively substantial number of agents is complex and extensive enough to coalesce into an environment in which individual agents have their subjectivities systematically defined in statistically significant and discernible ways, the notion of power is of relatively little use as an instrument for developing genealogies. When it does become useful, then, it may appear that something new has arisen.

The crucial point is that the term "power" denotes act-enabling and inhibiting actions or the complex web of interactive strategies within which we are agents and patients. What "power" denotes is real enough, but as has been stressed, power is not itself anything; power just is all the action-constraining actions that occur. It is to (wrongly) reify power to ask about its history as if that history were separate from the history of the interactive strategies denoted by the term. However, the *idea* of power has a history. The idea of power is an invented or fashioned instrument for dealing with history; it is a tool that facilitates conceptual objectification, and so treatment, of what power comprises. As a tool that enables us to think and talk productively about the environment within which we are agents and patients, and within which our individual acts are the actions they are, the notion of power helps us map that environment or the relations among the actions that occur in and shape that environment. The apparent historical novelty of power, then, should be understood as the way numerous strategies, development of discourses, and establishment of institutions become more visible and more amenable to mapping and investigation when there is enough history to provide contrastive raw material and enough people behaving in broad patterns. It is not power that is novel, not as something in itself, but rather employment of the idea to trace and map strategies, discourses, and institutions of a new order of complexity.

The question of power's history, therefore, is not one about the history of a particular phenomenon. It is a question about the utility of Foucault's instrument or device for investigating institutional development, measures of control, and ways of averring and assessing truth and knowledge. Had Foucault lived in the twelfth century, he could have written a genealogy of, say, the papacy, contrasting it with previously localized religious seats of authority. The notion of power would have been an effective instrument in such an exercise. But clearly the wealth of complexity and scope that another eight centuries add to genealogy's raw material makes the twentieth-century notion of power a hugely more effective instrument and its employment vastly more productive. That complexity and scope also make it much more likely that the instrumental notion Foucault so brilliantly articulates would be fashioned in the twentieth century rather than the twelfth. We must bear in mind the paramount importance of history in considering Foucault's genealogical analytics; we must also bear in mind that the notion of power is not the name of a mysterious force but a device to deal with history, a way of producing accounts that are interpretations without being teleological "grand narratives."

As touched on previously, misconstruing power as having its own history, and what has been said in response, raises a question about the possibly theoretical nature of Foucault's notion. But it is the *idea* of power that has a history, not the comportment-constraining strategies that are power itself. However, this risks a perception of tension between my exposition of Foucault on power and his own descriptions and uses of the notion. Foucault rejects the idea that his conception of power is a theoretical one, that he offers a theory about "power" as some sort of determinative force or agency (Foucault 1980a:92–93, 97). His own use of power or power-relations is intended as, and for the most part is, an instrument employed to make a number of historical points. But a good deal of what I have said about power may suggest that I am treating it as a theoretical notion. The trouble is that exposition generally, especially of a notion as initially elusive as Foucauldian power, requires imposing artificial theoretical structuring that is quite independent of the underlying discussion. Without such a structure one is reduced to paraphrasing. It is also not at all clear that Foucault himself avoids treating power theoretically in spite of his claims: "I am no theoretician of power" (Foucault 1989:254). It is not my intention to "theoretize" Foucault's notion of power in discussing it as I do. The trick is to avoid doing so inadvertently. What I suggest here is that my difficulty—and Foucault's—should be productively used by the reader as an ever-present reminder that we must be nominalistic about power.

We can use the foregoing remarks, about how the changes Foucault investigates in *Discipline and Punish* as well as in *The History of Sexuality* occurred when large numbers of people were being managed by hegemonic practices, to refine Foucault's notion of power. He uses the term "government" to designate the management in question; this illuminates how power comprises all the interactive strategies that control and regulate large groups. Foucault tells us that power is basically "a question of government," but adds that the word "government" must be given "the very broad meaning which it had in the Sixteenth Century" (Foucault 1983a:221). This archaic sense was considerably more inclusive than the current, largely political, sense and did not refer only or even primarily to "political structures or the management of states." Instead the term designated the regulation and administration of anything amenable to being managed, and so "designated the way in which the conduct of individuals or states might be directed" (Foucault 1983a:221). This further illuminates how power becomes a viable tool in genealogical analysis, because power-relations emerge as an analytic concern only when there is appreciable government of the "modes of action" that in various ways structure and constrain "the possible field of actions of others" (Foucault 1983a:221).

The most important way in which power equals government is through the production of knowledges and disciplines and so the manufacture of experts who determine not only how we should act but what we are. Traditionally, subjects of intellectual inquiry are taken merely as so many given problematics that invite study for purposes of control or for their own sake. But for Foucault, every subject of disciplinary study is a product, an artifact. Traditionally conceived intellectual and empirical inquiry is reasoned effort at discernment of the nature of an objective subject of study. For Foucault inquiry itself both constitutes the subject studied and bestows on that subject whatever objectivity it is deemed to have. Subjects of study do not preexist study but develop as consequences of the discourse employed in inquiry. This is how "power perpetually creates knowledge" (Foucault 1980b:51–52). But knowledge is not only a product, for it reciprocally enables and sustains power-relations. This is why Foucault often speaks of "power/knowledge" and insists that "there is no exteriority" between "techniques of knowledge and strategies of power" (Foucault 1980a:98).

Development of the penal system, as laid out in *Discipline and Punish,* illustrates the reciprocity between techniques of knowledge and strategies of power by showing how juridical subjects were remade into psychological subjects when the soul was manufactured and punishment reconceived from retribution to normalization. *The History of Sexuality* illustrates the power/knowledge reciprocity by showing how the creation of a new field of study generated new sexual subjects. Foucault maintains that "sexuality was constituted as an area of investigation" because "relations of power had established it as a possible object." And "conversely, if power was able to take [sexuality] as a target, this was because techniques of knowledge and procedures of discourse were capable of investing it" (Foucault 1980a:98). Power enabled certain behaviors and relationships to constitute a structured whole of interest to experts—human sexuality. Foucault contends that sexuality as a term "did not appear until the beginning of the nineteenth century" (Foucault 1986:3). What had been some three hundred years earlier just so many disparate urges, inclinations, and activities, were delineated as a problematic set of traits and drives that supposedly define a central aspect of human nature. Power produced a knowledge and, to paraphrase Foucault's remark about Hume, Freud and Alfred Kinsey became possible. But instead of raising skeptical questions, Freud, Kinsey, and others proceeded, in their respective disciplines, to determine and to teach us what we are, to define us as sexual subjects (Kinsey 1948:53).

We can close this section, and this chapter, by considering a difficulty with Foucault's account of how power produces knowledges. Its resolution is enlightening with respect to the notion of power in that it removes a lingering doubt about power's enabling or productive role. Foucault often speaks of "random" events and "accidents" in discussing the development of techniques of knowledge and strategies of power. As we saw in considering his conception of genealogy, Foucault opposes lowly accidental and random beginnings to the illusory Capital-O Origins sought by traditional history and claims that reasoned inquiry itself "was born ... from *chance*" (Foucault 1971:78; my emphasis). But what are these events that may be random? It is what agents do or do not do that is relevant to power; power ranges over acts and events comprising acts, not over events in the sense that an earthquake is an event. An earthquake, in a sense, is not even an event until it is deemed such. The random events at issue in Foucault's account cannot be only happenings, like earthquakes, which then prompt actions, because they could be only the occasions for power-constrained action. Recall Hacking's remark regarding the "tiny local events where battles are unwittingly enacted by players who don't know what they are doing" (Hacking 1981:29). Though earthquakes and other happenings do play their part, what concerns us are supposedly random *acts*. But if so, given what Foucault says about power constraining acts and not agents and about power's pervasiveness, what sort of "chance" or random acts could there be in the history of a knowledge or of an individual subject? If all acts, except a slave's, are constrained by power, if all acts are acts *within* power, how can some acts be random? Foucault's conception of power is not a deterministic one, but it is unclear how it allows for randomness if there are no acts that are extraneous to power.

Consider again the definitional passage on power discussed earlier. Power is a "multiplicity of force relations" that "constitute their own organization." Power is also "the process" that "transforms" these force relations. Thus power is both a dynamic structure and the way that structure changes. Power is also "the support which these force relations find in one another [and/or] the disjunctions and contradictions which isolate them from one another." Finally, power is "the strategies in which [force-relations] take effect" (Foucault 1980a:92–93). Power, then, is inherently fluid. Moreover, the changes that occur in the totality of power or "force-relations" are not consequences of the particular characteristics of each but of their interaction.

Because power is, from one perspective, how force-relations interact in contributing to the dynamic whole, the alterations of the multiplicity of force-relations are in part due to some constituent force-relations reinforcing one another and in part due to some constituent force-relations diminishing the effects of other constituent force-relations. As noted, the effect of any given constituent force-relation on the dynamic whole is not a function of something intrinsic to the force-relation itself, but of how that particular force-relation relates to other constituent force-relations. Changes in the dynamic whole, alterations of the multiplicity of force-relations, are therefore unpredictable. Predictability would require not only detailed knowledge of the properties of constituent force-relations, but impossible knowledge of the dynamic structure of force-relations in their entirety. Even if it were possible to map all or enough of the dynamic whole at a given time, its consequent state would not be predictable as some sort of computationally discernible successor to the mapped state. Aside from the unpredictability of force-relation influences on other force-relations, chance events, in the sense that earthquakes are events, enter the equation at this point. Particular force-relations will be affected by chance events in this mundane sense, and the repercussions will spread throughout the web of force-relations, altering it to some degree.

The importance of the unpredictability of alterations of the multiplicity of force-relations is that it shows how acts and events, in the act-comprising sense, may be random and accidental in the histories of power-shaped subjects and knowledges. It is not that individual acts or act-comprising events are somehow uncaused or themselves without histories; it is that their specific contributions to the multiplicity of force-relations cannot be anticipated. This points out that Foucauldian randomness contrasts, not with causal determination, but with what genealogy opposes: totalizing history. What Foucault calls "random" events are events that do not fit in any overall teleological pattern. Randomness in the workings of power amounts to preclusion of holistic theories of how things develop as they do or why things are as they are. The mechanics of power cannot be predicted; they can only be retrospectively traced through genealogical analysis, and that means precisely the "gray, meticulous, and patiently documentary" detailing of developments in the asylum, in the clinic, in the prison, and in what we will now turn to: the deployment of sexuality.

5 The Manufacture of Knowledge

In *The History of Sexuality, Volume One,* Foucault sets out to trace, articulate, and investigate the production of a particular conception of sexuality, one he contends has been accepted as "natural" and dictates values and behavior across a spectrum encompassing much, if not most, of human activity. In describing what he calls the deployment of sexuality, Foucault lays out how a norm-based sexuality was developed and made into the truth about sex. In doing this, he provides a portrait of the workings of power-relations, of how power manufactures a particular subjectivity that is internalized and made the truth about oneself by most members of our culture. Foucault's is a multivolume project, but it is in the first volume that we find the genealogical treatment of sexuality. The second and third volumes, *The Use of Pleasure* and *The Care of the Self,* are ethical works in Foucault's rather proprietary sense.

The easiest way to understand *The History of Sexuality* is to view the book as about our beliefs and perceptions, as distinct from about what there really is. This is to read Foucault as if he was concerned with how we construe and understand our objective sexual nature and as if attempting to correct a misconstrual. This is a serious misinterpretation, but it also is one that I have encountered often among those whose first exposure to Foucault is through *The History of Sexuality.* In spite of Foucault's explicit questioning of the idea of an objective sexual nature, the book is sometimes read as only about how culture organizes and regulates perception, valuation, and use of an objective sexual nature. But "it is precisely this idea of sex *in itself* that we cannot accept without examination" (Foucault 1980a:152). The irony is that this misinterpretation is attributable in large part to the success with which the sexuality Foucault investigates has been deployed. Some readers are simply unprepared to take seriously that Foucault's investigation could reach all the way down to what they see as natural and unquestionable. But *The History of Sexuality* is not about the culturally determined construal of a biological given. What is hard to grasp, and harder to accept, is that for Foucault the very idea of an objective sexual nature that underlies sexuality is itself an historical product, and so a subject of genealogy. For Foucault, the idea of an objective sexual nature is an idea the descent and emergence of which is to be investigated as a part of the investigation of sexuality. The point of *The History of Sexuality* has much to do with how believing that there is an objective sexual nature (which is supposedly then the subject of a complex cultural interpretation) is itself a result of the discourses that regulate sexuality. Foucault asks whether our putative objective sexual nature is "really the anchorage point that supports the manifestations of sexuality, or is ... rather a complex idea that was formed inside the deployment of sexuality." His answer is that "the deployment of sexuality ... was what established this notion [of objective] 'sex'" (Foucault 1980a:152).

It is prudent to forestall confusion at this point. Foucault's claim, that the notion of an objective sexual nature is itself a product of the deployment of sexuality, does not mean that strictly physiological and anatomical differences between men and women are somehow not real. A product of deployment is the conception of those physiological and anatomical features as definitive and integrated elements constituting particular kinds or types: "the masculine," "the feminine." There is, though, a difficulty raised by this clarification. That is to distinguish between the mistaken view that Foucault is dealing only with how we construe objective sexuality and what I take to be the correct understanding: that Foucault is not denying that male and female bodies exist in the strictly biological sense. However, it is not clear that the distinction is consistent with Foucault's views, because there is a serious question regarding what, if anything, can be said about brute reality. However, not drawing the distinction opens the possibility for a hasty rejection of Foucault's historicist claim about our "objective" sexual nature simply on the grounds that the reality of the human body precludes the claim's being taken seriously.

Reference to "brute reality," an admittedly dicey way to try to indicate how things are outside language or power-shaped discourse, is used as a heuristic device for exposition. The point is that misinterpretation of *The History of Sexuality* as about construal of an objective sexual nature has a deeper source than our belief in an objective sexual nature. That source is the familiar idea that there is the world on one hand and what we make of it on the other, and that therefore it is the world that makes our beliefs and descriptions true or false. This is a view Foucault opposed long before investigating sexuality. As we saw earlier, Foucault rejects the idea that "'things' anterior to discourse" are what make what we say true, agreeing with Davidson that "[n]othing ... no *thing*, makes sentences and theories true" and with Rorty that "the world" is "either the purely vacuous notion of the ineffable cause of sense ... or else a name for the objects that inquiry at the moment is leaving alone" (Foucault 1972:47; Davidson, D. 1984:194; Rorty 1982:15). For Foucault, "the world," as the objective standard to measure what we say, is an apparent absolute that discourse generates in the process of structuring and legitimizing various practices. It is, as such, as much the target of genealogical investigation as the institutions and disciplines in which the notion is embedded and which it serves. For Foucault it makes no sense to speak of a neutral, natural sexuality, because it makes no sense to think or talk about an objective nature, an essence, that underlies our discourses and interpretations and is accessible only indirectly through representation in those discourses and interpretations.

But as stressed in Chapter 1, there is no denial of brute reality here. It would make no more sense to deny reality than it does to affirm its inaccessible existence. The point is that brute reality plays only a causal role with respect to our beliefs and activities; it plays no epistemic, justifying role. The very idea of objective reality as that which justifies beliefs and makes descriptions true is a product of doing the kind of philosophy Descartes did, and it immediately provokes the hopeless Cartesian epistemological quest to establish our beliefs as justified and our descriptions as objectively true. Foucault disallows a distinction between how things are in themselves and how we take things to be; he sees the distinction as having no content because he understands that we are unable to step out of our theories and descriptions to see how they fit the world (Rorty 1979b:85). Foucault understands what Lawson articulates as the paradox of reflexivity: the wholly inescapable "turning back" on ourselves that occurs in all inquiry (Lawson 1985).

However, if one gross mistake is avoided—if one understands that *The History of Sexuality* is not about the cultural face of sex in contrast to its natural reality—a second, more subtle interpretive mistake also needs to be avoided. In an important sense, the book is not really about its title any more than it is about objective sex. It is an Aesopian book about sexuality. At a deeper level, *The History of Sexuality* is primarily about how a particular institutionalized ideational construct came to be the truth and to constitute knowledge; it is about how that construct came to be taken as natural. The trouble is that *The History of Sexuality* may look to some readers like an historical exposé, appearing to offer only a more accurate account of certain independent developments which were somehow distorted. Even if one agrees that Foucault is not concerned only with the cultural face of an objective sexual nature, because he denies the repression of sexuality it could be interpreted that he is concerned with objective events that were deliberately misrepresented. But we saw in Chapter 4 that power is not "subjective" and hence is not conspiratorial. Foucault is not arguing that the presently dominant view of sex, as largely repressed since the Victorian period, is the result of a conspiracy, but rather that it is a product of one set of power-relations. To

show this he recounts an alternative history of sexuality crafted to reveal
the roles played by those power-relations, highlighting just the things
those operant power-relations obscured. This is not exposure of a conspiracy; it is a genealogical analysis of sexuality.

The character of Foucault's own intellectual and political background
tends to bolster the wrongheaded view that *The History of Sexuality* is an
exposé of covert manipulations relating to sexuality. Some read Foucault
as in the Marxian tradition, and so as arguing that power disguises what
actually happens with a deceptive façade of its own making designed to
foster the ends of those with power. Some take him as thinking that history is distorted by power; as thinking that history is "the ruse of reason"
and that "power is the ruse of history" (Foucault 1980a:95). And though
Foucault does refer to capitalism and the bourgeoisie in *The History of
Sexuality* and elsewhere, this would be an erroneous interpretation of
The History of Sexuality in particular and Foucault in general because it
requires understanding power as covert domination. Unfortunately, this
misinterpretation is common, and Foucault is well aware that too many
take him to be arguing that knowledge is "no more than a thin mask
thrown over the structures of domination." Foucault scorns this view, re-
marking that those "who say that for me knowledge is the mask of power
seem to me quite incapable of understanding" (Foucault 1988b:264).

Precisely because this is a fairly common and superficially support-
able interpretation, it is worth reiterating that it is wrong to think that
power is only subtle or covert manipulation or domination and to read
Foucault as saying merely that we are indirectly and cunningly manipulated as opposed to obviously so. This misconception casts power as
conspiratorial or, worse still, as a dark force shaping events. As we saw in
Chapter 4, Foucauldian power is no one's power nor any kind of force.
Our present sexuality is not a product of power in the sense of being the
consequence of a successful conspiracy or the effect of an irresistible
mysterious force. But to better understand how sexuality is a product of
power, we have to look at *The History of Sexuality* in detail.

The Will to Knowledge

To begin, we must recall that which is detailed in *Discipline and Punish*,
namely, how power forms subjects by disciplining individuals to believe
themselves to be persons having a certain nature. The formation of a
subject requires that it seem to each power-shaped subject that she or
he is that subject naturally. If there is reflection on one's subjectivity, on
what sort of subject one is, the aim must be to discover something about
one's given nature, not to understand how one was produced as a subject. When it occurs, reflective introspection must be engaged in by an

individual with a view to getting past the effects of enculturation to the "real self." And among all that subjects are disciplined to take as natural, there is nothing in the contemporary Christian and post-Freudian view more fundamental than sexuality: "Since Christianity, Western civilization has not stopped saying, 'To know who you are, know what your sexuality is about'" (Foucault 1989:138). As Hekman remarks, Foucault is maintaining that "the essence of ... the subject is to be found in sexuality because, in the west, subjects fin[d] their 'truth' in their sexuality" (Hekman 1990:70). Foucault's treatment of sexuality, therefore, is the cardinal application of his genealogical analytics and of his views on the constitutive and enabling aspects of power-relations.

The History of Sexuality begins by describing us as inheritors of the Victorian Age. The point is to characterize the accepted view of sexuality as repressed, which Foucault questions and ultimately rejects. In contrasting his own view with the accepted one, Foucault draws a crucial distinction: On one side is a regime of sexuality in which questions about sex and sexual behavior have to do with what is licit and illicit, what is in accordance with or in contravention of the law. On the other side is a regime in which questions about sex and sexual behavior have to do with what is normal and abnormal. The crucial difference is that in the first regime sexual activity is regulated by imposed codes and in the second social beings become self-regulating sexual agents by adopting norms that become continuous with their own values and desires. In the regime of law, adherence to rules or conventions is externally coerced behavior. Where behavior is governed by internalized norms, individuals need not be coerced, because they behave according to those norms by their own desire; their wills become that of the community.

The law regime is described by Foucault as a "deployment of alliances." Law-based regulation of sexuality includes alliances or compacts that legitimize and enforce standards of conduct and redress delinquent behavior falling short of outright illegality. The alliances are relations among families. In the law regime, socially recognized sexual union, that is, marriage, is deemed less a matter of mutual attraction leading to the sexual bonding and cohabitation of two individuals than a procreative partnership and so the contractual bonding of two families. Alliances of this kind involve complex rules about sexual behavior. For instance, brides must be virginal and wives totally monogamous to ensure that offspring are genetically as well as legally "legitimate." Sanctions include disinheritance and disownment. The law regime is one in which legal prohibitions supervene various regulatory affiliations and associations that develop to govern individuals' behavior through the enforcement of standards. The law is construed as articulating and institutionalizing aspects of broad standards for desirable conduct and is considered necessary because those standards are taken as essentially running counter to "natural" inclinations. The alliances are the first line of defense against "immoral" or unacceptable conduct; the law only crystallizes the more central prohibitions.

In contrast to the law regime, the norm-governed regime is described by Foucault as the "deployment of sexuality." The thing deployed is a particular conception that, once adopted, first determines what is sexual and then regulates every aspect of thought, discourse, and behavior regarding the sexual. The regulation of sexuality, then, is not through coercion but through the shaping of perceptions, desires, and agents themselves. The deployed sexuality regulates sexual behavior by manufacturing sexuality as a particular nature. Deployment of sexuality makes individuals into self- and other-perceived subjects having specific needs and wants, through individuals' acceptance of the deployed nature as their own.

The differences between the deployments of alliances and of sexuality can be clarified by considering that in the alliances-deployment case sexual activity is taken as a very diverse given and particular acts are legally proscribed. "Allowable" sexual activity is delineated more or less by default through the prohibition of specific sexual acts that are deemed against nature. Acts not proscribed then appear to be unproblematic because of their naturalness. Typically heterosexual intercourse is acknowledged as "natural" and in effect sanctioned by the legal proscription of "unnatural" homosexual sodomy. But in the sexuality-deployment case, heterosexual intercourse becomes more than a natural and so allowable form of sexual activity; instead it becomes the defining expression of human sexual nature and, as such, the norm. Acts like homosexual sodomy then become departures from the norm: "The sodomite had been a temporary aberration; the homosexual was now a species" (Foucault 1980a:43). Thus the desire to engage in such acts is not only a desire to engage in an unnatural act, but a manifestation of something deeply amiss in the agent's nature. In the alliances-deployment case, a homosexually active individual is a criminal, mainly concerned with not getting caught; in the sexuality-deployment case, a homosexually active individual is a pervert, mainly concerned with having a shameful affliction.

With respect to differences in modes of regulation between deployments, in the case of alliances nothing need be hidden. On the contrary, laws must be publicly promulgated, and alliances are overtly deployed to complement and reinforce those laws. In the case of sexuality-deployment, a great deal must be hidden, because otherwise the deployment will fail. But this is not to say that some person or group conspires to camouflage and conceal the deployment. The point is that power constrains actions or comportments in ways that are not evident. Unlike in the deployment of alliances, no regulations are explicitly laid down; rather, self-defining values and conceptions are deployed. Recall the point running through *Discipline and Punish*, the point central to the deployment of sexuality: The individual must come to take herself or himself to be a certain sort of being with fairly specific needs and inclinations that can be satisfied in proper and improper ways, and the individual must come to want to satisfy those needs and inclinations in the proper ways. Since the key to regulation by norms (as opposed to coercion) is getting the subject to participate in his or her own surveillance, the subject must not be aware that he or she is being made to adopt or internalize certain norms. Subjects must believe that those norms are manifestations of their own nature, and so despise in themselves any inclination to contravene them.

Foucault contends that there was a major shift in attitudes about sex in the seventeenth century. The change was one from candor and relative openness regarding sexuality toward a view of sexuality as properly restricted to the familial context. Sexual activity was localized, in the sense that "[a] single locus of sexuality was acknowledged ... the parents' bedroom" (Foucault 1980a:3). The circumscription, of course, was not purely locative, because the sanctioned location was defined by legal status. As important as the circumscription of sexuality was the consequent circumscription of deviancy to certain locales: "The brothel and the mental hospital would be ... places of tolerance." The circumscription of deviancy involved the classification of individuals into types: "the prostitute, the client, and the pimp, together with the psychiatrist and his hysteric." Through circumscription and classification the deployment of sexuality "surreptitiously transferred the pleasures that are unspoken into the order of things that are counted" (Foucault 1980a:4).

The contention about the quantification of "pleasures that are unspoken" may be read as adding or revealing a normative dimension of Foucault's claims and raises a point that needs to be acknowledged in passing. Some see Foucault's claims in the area of sexuality as, at least in part, rationalizations of his personal sexual orientation and preferences. Certainly there are problematic passages in his works, such as the insensitive and abuser-centered portrayal of child molestation in *The History of Sexuality*, that appear to be clearly tendentious and self-serving in ways having little to do with the philosophical or historical points at issue (Foucault 1980a:31–32). There is also an ongoing discussion of how Foucault's own sexual orientation and his questionable interest in sadomasochism and necrophilia may have colored his work (Foucault 1989:212–31; Miller 1993). Thus we need to separate Foucault's own predilections, together with the difficult ethical and political problems they raise, from his attempts to rethink the accepted and familiar. It is not my intent to clarify, much less justify, dubious things Foucault said and wrote about sexual matters. The point is to explain Foucault's genealogical views, not condemn or exonerate unfortunate but philosophically unimportant digressions.

Foucault states that the deployment of sexuality aims "to define the regime of power-knowledge-pleasure that sustains the discourse on human sexuality" (Foucault 1980a:11). His genealogical aim, therefore, is to trace the interrelated strategies and devices operant in that deployment, to describe the means by which variegated sexual activity is integrated and objectified into something then perceived as in need not only of specialized investigation, but of rigorous control. Foucault raises three questions: (1) Has there been, in fact, repression of sexuality? (2) Do "the workings of power ... really belong primarily to the category of repression?" (3) Did "the critical discourse that addresses itself to repression ... act as a roadblock to a power mechanism ... or is it ... part of [what] it denounces"? (Foucault 1980a:10).

The first question, which relates ostensibly to the book's main concern, challenges the familiar view that sexuality has been restricted and hidden since the Victorian period. This is typical Foucault: taking the accepted or obvious and asking whether that obviousness might not obscure the opposite of that taken to be the case. Foucault answers this first question by presenting a very different picture of what goes undisputed—maintaining that apparent repression of sexuality was actually an explosive increase of interest in sex, and the bulk of his subsequent discussion in the text sorts out the ways that interest was disguised. The second question, by challenging the view of the exercise of repressive power over sexuality, provides a context for expanding the reconception of power Foucault presents in *Discipline and Punish*. The answer to the second question is philosophically the most intriguing one, being the claim that the ages-old conception of power as domination and prohibition—and in the case of sexuality as coercive repression—falls well short of capturing the complexity and productive and enabling nature of power-relations. The third question raises the possibility that talk about repression of sexuality serves not to introduce candor by countering repression, but instead advances, extends, and consolidates the deployment of sexuality. Foucault's point is that learned talk about the repression of sexuality may be not liberating but integral to the deployment of the sexuality our culture takes as manifest and natural.

As these questions make clear, the focus of *The History of Sexuality* is not sexuality as such, for that would be to chase an apparition rather than to trace sexuality's emergence and descent. Foucault sets out "to account for the fact that [sex] is spoken about, to discover who does the speaking." We are told that the issue addressed is "the way in which sex is 'put into discourse'" (Foucault 1980a:11). Foucault is not concerned "to formulate the truth about sex," nor, as stressed above, to expose the "falsehoods designed to conceal that truth" (Foucault 1980a:12). The aim is to understand the will to knowledge that shapes and supports what then are taken as truths and falsehoods about sex. That is, the aim is to understand how learned discourse and disciplined inquiry produce a certain conception of sexuality that is then hailed as the discovered truth inquiry sought. This is a difficult idea to grasp for those new to Foucault, who think that if there is a question about sexuality, the correct procedure must be to look more carefully at sexuality; they are not prepared to accept as an initial premise that sexuality is the product of discourse. As noted earlier, this premise will be seen as idealist or irrealist, as hopelessly relativistic. But the premise must be tentatively accepted if we are to proceed, because it is only by working our way through *The History of Sexuality* that the premise can be clarified and its force demonstrated.

The pivotal importance of the premise that sexuality is a product of discourse is suggested by Foucault's use of the phrase "the will to know" as the French title of *The History of Sexuality, Volume One.* The point is that sexuality is the outcome of a will to know. The irony is that since there is no timeless, objective truth to be discerned (and the discernment of which would constitute knowledge), the will to know is a blind and futile drive to learn what is illusory and thus unattainable. That drive, then, can only be satisfied when disciplined inquiry and learned discourse produce what counts as knowledge and as truth. The will to know is in effect a drive to manufacture truth and knowledge. Foucault wants us to understand how we developed our discourse on sexuality and so made certain notions and ideas about our sexual nature into truth and knowledge. He wants us to understand how we manufacture the truth about sexuality and then appropriate the result as knowledge about ourselves.

Despite the foregoing warning that it is a mistake to read *The History of Sexuality* as an exposé, a key point regarding power and sexuality needs to be repeated. Having considered power in Chapter 4, the point can be made briefly. The traditional conception of power is of might or force held by some and exercised over others. So conceived, power is inherently coercive and prohibitive; it is the ability to make others do what one wants done or not do what one does not want done. Power so conceived is "subjective"; it is possessed and wielded by agents to achieve desired and envisaged ends by coercing other agents to act or not act. But as we have seen, one of Foucault's most perceptive and controversial insights regarding power is that power is "intentional and nonsubjective," that it is impersonal (Foucault 1980a:94). The deployment of sexuality is the work of power, but that deployment is no one's work. The change from alliances to our present sexuality is not to be thought of as a vast conspiracy. *The History of Sexuality* is a study of how impersonal power, not scheming individuals or groups, produced a sexuality so successfully deployed that it was and continues to be taken as manifest truth by many millions of people.

Two short chapters, "The Incitement to Discourse" and "The Perverse Implantation," offer the basic thesis of what Foucault calls the repressive hypothesis or the view that sexuality has been repressed. Foucault does not simply deny the repressive hypothesis; he acknowledges its actuality in a limited domain (Foucault 1980a:17–18). The point is that the repressive hypothesis is not the dominant truth of our era. Foucault does not deny that there was, roughly from the latter half of the seventeenth century onward, a new and increasingly extensive policing of sexual activity; he does not deny that there was, for example, censorship. Foucault aims to show that the policing was not primarily repressive, that instead of sexuality being repressed, there was "a veritable discursive explosion" about it (Foucault 1980a:17). The multifaceted policing of sexual activity—social, political, medical, and religious—is shown not to be repression at all by the fact that at the level of discourse "the opposite phenomenon occurred. There was a steady proliferation of discourses concerned with sex." However, Foucault feels that even more significant than the sheer expansion of talk about sexuality was "the multiplication of discourses concerning sex in the field of exercise of power itself" (Foucault 1980a:18). The newly generated discourses themselves became regulatory instruments; they augmented the mechanisms that gave rise to them. Every element of the policing of sexual activity carried with it more talk about its subject matter, and talk in turn tightened the control over subject matter. There was proliferation of studies, elaboration of reasons for the need for control, development of accounts of the nature that prompted specific activities, explanation of the benefits of control, survey of reactions, and ever more extensive canvassing and inventorying of attitudes and views.

Foucault uses the institution of confession (whether medical, religious, or other) as an example of how discourse grew, how individuals were made complicitous in their own control, and how sexuality was more and more objectified, quantified, and codified. Confession not only required disclosure of violations against sexual codes and norms, it required detailed examination of those violations and their motivation. Disclosure and examination were justified as integral to an understanding of one's sexual nature; understanding was considered to be a requisite to mental and physical health. Disclosure and examination not only advanced and extended the discourse on sexuality, they engaged the sexual agent in the increasing circumscription and scrutiny of her or his sexual activity. Agents, whose sexual activity was coming under ever greater control, were made participants in that control through devices, such as confession, made to appear as beneficial self-examination. People were "drawn for three centuries to the task of telling everything concerning ... sex"; the inducement to tell all involved an "optimization and an increasing valorization of the discourse on sex" with the objective of "displacement, intensification, reorientation, and modification of desire itself" (Foucault 1980a:23). The process of revelation, classification, and displacement reshaped and redirected the sexual agent's desires. The new perception of sexuality and of oneself as a certain sort of sexed being changed what the agent could allow herself or himself to want and thus, eventually, that which was actually wanted.

Foucault describes sexuality as coming more and more under broadly political control. But what came under control was not a sexuality that previously had been uncontrolled or differently controlled. Sexuality was defined and produced through technical vocabularies employed in the imposition of a kind of control that assimilated formerly diverse acts and inclinations into a unitary kind. The techniques projected and objectified a particular sexuality that automatically came under the authority of those same techniques; in accepting that sexuality as *their* sexuality, individuals collaborated in their own control.

As a consequence of objectification sexuality became "not something one simply judged; it was a thing one administered" (Foucault 1980a:24). Discursive treatment of sexuality defined, circumscribed, and controlled sexual attitudes, values, and behavior; it made attitudes, values, and behavior proper objects of regulative administration by scientific, political, and religious institutions. Given acceptance of the nature of sexuality, there was a resultant perception of a need to impose controls to inhibit supposedly natural but unwanted activities, such as promiscuity. Promiscuity was seen in some as an inclination, a kind of exaggeration of an instinctive tendency, but nevertheless a potentially socially disruptive inclination. Therefore, institutionalized curbs were deemed necessary. But they were different from more extensive legal, social, and religious prohibitions. This is central to the contrast between the deployment of alliances and of sexuality. When sexuality was made a matter of truth and knowledge about a nature, its administration required increasingly more extensive information to support effective control. In this way, by making sexuality a proper object of scientific study, discursive treatment rendered sexuality pliable regarding the results of theoretical development. The control of sexuality not only required theory-shaped information, it had to be adjusted in conformity to the fruits of further theorizing. There could be "discoveries" about the nature of sexuality; sets of accepted standards could be overturned by new "discernment" of some aspect or factor supposedly previously missed. Thus control could not be static. It had to be administrative in the sense of regulation through an ongoing application of a growing body of knowledge about sexuality.

Part Two of *The History of Sexuality* characterizes contemporary sexuality as a product promulgated through technicalized discourse. Foucault aims to ensure recognition that something taken as natural is actually an artifact, a construct. But he partly aims to ensure further recognition that not only is sexuality an artifact, it is one designed to require and facilitate regulation. If there had been plotters behind the deployment of sexuality, if there had been designers of sexuality, they could be credited with having carefully developed a conception of sexuality the very nature of which supported and indeed demanded extensive and quite complex control. But because there were no plotters, Foucault's ingenious point emerges clearly: The conception of sexuality was the result of the imposition of controls. In this sense, the control comes before that which is controlled; it was the imposition of various forms of regulation, dependent on equally various learned discourses about sexuality, that manufactured and deployed a unified conception of sexuality. The key to this apparently paradoxical contention is in Foucault's conception of power, because the control was not repressive or prohibitive; the control imposed was productive regulation that only wore the mask of repression while enabling huge expansion of discourse about sex. That discourse unified disparate regulatory practices, coalescing them into a cohesive conception of sexuality that reflexively legitimated those practices.

Part Three of *The History of Sexuality,* "Scientia Sexualis," deals with how sexuality was made the subject of scientific inquiry and how sexuality became "not only a matter of sensation and pleasure, of law and taboo, but also of truth and falsehood." The focus is how "sex was constituted as a problem of truth" (Foucault 1980a:56). The title is intended to indicate that our culture largely lacks an *ars erotica,* a tradition of artful treatment of sexuality intended to explore and enhance a dimension of human experience. In our culture erotica is at best a dubious commodity. Erotica is always in danger of sliding into pornography, and its purpose is usually seen as titillation rather than providing insight into sexual reality and possibility (and so augmenting sexual pleasure and practical—as opposed to theoretical—understanding). In our culture sexuality is cast as the proper subject matter of scientific investigation, not of artistic embellishment. Sexuality is not something to be imaginatively enriched; it is something to be studied. Therefore its portrayal, whether artistic or clinical, should be not for its own sake, as it sometimes is in literature and film, but for the sake of serving investigative ends. What Foucault views as most important, in sexuality being a scientific instead of an artistic domain, is that in our culture sexuality is something about which there are truths to be discerned. Rather than sexuality being an aesthetic and moral concern, it is a scientific one. Sexuality is a problem of truth and knowledge, so its aesthetic and even moral aspects are seen as consequent and secondary to what its scientific study reveals.

One result of sexuality's becoming a problem of truth is that new power-relations developed that turned on greater or lesser knowledge about sexuality. It became possible for some people to be more technically knowledgeable about sexual behavior than others, to be expert about sexuality, and so to be capable of considering and explaining sexual behavior in theoretical terms not recognizable to most people, regardless of how sexually active and practically knowledgeable. Correspondingly, it became possible for less knowledgeable individuals to accept theoretical accounts as accurate depictions of intimate events in their lives. Experiences that were once merely gratifying were redescribed and reconceived not as pleasing in themselves, but pleasing because they satisfied various drives and other unrecognized or introspectively inaccessible determinants. Sexually active individuals thus came to feel a need for explanations of those drives and determinants in order to understand their own pleasure. But the most important consequence of sexuality becoming a problem of truth was that expertise about sexuality enabled and supported claims about discerning the differences between normal and abnormal. Suddenly all sexually active persons were vulnerable to classification based on conformity to or deviance from norms generated by an objective sexual nature. This vulnerability in turn engendered a deeper vulnerability to self-classification as a certain sort of sexual being.

Discipline and Punish shows how prisoners are disciplined to perceive themselves as persons of a particular sort through the implementation of theory-supported techniques that regulate their lives and gain their compliance in their own surveillance. *The History of Sexuality* shows how members of a society are trained to perceive themselves as having a certain sexual nature through the deployment of theories and practices that define that nature and so determine the realms of the normal and abnormal. What establishes the deployed theories and practices as authoritative is that, in being the object of scientific study, sexuality is taken to be something discovered and unveiled rather than constructed and imposed. The self-surveillance gained in the case of sexuality, then, is individuals' vigilance regarding whether their sexual inclinations and activities are proper expressions of their sexual nature or are somehow deviant. The other side of the coin is that some members of society perceive themselves as empowered by special knowledge to exercise control over sexuality to prevent and correct deviancy.

Keeping in mind the earlier remarks about separating Foucault's sexual escapades from his analysis of sexuality, it seems his admiration for California's permissive subculture revealed something like indignation with any presumption of the right to identify and control deviancy. This point emerges particularly clearly in Miller's biography (Miller 1993). Its relevance at this juncture is that though we must separate sex from an analysis of sex, we must acknowledge an argument made by many feminist writers: It is often the marginalized or oppressed who most clearly see what is amiss in a given social order.

Interestingly, Foucault points out that had sexuality become the object of scientific study in the usual way, the consequences might have been less constraining. That is, the technicalization of sexuality might have remained arcane and had only a marginal impact on most people, the way botany has little direct impact on gardening. But as we are told early in Part Three of *The History of Sexuality,* in the nineteenth century disciplined interest in sexuality went beyond the study of reproduction, biological, and physiological matters. Standard scientific procedures and the limitations they imposed were overridden; there developed a "medicine of sex" supported only by a "distant and quite fictitious guarantee" tenuously connected to the scientific study of sexuality (Foucault 1980a:55). Unfortunately, the line dividing science and the "medicine of sex" was blurry. The literature of the time shows how even the most scientifically meticulous biologists and physiologists mixed dubious editorial asides with expert pronouncements on sexual traits. Feminists are well aware of how science, particularly medical science, was and is bent to generate, maintain, and enhance sexual stereotypes (Ehrenreich and English 1973).

In connection with development of the medicine of sex, Foucault again displays his ability to rethink the familiar. He claims that Freud's work threatened rather than expedited the deployment of sexuality. (Remember: The distinction between the deployment of alliances and of sexuality is one between regimes based on law versus internalized norms.) According to Foucault, Freud's psychoanalytic work "rediscovered the law of alliance, the involved workings of marriage and kinship" (Foucault 1980a:113). This meant that Freud offered the "guarantee that one would find the parents-children relationship at the root of everyone's sexuality." Foucault argues that this rediscovery could have "made it possible ... to keep the deployment of sexuality coupled to the system of alliance" and forced recognition that sexuality was "constituted only through the law" and was not an objective nature (Foucault 1980a:113). The deployment of sexuality would then be seen for what it was: imposition of a sexual nature through the development of a discourse. In spite of his ambivalence about Freud's work, Foucault contends that Freud threatened the conception of sexuality as defined by heterosexual procreative intercourse and the reconception of other sexual activities as perversions of the paradigm. Freud showed sexuality to be diffuse, its manifestations to have discernible causes, and its regulation to be a matter of what is civilly tolerated. Deployment of a conception of sexuality as natural, its regulation a matter of preventing deviant expression, thus looks highly problematic to those who have understood Freud.

The developments Foucault describes in Part 3 of *The History of Sexuality* brought together two previously distinct generative interests—human beings as a species and the workings of the human body (Dreyfus and Rabinow 1983:134–35). Human nature had been problematic only with respect to whether it was created by God or evolved naturally. In the changes Foucault describes in *The History of Sexuality,* as well as in *Madness and Civilization* and *The Birth of the Clinic,* human nature became problematic in other ways. The *nature* of human nature became an object of scientific study and debate. In other words several human natures were created in learned discourse, and each competing theoretical construct had practical consequences regarding the regulation of behavior and hence the control of human beings. As we saw in Chapter 4, this control was initially most evident in specific areas such as the clinic and prison, where theory served the management of well-defined groups of individuals excluded from society on the basis of shared traits and gathered together. The deployment of sexuality extended control globally, not on the basis of some set of abnormal traits or practices, but on the basis that male and female human beings are members of a species instantiating a single nature amenable to productive disciplinary investigation.

An Interim Retrospective

In order to provide the clearest explanation of Foucault's views, a certain amount of repetition is required. It may prove useful at this point to summarize what has been said.

Foucault maintains that beginning in the seventeenth century human beings came under scientific scrutiny in a new way—as entities possessed of a particular nature. Previously they had been scrutinized juridically, politically and, in a looser way, socially, but always as individuals capable of acting in various ways: as law-abiding or law-breaking agents, as observers or violators of various secular or ecclesiastical pro-

BELMONT UNIVERSITY LIBRARY

hibitions, as parties to marital contracts. Scrutinized as entities instantiating a particular nature, human beings came to be governed less by
laws that prohibited fairly specific actions and more by norms that determined the natural propriety and unnatural impropriety of actions.
Acceptable and unacceptable behavior was reconceived, less as the diverse actions of individuals and more as the proper or distorted manifestations of the drives and needs inherent in the nature shared by those
individuals. As scientific theories developed about human nature, juridical, political, and social regulatory practices became increasingly integrated and facilitated by recasting control as regulation of natural inclinations and limitations, rather than as a disparate collection of coercive
prohibitions. As we saw in *Discipline and Punish,* earlier repressive measures, which had been legitimated solely by the power of the monarch,
were displaced by consolidated regulatory devices, which were judged
to be necessitated by the putative nature of those to be controlled. Those
regulatory devices were thus legitimated by that nature. Lawbreakers
came to be considered—and to consider themselves—as beings possessed of certain tendencies, and therefore deservedly the objects of
constraint.

In the case of sexuality, men and women came to perceive of themselves as naturally possessing certain traits that carry the potential for
perverted expression, and thus perceived themselves as perhaps need-
ful of regulation. Alliances to regulate sexual behavior became redun-
dant when a new sexuality was deployed, which recast the individual as
a sexual being possessing a nature that automatically generates sexual
norms and the necessity of curbing deviance. The main burden of regulation is transferred to the individual, who seeks to attain and maintain
her or his proper or natural sexual identity by acting in specified ways
and refraining from acting in ways recast as aberrant. Most central to the
legitimation of control by appeal to natural traits and proclivities is the
complicity of subjects in regulating their own behavior. Only when we
fully appreciate the necessity of that complicity can we understand Foucault's view that the exercise of power is most effective and best tolerated when masked. The exercise of power is masked when those constrained believe something about themselves requires constraint. The
most effective way to achieve this cognitive end, to get people to believe
their very own nature calls for regulation, is to promulgate a scientific
conception of human beings as having a specific objective nature, one
that is replete with possibilities for unnatural and deleterious expression.

This is what Foucault calls the deployment of sexuality. Through deployment, control seemingly serves nature and necessity and does not

clearly arise from a particular historical conglomeration of values, theories, and practices.

Regarding the specific devices that are integral to the deployment of sexuality, Foucault focuses on the institution of confession, which may be instantiated in a psychiatric, medical, sociological, or religious context. In confession individuals are required to objectify and discuss their own inclinations, desires, pleasures, and fears in ways that make these the subjects of theoretical analysis and assessment and the bases for behavioral constraints. Confession juxtaposes the confessing individual with one or more other individuals, who assume a significant measure of authority over him or her. Confession "unfolds within a power relationship, for one does not confess without ... a partner who is not simply the interlocutor but the authority who requires the confession" (Foucault 1980a:61).

The Mechanics of the Will to Power

To continue our explanation, Foucault lists five devices used to shape individuals into sexual beings of a particular sort, to produce a subjectivity that incorporates the conception that "subjects fin[d] their 'truth' in their sexuality" (Hekman 1990:70). The devices are the "clinical codification of the inducement to speak," the "postulate of a general and diffuse causality," the "principle of a latency intrinsic to sexuality," a "method of interpretation," and the "medicalization of the effects of confession" (Foucault 1980a:65–67).

Clinical codification of the inducement to speak is the integration of confession and examination to enhance the individual's complicity in regulation. Everything from medical questionnaires to interrogation contributes to the erosion of the difference between a third-party record of an individual's treatment and that individual's own perceptions. The individual's most intimate thoughts are made relevant to a medical or psychological record. Rather than keeping some ideas or desires private, the subject is convinced that total disclosure is the only avenue to normality, a goal more valued than an individuality that comes to be perceived as suspect, if not perverse. The subject comes to want to tell all, because doing so is seen as requisite to achieving normality. Everything told is categorized and assimilated into a record, which then assumes a greater authority about the individual's states of mind than any introspective conviction she or he may hold. In this way, the subject is constituted as an object of knowledge by the relevant disciplines, and any "internal" counterinfluences to adopting the resulting conception by the individual are minimized.

Much of the force behind the inducement to speak, the encouragement of revelation, derives from the postulation of a diffuse causality, the view that sex can be the cause of almost anything that might prove detrimental to the individual. For instance, even blindness or crippling pain can be due to hysteria, and since hysteria supposedly is a sexual disorder there is no antecedent criterion for determining what maladies are and are not related to sexual problems. A notorious and deplorably common case in point is the persistent diagnosis of women's complaints as due not to somatic factors but rather the psychological effects of menopause. The perception of sex as the possible cause of almost any sort of distress reinforces the view that the most intimate and private idea or desire may be relevant to diagnosis and treatment. There are no limits imposed by modesty or propriety on questions that health practitioners may put to patients, or even on what the patient may tell the practitioner. The patient cooperates willingly, sharing the assumption that only total candor can enable effective diagnosis—and thereby facilitate the achievement or reachievement of normality.

The third device, the principle of a special latency intrinsic to sexuality, adds force to the inducement to speak. It makes it possible for practitioners and agents themselves to pursue the most elusive and apparently peripheral notions and desires, on the assumption that the causes of sexual behavior are deeply buried. Virtually anything the patient thinks or says is taken as potentially crucial. Again, the patient is compelled to tell everything, and the practitioner must consider every utterance relevant to diagnosis and treatment. One result is that the superabundance of material, provided by the patient and recorded by the practitioner, ensures that interpretation of that material can satisfy practically any theoretical expectation. Because of the abundance, because nothing related by the patient can be excluded, and because nothing can be taken as evidently more or less important, anything in the patient's record can be focused on and given importance and so made to meet theoretical expectations. But rather than being recognized as guaranteeing that the operant theory goes unchallenged, this interpretive indeterminacy itself is seen as evidence of the elusiveness and complexity of sexual motivation and causality, and so as corroboration of the theories that foster it.

The fourth device, the method of interpretation, focuses on how confessions are treated and dealt with. That which is confessed is not limited to the particular case in which it occurs; it is interpreted to fit preexistent theory–described general patterns. Confessions thus serve the deployment of sexuality in two ways: First, they further embroil both patient and practitioner in the operant discourse, and second, because they are supposedly revelatory of an underlying common and unitary sexuality, confessions authenticate the deployed sexuality. Though the appearance is that of carefully discerning the nature and scope of sexuality through analysis of confessional revelations, actually confessional revelations are interpreted and structured by the operant theory in ways that make them confirming instances of the theories behind the deployed sexuality and hence confirmation that the deployed sexuality is indeed an objective nature slowly being limned and comprehended.

Finally, the fifth device, the medicalization of the effects of confession, is the reconception of confession as having less a cathartic than comparative purpose. This reconception follows from the others; central is that confessional revelations are assessed not in terms of acknowledgment of perceived right and wrong actions, but in terms of the characterization of normal and abnormal behavior. Their purpose, then, is not cathartic in the traditional purgative sense; rather it is to provide an intimately detailed picture of the patient that can be compared to the deployed paradigm of the "normal" sexual being, namely, a heterosexual individual concerned primarily with procreation and only secondarily with gratification. Whereas at one time the sanctity of confession depended on the morally accountable discretion of the confessor, its sanctity now is a matter of bureaucratic propriety—the sanctioned use of diagnostic material and maintenance of the anonymity of the confessing patient outside the context of diagnosis and treatment.

Foucault sees the cumulative effect of these devices as follows. Where other cultures conceive of sexuality as a multifarious aspect of life that defies comprehensive understanding and is best dealt with artistically, Western culture conceives of sexuality as a complex but essentially unitary defining aspect of human nature best dealt with a *scientia sexualis* capable of fully mapping that complexity. Instead of repressing sexuality, or enhancing it artistically, our culture has made sexuality an object of intense and extensive disciplinary research and study. More specifically, our culture has imposed on itself, and then pursued, the task of "producing true discourses" pertaining to sexuality. What emerged "in the nineteenth century" was not the "refusal of recognition" of sex but rather extensive and complicated "machinery for producing true discourses concerning it" (Foucault 1980a:67–69). Those discourses determined the nature of our supposedly inherent sexuality and shaped what it is we take ourselves to be as sexed creatures.

This may look to many like an account of deliberate deception; *The History of Sexuality* will thus look like a liberating exposé. This is a view Foucault is most anxious to defeat, namely, that "truth is intrinsically opposed to power and therefore inevitably plays a liberating role" (Dreyfus and Rabinow 1983:127). But this clash productively highlights the deepest philosophical implications of *The History of Sexuality*. Here

we see that Foucault's rejection of the repressive hypothesis goes beyond rejection of a particular construal of our sexual history. The
claimed repression of sexuality is contested, not only as the dominant
truth of an era, but as the embodiment of a fundamental conception of
the nature and role of truth.

For traditionalists, truth is objective and its discernment is the means
of liberation from error, skeptical doubts, confusion, ideological and
cultural distortions, and self- or other-imposed deception. But Foucault's discussion of the five devices is not intended to expose deceptive
manipulation in order to enable circumvention or defeat of that manipulation. The point is to show how power-relations operate in the deployment of sexuality. Once that is accomplished, there should be realization
that awareness of the operations of power yields only the possibility of
change to some other set of subjectivity-shaping and practice-determining power-relations, not liberation. There can be no absolute liberation; the truth cannot make us free (Allen 1993:182). There is no dis-
course-independent truth the discernment of which can free us from
power.

Some think the inescapability from power renders the notion of power
incoherent, because power is without contrast, because one can only escape from one particular configuration of power-relations by entering
some other configuration: "There is no escaping from power ... it is always already present, constituting that very thing which one attempts to
counter it with" (Foucault 1980a:82; compare Taylor 1984). However, if
the claim that it is incoherent to conceive of power as all-encompassing
looks compelling, what is called for is reflection not on the notion of
power, but on the notion of liberation. What would it be to be free of all
constraints on thought and action, including the constraints imposed
by our own values and perspectives? Surely such "liberation" could only
be attainment of a wholly impossible Cartesian solipsistic autonomy. Attainable is what Foucault clearly valued and worked for, as is evident in
his political activism (Miller 1993). Attainable is change from more restrictive to more permissive power-relations or sets of constraints. Our
lot *can* be improved, but only in relative terms. As Kant's dove could not
fly without what it thought of as speed- and grace-restricting air, we cannot interact with one another and be free of power.

In Part Four of *The History of Sexuality,* "The Deployment of Sexuality," we find Foucault's most focused discussion of power-relations.
Foucault describes the manufacture of a norm-based conception of sexuality, and in so doing provides a detailed working model of how power-
relations enable and produce truth and knowledge. More significant
still, Foucault provides an account of how power-relations produce a
given subjectivity (and does so more effectively than in *Discipline and*

Punish, where the subjectivity produced is more limited in scope). However, in considering the account we must bear in mind three cautionary points. First, we saw in Chapter 4 that a good deal said about power or power-relations is negative. This is partly due to Foucault's nominalistic treatment of power-relations and partly due to the need for him to constantly contrast his conception of power with the established conception of power as domination. Second, power is not, after all, the main topic of discussion; power is the means to the production of subjectivity and therefore should not be given quite the centrality so many readers of Foucault give it. Of central importance is how power shapes subjectivity: "It is not power, but the subject, which is the general theme of my research" (Foucault 1983a:209).

The third cautionary point relates to the earlier notion that Foucault knowingly or inadvertently offers a theory of power. Foucault is adamant that he is not offering a theory of power; he insists that if one "tries to erect a theory of power one will always be obligated to … reconstruct its genesis" (Foucault 1980b:199). That would be to search for essences, which is why "Foucault's account of power is not intended as a theory" (Dreyfus and Rabinow 1983:184). Instead of a theory of power, Foucault develops what he calls "analytics" of power-relations, something we can best think of as a dynamic mapping of power or power-relations (Foucault 1980a:82). We have to understand that since power "is in reality an open, more-or-less coordinated … cluster of relations," we do not need a theory of power but rather "a grid of analysis which makes possible an analytic of relations of power" (Foucault 1980b:199). An analytics of power, a dynamic mapping of power-relations, is a genealogical exercise and so must remain wholly historical. It cannot be intended or construed "as a context-free, ahistorical, objective description" (Dreyfus and Rabinow 1983:184). The discussion about power or power-relations in Part Four of *The History of Sexuality,* then, is all there is to explain the notion of power. Beyond that, we must turn to the detailed descriptions of devices, strategies, and techniques in *Discipline and Punish* and *The History of Sexuality.*

The first chapter of Part Four, "Objective," describes not only what Foucault intends to establish in the first volume of *The History of Sexuality,* but the main point of six projected volumes (only three were published and part of a fourth completed). As I have stressed, the point is to trace and investigate the production of a certain sexual subjectivity. The discussion of power, then, is not conducted for its own sake, but to elucidate the mechanics of the deployment of sexuality and thus of the production of a certain subjectivity.

Contrasting it with his own conception of power, Foucault calls the traditional domination or coercive/prohibitive conception of power the "juridico-discursive" conception (Foucault 1980a:82). The point is to bring out how the traditional conception of power as coercive and prohibitive is exemplified in the state's promulgation and enforcement of laws. In this traditional conception, power is mainly proscriptive. Even when it is productive, in the limited sense of forcing something to be done, traditionally conceived power functions proscriptively by forbidding lack of compliance with promulgated prescriptive rules and laws.

Foucault attributes four defining characteristics to juridico-discursive power. First is the proscriptive or prohibitive character exemplified in the fact that with respect to "sex and pleasure ... power can 'do' nothing but say no to them" (Foucault 1980a:83). Juridico-discursive power over sexuality is exhausted by interdictions, exclusions, refusals, and taboos; it ranges over sexuality only with respect to what it prohibits. The unprohibited is ignored or at most sanctioned or tolerated by default rather than being explicitly enabled or condoned. In the premodern context the sexual was not unified as a kind in the realm of law; it was not an object of coercive and prohibitive power as a whole. The sexual was defined piecemeal, by proscriptive description in the identification of forbidden acts.

The second and related defining characteristic is the "insistence of the rule," which is conception of power as essentially regulatory in nature through the classification and prohibition of various acts as illicit. A key point is that the sundry acts judged to be illicit and regulated are, in being prohibited, separately identified. That is, in contrast to the deployment of sexuality, they are not acts classed and prohibited as intrinsically related aberrant expressions of a unified nature.

The third characteristic of traditionally conceived or juridico-discursive power is the "logic of censorship," which complements and enhances the prohibition of sexual acts and provocative material with effective denial of their existence. Foucault observes that "[t]he logic of power exerted on sex is the paradoxical ... injunction of nonexistence, nonmanifestation, and silence" (Foucault 1980a:84). It is not enough to prohibit certain acts and anything that might prompt or elicit them; the existence of some things must be denied. Some acts, and the respective motivating desires and anything that caters to those desires, must be systematically overlooked; their occurrence cannot be admitted. When these unthinkable acts cannot be ignored because reality forces itself on people, previous denial, rather than being exposed as deceptive or at least ineffectual, actually serves to make what has been denied appear more monstrous, making punishment, prevention, and continued denial even more compelling. Prohibition-through-denial not only survives intermittent lapses by making the acts it hides seem too bizarre to be real possibilities, it makes many of those tempted to perform those acts see themselves as in need of help to avoid violating their nature.

What Foucault captures in the third characteristic is that the most effective sort of prohibition is preclusion of awareness of certain possibilities. That sort of preclusion requires what is provided by the fourth juridico-discursive characteristic, the "uniformity of the apparatus." This is the consistency of denial, taboo, and prohibition across class and other societal distinctions. At least in theory, no one is exempt from the preventative application of traditionally conceived censorial power to sexual matters. The reality, of course, may be quite different, in that privilege grants some measure of impunity in the commission of forbidden acts.

Central to the four characteristics is that traditional power is deemed always to operate juridically; it is thought to be power "centered on nothing more than the statement of the law and the operation of taboos" (Foucault 1980a:85). The thrust of Chapter 1 of Part Four, then, is the point so thoroughly developed in *Discipline and Punish,* namely, that the traditional conception of power is coercive restraining force best exemplified by prohibitive law. The traditional conception of power is a thou-shalt-not conception, and the compulsion behind the prohibition is ultimately brute force, as in the physical restraint of the criminal or the imposition of pain or death. Significantly, power so conceived allows that those subjected to power may be liberated. Liberation can come from a greater, opposing power, or from exposure and consequent understanding-facilitated dismantling of the operant power structure. Foucault is careful to tightly link the idea that the truth can free us by revealing how we are manipulated to the traditional coercive/prohibitive conception of power. As indicated, it is fundamental to his own conception of power that though liberation can occur against particular instances of domination, escaping one set of power-relations can only be to enter another set and that, as we saw earlier, the only alternatives to immersion in power are an impossible solipsism, total enslavement, or death.

In Chapter 2 of Part Four, "Method," we find the most positive and extended description of Foucauldian power given in *The History of Sexuality*—the definitional passage we considered in some detail in the section on power in Chapter 4. It suffices to rephrase one or two central points. One concerns the relational nature of power. In an interview Foucault stresses that he "hardly ever" speaks of power; he claims that when he does speak of power, "it is always a short cut," a gloss on power-relations or relationships of power (Bernauer, J. and Rasmussen 1988:11). This underscores how power is wholly relational, how power is nothing but a "multiplicity of force relations." Those force-relations are not, of course, relations among forces in the sense of forces that are different from what they govern and structure, nor are these force-relations themselves governed by anything separate. Force-relations are "immanent in the sphere in which they operate and ... constitute their own organization" (Foucault 1980a:92). Force-relations are immanent in what they govern and structure in that they are nothing over and above the interrelatedness of past and present comportments that, in their interrelatedness, facilitate or inhibit ensuing comportments.

Force-relations are also self-sustaining; their immanence in what they govern and structure itself constitutes "the process which ... transforms, strengthens, or reverses them." As suggested with the magnet-analogy used in Chapter 4, what changes or cancels force-relations is nothing external but rather actions of agents who act in the environment those force-relations provide. Because they are not something other than what they structure, force-relations are identical with or are exhaustively instantiated in "the strategies in which they take effect." The multiplicity of force-relations is not a structure imposed on the actions of agents; it is the interactive totality of those actions. Nor are force-relations independent of one another or related only in a mutually exclusive way; power is also "the support which these force relations find in one another" (Foucault 1980a:92). This is how power is enabling, because the distribution or organization of some of the force-relations will facilitate or promote some actions and inhibit others.

Chapter 3 of Part Four, titled "Domain," focuses on four elements that Foucault identifies as pivotal in the deployment of sexuality. These are, first, the "hysterization of women's bodies"—the conception of women as essentially sexual beings, as "saturated with sexuality" and hence prone to a multitude of related infirmities; second, the "pedagogization of children's sex"—the conception of children as protosexual beings requiring strict control to prevent the development of abnormality; third, the "socialization of procreative behavior," or the installation of the heterosexual couple as the fundamental societal unit; and fourth, the "psychiatrization of perverse pleasure," or the creation of categories of abnormality and the related establishment of corrective techniques (Foucault 1980a:104–05). These strategic elements amount to "the very production of sexuality" (Foucault 1980a:105). The elements do not merely characterize but contribute constitutively to the establishment of what is then deemed a definitive aspect of human nature. Chapter 3 of Part Four also contains the gist of the socio-historical thesis of *The History of Sexuality,* which claims that the elements were produced by discourses initiated in the late seventeenth century. This is where we find explicit statement of the constructivist claim that contemporary sexuality is a product of discourse. The claim is articulated in terms of denial that there was repression of sexuality and description of the illusion of repression as masking the initiation and development of the new discourses that deployed our present sexuality.

Chapter 4 of Part Four, "Periodization," describes the historical progression of the development of late and post–seventeenth-century sexuality, emphasizing the role of social classes in that development. Contrary to the ideological climate of France and most of Europe at the time *The History of Sexuality* was written, Foucault argues against mainstream Marxists: Rather than being downwardly oriented and constituting the repression and exploitation of the working class, the deployment of sexuality is primarily a "self-affirmation" on the part of the bourgeoisie (Foucault 1980a:122). Most Marxists see bourgeois sexual values and practices as designed to restrict sex to the productive business of procreation and to diminish its potential as a counterproductive distraction. Against this view, Foucault maintains that, in deploying sexuality, the bourgeoisie is less concerned with manipulation of the working class than with institutionalizing its own special status. Foucault contends that in deploying sexuality the bourgeoisie "provided itself with a body to be cared for," a body defined and catered to by "a technology of sex" (Foucault 1980a:122).

Part Five of *The History of Sexuality* echoes the message of *Discipline and Punish* and stresses that the deployment of sexuality reflects and expresses a crucial change, from the government of people as primarily a matter of "dealing simply with legal subjects over whom the ultimate dominion was death" to a "taking charge of life." Government, used in the broad sense, changed from prohibiting specific acts to subject-shaping management of action (Foucault 1980a:142–43). As we saw in Chapter 4, and see here, the development of contemporary penality and sexuality are instances of the shift from the governing of populations as circumspect regulation to positive, productive administration through inculcation of values and perspectives. Rather than merely trying to stop people from doing what is deemed unacceptable, modern and contemporary administrative efforts are aimed at making them the sorts of persons who incorporate desirable aspirations and aversions as integral elements of their subjectivity.

Foucault's Truth-Claims

At the end of *The History of Sexuality* one is left with a three-layered problem: First, there are the largely historical issues raised by the claim that, rather than being repressed, sexuality has mushroomed into a monumental topic of discussion and study. Second, there are the more philosophically significant issues raised by Foucault's claims about the devices through which sexuality allegedly was deployed. These issues include the complex one of whether the devices he describes can or need be understood as instances and functions of something called "power," since one can accept much of what Foucault offers in critique of the established socio-historical accounts of sexuality and penality without accepting his more problematic notion of power. Third, there are the deeper and still more philosophically significant issues raised about truth and subjectivity.

All three sets of issues are intriguing, and considering them is important for understanding Foucault. But the issues about truth and subjectivity are the most fundamental; of the two, issues about truth are most pressing. Given seminal critiques by Hume, Nietzsche, Freud, and Mead of the deeply entrenched conception of subjectivity as inherently unitary, and more recent contributions by Daniel Dennett, Davidson, Derek Parfit, and Ricoeur, Foucault's emergentist conception of the subject, however novel and interesting, is a contribution to an ongoing, productive philosophical discussion (Dennett 1991; Davidson, D. 1989; Parfit 1984; Ricoeur 1992). Those new to Foucault may find his views on subjectivity too extreme, but not wholly unfamiliar or too eccentric to take seriously. Even though Foucault's conception of truth as a product of power may also appear to be a contribution to an ongoing, productive discussion, that appearance is quite misleading. Debates between traditionalists and postmoderns on truth range mostly from vociferous reiteration of familiar charges and countercharges to name-calling and are anything but productive. In fact, it is a controversy at an impasse. Therefore those new to Foucault, especially those influenced by or trained in analytic philosophy, may too quickly take sides on the issue of truth and not consider Foucault seriously enough because of his relativism. It is of primary importance, then, that any introduction to Foucauldian genealogy make out a reasonable case that Foucault's views on truth are neither incoherent nor self-vitiating.

Understanding Foucault's conception of truth is too large a matter to pursue in the balance of this chapter, so it is the sole topic of the next. Considered here is the closely related matter of Foucault's apparent inconsistency regarding his historicist views on truth and the ahistoricist manner in which he presents some of his genealogical claims. As noted earlier, Foucault sometimes appears to contravene his own historicist account of truth as a product of power by seeming to exempt his analytics from the historicism he endorses. Given our better understanding of genealogy, we can clarify the apparent inconsistency regarding historicity.

Someone new to Foucault's genealogical analytics may dismiss them because of a perception that though truth is made a function of power, objective or ahistoric truth-claims seem to be made regarding the putative machinations of power. A basic problem is that though some first-time readers may think themselves broad-minded and prepared to consider the possible historicist nature of truth and knowledge, they unreflectively continue to take philosophical discussion as truth-establishing polemical debate (Moulton 1983). This means they read Foucault as saying things to establish his view as the correct one. How can he, then, claim that truth is a product of power? What point could there be to producing a new "truth" if doing so is merely changing one construct for another? Failing to see the point, these readers then take it that Foucault must be either inconsistent or disingenuous. This misinterpretation and consequent dismissal are specific instances of the traditionalist's puzzlement about intellectual inquiry: What can the point be if it is not discernment of objective truth? The preclusive question being asked is: How could philosophy in particular, and intellectual inquiry in general, be historicized without thereby losing intellectual import and any possibility of claiming cogency for argumentation?

It is a serious bar to understanding Foucauldian genealogy to think that he is engaging in polemics in the sense of trying to replace philosophical conclusions, assumptions, methods, and objectives he thinks erroneous with those he believes he has discerned to be the correct ones. The point of Foucault's work is to provide productive genealogies of accepted conclusions, assumptions, methods, and objectives and of any established system of truth and knowledge in order to understand how the elements of such systems, like the notion of objective biological sex, developed and came to constitute truth and knowledge. Once this point is appreciated, the question about disingenuous or inconsistent truth-claims should dissolve, for we see what Foucault has to say not as so much adversarial debate intended to establish favored theses, but as commentary enabling the productive intellectual activity he describes as genealogy's struggle. In "Two Lectures" Foucault maintains that genealogies are "anti-sciences" and that they develop and exist not to "vindicate a lyrical right to ignorance," but rather to oppose themselves to "the institution and functioning of an organized scientific discourse within a society" (Foucault 1980b:83–84). It is always "against the power of a discourse that is considered to be scientific that ... genealogy must wage its struggle" (Foucault 1980b:84; compare Deleuze 1984:149). Genealogy opposes the "scientific" in the sense of countering authoritative disciplines that establish what is true and what is known. Genealogy, then, cannot aspire to be scientific; it cannot conduct its opposition by employing the methods and assumptions of its opponents. Genealogy cannot struggle against disciplinary truth-claims by making disciplinary truth-claims.

Genealogy is always oppositional and cannot pretend to be a new orthodoxy. Genealogy offers alternative-enabling awareness of power-relations through opposition to the products of power. That awareness is gained through constant problematization of established discourses. In an interview given not long before his death, Foucault acknowledges the importance of this point in saying that what is "common to the work I've done since *Madness and Civilization* is the notion of problematization" (Foucault 1989:295). As in the case of "effective" history opposing totalizing or essence-seeking history, it is integral to genealogy that it counter and oppose particular established truth-regimes and knowledge-systems by problematizing them. But that opposition can never be conducted on the basis of providing a competing theory itself claiming objectivity and universality. Genealogy is always local; Gutting tells us that Foucault's work "is at root ad hoc" (Gutting 1994:2). Genealogical analysis and criticism are "non-centralized" in that they are defined by their targets. The force and value of such analysis and criticism are "not dependent on the approval of the established regimes of thought" because those regimes are the targets of analysis and criticism (Foucault 1980b:81). Genealogy's critical basis is always the knowledge-system or truth-regime it opposes. It is in the history of what it opposes that genealogy finds the means for opposition—in the development of the targeted knowledge-system or truth-regime and in the subjugated knowledges that regime or system obscured and suppressed. Since there cannot be a universal system of knowledge because a totalizing description cannot be achieved, since there is no ultimate perspective-unifying objective truth to be attained, there can be no broad, discourse-spanning ground on which to base critiques of truth-regimes or knowledge-systems. There is nothing *of its own* that genealogy can attempt to establish. To construe Foucault as engaged in truth-establishing debate, then, is to misconstrue genealogy as totalizing in just the way the systems and regimes it opposes claim to be totalizing by discerning objective and universal truths.

To deflect an obvious objection, I must admit these remarks contrast genealogy's local nature with objectivity and universality in a way that, in linking the latter two very tightly, contrasts the local and the objective. This is misleading because locality does not exclude objectivity. My intention here is to stress the local nature of genealogy, not to make a blanket claim about locality. Genealogy opposes claimed objectivity and claimed universality jointly and separately; it claims neither for itself. This is precisely the trouble when Foucault sounds as if genealogy is universal and/or objective by speaking as if genealogy stands outside the historical sequence of regimes of truth and systems of knowledge. But genealogy *cannot* oppose truth-regimes and knowledge-systems on the basis of a proprietary theory. Genealogy must remain an analytic technique; it can only trace the descent of knowledges and problematize truths. Genealogy cannot proffer *competing* truths and cannot claim to have or constitute privileged knowledge.

Foucault's use of "struggle" in his remark that genealogy wages its struggle against the power of a discourse is at least as important as the local nature of genealogy. It is not merely a manner of speaking to portray genealogy as struggling against established discourses or systems of knowledge. Once we understand Foucauldian power, it becomes evident that power's internal development always tends toward ever greater and more pervasive control; the disciplinary techniques of penality undergo refinement, the science of sex grows increasingly authoritative. In both cases, the ranges of enabled comportments for those individuals who are subjects in regimes of truth grow increasingly limited as power-relations become more defined. Because there is no escaping power, the most productive role for the intellectual, then, is genealogical in character, being a perennial struggle waged against the expanding and increasingly restrictive doctrinal homogeneity that is the nearly inevitable result of the maturing of disciplinary techniques. "To change something in the minds of people—that's the role of an intellectual"; in what does philosophy consist "if not in the endeavour to know how and to what extent it might be possible to think differently, instead of legitimating what is already known?" (Martin et al. 1988:10; Foucault 1986:9).

It is a fair question to ask why Foucault thinks difference in thought is intrinsically desirable. Particularly as portrayed in Miller's biography, Foucault seems bent on change for its own sake (Miller 1993). I return to this point in Chapter 7, and a partial answer to Foucault's valuation of change will emerge when we consider "limit" experiences in Chapter 6, but the most important part of the answer is that novel turns in thought are the only effective means to resist power. Constant struggle against power's hegemony as the primary mode of productive intellectual being drives genealogy's persistent efforts to "emancipate historical knowledges from ... subjection, to render them ... capable of opposition" to established regimes of truth. This emancipation is not for the sake of those knowledges themselves; the point is not to refurbish abandoned lores because of their inherent value. The point is to pit subjugated knowledges "against the coercion of a theoretical, unitary, formal and scientific discourse" (Foucault 1980b:85). Since escape from power-relations is impossible, internal resistance is necessary to gain those measures of intellectual freedom and well-being that are achievable by altering dominant relations. As we saw the way Foucault's genealogical accounts challenge established ones simply by being alternatives to them, alternity is all that intellectuals have to offer against the growing rigidity of a system of knowledge and its attendant disciplinary subject-shaping techniques.

But if providing genealogical alternatives cannot be a matter of claiming discernment of suppressed or overlooked Capital-T Truth, neither is it a matter of inventing suitably serviceable proxies. Resistance through problematization "doesn't mean the representation of a pre-existent object, nor the creation through discourse of an object that doesn't exist." Instead, problematization is the development of a discourse that "makes something enter into the play of the true and false, and constitutes it as an object of thought" (Foucault 1989:269). Just as an established regime is not opposed by providing some deeper truth, neither is it opposed by providing what we might describe as a simply invented holistic alternative. As the use of "struggle" suggests, genealogical problematization is always *engaged* problematization. This is the other side of genealogy's dependence on what it opposes for its subject matter. In spite of valuing change and striving to think the "unthought," Foucault does not seem to share Rorty's view that it is creative invention of new vocabularies *ad infinitum*, and consequent wholesale abandonment of old ones, that keeps "the conversation" going (Prado 1988).

Intellectuals resist regimes of truth not by constant and detached creation of new ones, but by deliberately and internally countering what power achieves blindly when it establishes new regimes of truth. What is countered is not something achieved "because power [is] omniscient, but because it [is] blind" (Foucault 1989:183). Power incognizantly or "nonsubjectively" establishes truths and knowledges—as when madness was unwittingly invented by being wittingly treated as a determinate ailment in the asylum, when delinquency was made the object of a surveillance-based disciplinary penality, and when diverse sexual activities were selectively codified into a "natural" norm-generating sexuality. Intellectuals problematize in resisting the establishment of a regime of truth and knowledge and in attempting to undermine an already established regime of truth and knowledge. That resistance may be facilitated with striking and perhaps novel contributions by people of genius—Newton, Darwin, Freud—but it does not proceed by virtue of flashes of entirely new thinking; it proceeds by continuous problematization of whatever is taken as not problematic in discourse.

The genealogical objective, then, is to problematize accepted knowledge and truth in order to enrich, to enhance, to embellish, to amplify, to augment, and to empower by providing alternity. Foucault asks "what is philosophy today ... if it is not the critical work that thought brings to bear on itself?" (Foucault 1986:9). Genealogy's task is to "separate out, from the contingency that has made us what we are, the possibility of no longer being ... what we are" (Foucault 1984a:46). Greater sophistication with respect to subjectivity-shaping power-relations should enable more rewardingly flexible and diverse discourses and practices.

Changing whatever we might be through genealogical problematization will appear to traditionalists as pointless if all that is provided is alternity. They will see such change as meritless so long as they believe there is objective truth to be discerned and Platonic or Cartesian knowledge to be achieved. Though such knowledge is thought achievable, all philosophical discussion will be seen as straightforwardly or disingenuously polemical. For this reason, traditionalists insist on reading Foucault as if advancing theses he deems to be *correct* even though he claims only to counter the supposedly stifling homogeneity that results from acceptance of something as objective truth. And though it may be clearer at this point that Foucault's genealogical claims are not intended as polemical truth-claims about the machinations of power, he does say a good deal about those machinations and clearly intends it to be taken as in some way preferable to continuing to view sexuality as natural and as suppressed. So even if Foucault is more concerned with opposing intellectual rigidity than establishing a particular position, questions remain about the cogency and force of what he says in *The History of Sexuality*. Moreover, these questions are complicated by Foucault's explicit claim that if his books are to be of value they must assert what is true (Foucault 1991a:36).

There can be no question that Foucault rejects outright the traditional objectivist conception of truth and conceives of truth as a product of power, as "produced ... by virtue of multiple forms of constraint" (Foucault 1980b:131). It is one of his central contentions that truth is a result, an outcome, of every society having "its regime of truth." Every society has discourses that "it accepts and makes function as true"; every society has "mechanisms and instances which enable one to distinguish true and false statements" as well as attendant "techniques and procedures accorded value in the acquisition of truth"; every society has its experts "who are charged with saying what counts as true" (Foucault 1980b:131). Rather than discovering truth through investigation, we are "subjected to the production of truth through power" (Foucault 1980b:93). Yet Foucault is attempting to demonstrate the manufactured nature of the sexuality we take to be fundamental to our nature. How then does *The History of Sexuality* assert what is true? Does it, in the end, supply merely another construal of sex?

From a traditional perspective, the contention that truth is produced is a fundamental claim and should take priority over every other philosophical issue, since it must condition exactly those standards and procedures that guide philosophizing in particular and intellectual inquiry in general. Thus one would expect Foucault to take great pains to clarify his position on the sense or way in which he takes his claims about the deployment of sexuality to be true and how his books state what is true. But Foucault does not give the question of truth priority (at least in the sense of providing a sustained treatment of it). Instead he gives priority to the question of subjectivity. Less than two years before his death, Foucault made the claim quoted in Chapter 4 that the real goal of his work during the twenty years prior had "not been to analyze the phenomena of power," but rather "to create a history of the different modes by which ... human beings are made subjects." As mentioned earlier, Foucault forthrightly put subjectivity at the center of his work: "It is not power, but the subject, which is the general theme of my research" (Foucault 1983a:208–09). In spite of the need for caution regarding Foucault's revisionary reconstructions of his own work, during most of the genealogical period his motivation for trying to understand power is primarily to understand how subjects are shaped through certain discursive deployments. In *The History of Sexuality* the priority of subjectivity is quite evident, even more so than in *Discipline and Punish.*

The priority given to subjectivity, and relative neglect of truth, relate to Foucault's fundamental conception of subjectivity that we are not subjects that preexist the influences that impose beliefs on us. We are wholly historical in being constituted by subjectivities deployed by discourses and practices. For Foucault "the individual is not a pre-given entity"; rather the individual "is the product of a relation of power exercised over bodies, multiplicities, movements, desires, forces" (Foucault 1980b:73–4). The elemental Cartesian conception is mythical: The subject "is not to be conceived as a sort of elementary nucleus ... on which power comes to fasten or against which it happens to strike." Instead, it is "one of the prime effects of power that certain bodies, certain gestures, certain discourses, certain desires, come to be identified and constituted as individuals" (Foucault 1980b:98).

The most relevant consequence of subjects not being preexistent entities but "one of the prime effects of power" is that truth cannot be anything but historical and perspectival for Foucauldian subjects. If subjectivity itself is a product of power, there can be no important practical or pragmatic difference between what is true and what passes for true (Allen 1993). Even if Foucault could allow the bare conceivability of objective truth, it could be nothing to us; it could play no role in cognition, for what are available to us are only historical truths that in part define our subjectivity. *The History of Sexuality,* in showing us how our present sexual subjectivity is shaped, forces us to rethink truth and to see how issues of truth are issues about what comes to pass for true in a given discourse and for a given subjectivity. Therefore it is paramount to understand how subjectivities are shaped by power and discourse. Only then can questions arise about what passes for true. It is only then that we can identify and address the truths that are the elements of a particular regime within which some individuals are subjects. The claims made in *The History of Sexuality* are genealogical redescriptions, and they include as a major component reconstrual of what passes for true within the deployed subjectivity they depict. The force or cogency of these genealogical claims, then, has to do with the production of a new subjectivity, not with disingenuous or inconsistent truth-claims. The key test is not conformity to some objective standard, nor even Rortyan "uptake"; the key test is the success or failure of the attempt to produce subjects for whom the dominant truth is that sexuality is deployed rather than natural.

Nonetheless, doubts will persist, and the issue of Foucault's possibly inconsistent truth-claims will not look to many to have been dealt with. We must turn now to a more detailed consideration of truth in Foucault's thought.

6 The Faces of Truth

To most readers with an analytic background, Foucault's views on truth initially appear diffuse, philosophically unrigorous, and at best inchoate or at worst inconsistent. As mentioned in Chapter 1, this amounts to perception of his views as merely a modish postmodernist relativism and too often precludes serious consideration of Foucault's work. An introduction to Foucault's genealogy must prevent or dispel this perception. Moreover, though Foucault's reconception of subjectivity and his conception of power are the topics that rightly appear most central to his genealogical analytics, his views on truth claim priority over those conceptions because they underlie and enable genealogy. The matter of truth, then, is a priority for us. My aim in this chapter is to clarify what Foucault says about truth and to show how his is not a confused relativism. What I do later is to winnow out the several different ways he uses truth and to propose how those uses are most productively interpreted.

In spite of the common impression referred to earlier, that Foucault dismisses the matter of truth out of hand, as well as the point made in Chapter 5 that he does not give truth the priority he might, Foucault says a lot about truth. He does so because countering the traditional objectivist conception of truth is integral to his vision, but also because he is aware that many think he espouses some form of self-vitiating relativism. As we saw, Foucault feels it necessary to avow his concern with truth, describing those who take him to be denying truth in some holistic way as "simple-minded" and insisting that someone claiming to be a philosopher could not be considered such if he or she "didn't ask ... 'What is truth?'" (Foucault 1989:295; 1980b:66).

The trouble is that Foucault says many *different* things about truth. This is because he explicitly contends that *"there are different truths and different ways of saying [the truth]"* (Foucault 1989:314; my emphasis). Unfortunately, some of the different things Foucault says or implies about truth look to many as inconsistent. Most notably, as we have seen, Foucault describes truth as relative to discourse and as the product of power, and so as historical, but at the same time he seems to make ahistorical truth-claims in his archaeological and genealogical works. On occasion he also seems to acknowledge an objective sort of truth in science and in mundane contexts.

Demonstrating to newcomers that Foucault is not inconsistent in his claims and uses of truth is not easy, because it is not simply a matter of listing claims and uses and then testing them for consistency. Since Foucault does not offer a theory of truth—something I will continue to stress—his various claims about and uses of truth are not components of a unified conception that might be articulated and serve as a standard against which to check problematic remarks. Moreover, the question of whether the diverse things Foucault says about truth are mutually consistent is complicated by the fact that it is one of his objectives to impugn traditional philosophical correctness-criteria. We cannot assume that pronouncements or uses that may be at odds with one another on a traditional unitary understanding of truth are incompatible in Foucault's revisionary and pluralistic treatment of truth. More particularly, given his pluralistic approach to truth, it is not at all clear that the different things Foucault says about truth and the different ways he uses "true" and "truth" are similar enough to be compared for consistency. Moreover, it is difficult to assess consistency because it is often not clear which face of truth Foucault is working with or discussing at any given time. Thus the best way to proceed is to separate out as clearly as possible the most significant ways Foucault treats truth—Foucault's faces of truth. What follows, then, is an analytic list of Foucault's claims about and uses of truth. (I must add that I offer this list well aware of the specter of Jorge Luis Borges's "animal" list with which Foucault begins *The Order of Things*.)

One necessary caveat is that I will use the vague word "notion" to refer to the various claims regarding truth and uses of "true" and "truth." A flexible term is called for because though the claims and uses considered differ in each of the several cases, the cases themselves are too interrelated, overlapping, and complementary to be diverse conceptions of truth. Yet they need to be accurately presented as individually too robust to be only aspects of a unitary conception of truth.

The Relativist Notion of Truth

The first of Foucault's notions to consider, but which admits only brief treatment on its own, is the decidedly relativistic notion of truth variously alluded to earlier. This is the notion evident in explicit claims like those noted in Chapter 5, to the effect that each society "has its regime of truth." Each society not only has "types of discourse which it accepts … as true," each also has "mechanisms … which enable one to distinguish true and false statements, … means by which each is sanctioned;

... procedures accorded value in the acquisition of truth; [and] ... those who are charged with saying what counts as true" (Foucault 1980b:131). This notion of truth, when taken in isolation, causes Foucault to be summarily lumped with the postmoderns in the minds of analytic philosophers; it is the notion most philosophers focus on, if they even recognize there are others, when summarily dismissing his work on the grounds it is supposedly vitiated by self-defeating relativism.

Those who reject Foucault's work out of hand construe his relativism as self-defeating in implicitly claiming to be a theoretical account of truth (thus amounting to the hopeless claim that it is absolutely true that truth is relative). But to reject Foucault's relativism in this way is to miss that this first notion is criterial in nature. That is, the first complexity in understanding Foucault's relativism is that, when he uses this relativistic notion of truth, he seems to be concerned with what counts as true or truth in a disciplined or learned discourse or, more broadly, in a given society. Depending on the scope of the relativistic notion, a criterial relativism having to do with the "mechanisms" that determine what "counts as true" could be compatible with, say, an objectivist view of the hard sciences (Foucault 1980b:131). If the criterial character of this first notion is missed, and if his explicit relativist claims are taken as jointly constituting the whole of Foucault's view on truth, that view does look self-defeating. Thus many of the other things Foucault says about truth would look inconsistent with what appears to be, based on this mistaken interpretation, only a familiar sort of holistic and likely self-vitiating relativism. But this first notion is only one face of Foucault's truth, and it must not be taken as exhaustive or essential. At the same time, one must not go too far and interpret the criterial character of Foucault's discourse-relativism as implying that he is concerned only with how ideology shapes discourses and societies and believes that what counts as true is deliberately manipulated sets of ideas and beliefs that cloak deeper, suppressed truths.

The Constructivist Notion of Truth

The textually most prevalent notion of truth is the constructivist idea that power produces truth. Whereas critics err by focusing on the relativist notion to the exclusion of others, adherents make too much of the constructivist notion and avail themselves of it too readily and sometimes indiscriminately (compare Burrell 1988; Hooper and Pratt 1993). When the criterial nature of Foucault's relativist notion of truth is appreciated, his various constructivist claims and remarks describing truth as a product of power can be seen as being about how what is true in a discourse comes to be so. The constructivist notion is the claim that truth is not only relative to discourses, but that truth is produced in discourses by power-relations because we are constantly "subjected to the production of truth through power" (Foucault 1980b:93). Though constructivist claims are seldom distinguished from discourse-relativist claims (and were not distinguished in the earlier chapters), it should be clear that if each society has its own regime of truth, truths must be somehow produced in a way that makes them specific to their regime. If the truths of a discourse are as they are, and vary from those of other discourses, something must shape and determine what is true in a particular regime of truth.

Perhaps even more so than the discourse-relativization of truth, the constructivist notion of truth as a product of power baffles some, alienates others, and prompts serious misinterpretations. Foucault is well aware that one of the most important of these misinterpretations is that some of his critics and adherents understand his power-produces-truth claim to be one about the role of ideology. Under this reading, Foucault is supposedly concerned with the ideological nature of what passes for true, or the way ideology shapes and distorts truth. Under this reading Foucault's target is not really truth, the objectivist conception of which is supposedly retained, but how power twists and obscures objective truth. Foucault responds by stating that when he claims there is "a relation between truth and power," traditional philosophers and others say: " 'Ah hah! then it is not the truth' " (Foucault 1989:17). Foucault's point is that many of his critics, and some of his adherents, are unwilling or unable to understand the genealogical or historicist analysis of truth as being about truth itself. In other words, some critics and adherents alike insist on distinguishing between what is true and what passes for true and read Foucault as concerned only with the latter. They then understand genealogical analysis as dealing with something less than truth, as dealing only with shared belief imposed by and through an ideology.

Here we see the sort of problem that Foucault's different truths raise for first-time readers, especially those with an analytic background. Foucault contends it is wrong to interpret his constructivism—the production of truth by power—as limited to what only passes for true in a given discourse or society and that contrasts with what is true (Foucault 1980b:118; 1989:17). Foucault's constructivism allows no distinction between truth and apparent truth. Though his relativist notion of truth, interpreted as criterial regarding what passes for true in given discourses and societies, initially looks compatible with some form of objectivism, the constructivist notion should eliminate that possibility. If power *produces* truth rather than merely distorting or hiding it, Foucault's constructivism should be exhaustive. It should not allow more to the concept of truth than what genealogy inventories in the production of truth.

But if *all* that is truth is produced by power, then Foucault seems unable to avoid the dilemma Hoy poses, that he must either be inconsistent in doing genealogy (or archaeology or ethics) or admit to offering only one more construal among others.

Understanding the relativist and constructivist notions of truth requires one to grasp just how Foucault relativizes truth to discourses and their criterial standards and assessment procedures. A discourse, what Rorty would call a "vocabulary," is not something purely verbal. A discourse is verbal in being an integrated set of things we say. But two qualifications are necessary. First, as Wittgenstein needed to remind us, the things we "say" include strictly nonverbal but still communicative elements, like gestures and even silence. Second, besides the verbal and nonverbal communicative elements of a discourse, there are practices that, though integral to and constitutive of a discourse, are not in themselves communicative. These practices include conventions determining who may speak and when and also in what contexts decisions and responses constitute the establishment of something as true. Truth is not relative only to the integrated things we say and related communicative acts; truth is also relative to the "mechanisms ... which enable one to distinguish true and false statements," to the "techniques and procedures accorded value in the acquisition of truth," and even to persons deemed expert and "charged with saying what counts as true" (Foucault 1980b:131). These mechanisms, techniques, and procedures, then, include considerably more than utterances, gestures, and strategic silences. In terms of scope, a discourse and its regime of truth are more like a Wittgensteinian form of life than a delineable language-game, a point that relates directly to how power constitutes an environment.

But in spite of the scope just stressed, discourses are not "conceptual schemes" the truths of which are functions of how each scheme organizes or "cuts up" a noumenal but unitary reality. Recourse to conceptual schemes is an easy way of understanding relativism, but it is a trap in the case of dissecting Foucault's relativism. His relativism differs from more familiar forms that do no more than multiply truth by the number of subjects or the number of conceptual schemes. Foucauldian power does not produce truth in the sense of generating beliefs, nor does it produce truth by functioning as do "categories" that organize a Jamesian blooming, buzzing confusion. Power produces truth blindly, non-subjectively, and unsystematically, and it does so not by causing beliefs or codifying perceptions but in and through *actions*. As Hacking puts it, acts that are unknowing with respect to consequences, and which occur "at the level of tiny local events," determine the content and shape of a discourse—and a discourse's criterial practices determine what counts as true in that discourse (Hacking 1981:29). Every hypothesis offered, every assumption of authority, every denial or exclusion, is a contribution to the construction of a discourse and the establishment of its various truths. We saw with *Discipline and Punish* and *The History of Sexuality* how these truths, which are initially established at the level of expert discourse, are promulgated throughout a population via the institutionalized disciplinary techniques employed in government.

Truth is relative to discourse in that what is true in given discourses is determined by the various criterial procedures of those discourses. Though with varying degrees of formality, procedures in part constitutive of discourses determine what may be said within their domains. But what is established as true in a given discourse, what a discourse's criterial procedures determine as truth, does not simply happen. What is established as true is what participants in a discourse do at the level of tiny local events. And what they do is done because of how power-relations constrain the comportments of discourse-participants—so truth *is* a product of power.

Of course, power is not anything different from the structured interactions in which participants in a discourse engage. Power is not a determining force exerted on discourse-participants but is the environment in which they act. Power, as the interactive strategies that constrain discursive and nondiscursive acts, is merely the employment of language and engagement in practices in particular ways by individuals. The truth power produces is wholly linguistic in being the correctness of discursive acts, where correctness is to be understood on the model of how positioning pieces on a gameboard are licit moves if made in accordance with the rules that define the game. Speaking the truth is making the right moves in a discourse, where "right" is that dictated or tolerated by a truth-regime's criteria for what is acceptable, that sanctioned or excluded by its mechanisms for distinguishing truth and falsity, and that which is in accordance with its belief-determining expert judgments.

We come now to a crucial question raised by the constructivist contention that power produces truth. Foucault's is neither a purely behavioristic nor deterministic view of the production of truth in discourse and so of beliefs in particular and subjectivity in general. The question, then, is this: How can we best explain the way the truths of a discourse become what individual participants in that discourse actually believe? This is the question of how individual subjects come to appropriate the truths of a discourse as their own. We need to understand how truth, as relative to discourse and a product of power, relates to what participants in a discourse themselves come to hold true. We need to understand how individuals make the truths of a discourse their own truth, rather than merely accepting those truths as one might follow certain conventions for prudential reasons. How do penitentiary inmates and sexed social beings accept the truths of their respective discourses as definitive of their own essence, of their very nature? This is, in effect, the large question of how subjects are defined, of how subjectivities are manufactured. Foucault's answer is the whole of *Discipline and Punish* and *The History of Sexuality*, but something considerably more compact is required here.

Discipline and Punish and *The History of Sexuality* describe how discourses develop and are sustained by the unwitting compliance of those who participate in them. Although obviously sustained by the compliance of those participants, developed discourses assume a measure of autonomy not only by gaining continuity and cohesion, but through the simple expedient of usually outliving any given participant in those discourses. Discourses and their truths, therefore, are given environments in which most individuals find themselves. Only a very few—the Darwins and the Freuds—have a hand in the initial development of a discourse. The question of how subjectivity is produced, then, is largely the question of how individuals appropriate the truths of the discourses in which they find themselves. We need to say briefly how those truths become constitutive elements of their subjectivity and hence their world through the sort of disciplining and habit-formation that we considered in Chapters 4 and 5.

In asking how individuals appropriate their discourses' truths, I am for the moment taking a position contrary to Foucault, treating participants in discourses as if they were subjects independently of those discourses, as if subjects prior to participation in discourse. The point of this heuristic ploy is to say how those subjects accept the word of a society's experts, how they internalize the favored ways of acquiring truth, how they come to respect the sanctions of a regime of truth, how they endorse the criteria for distinguishing the true and the false. My objective is to clarify how discourse-relative and power-produced truth relates not just to the behavior of individuals but also to their states-of-mind. However, in trying to say how a discourse's truths are appropriated by its participants, we must be careful not to simply collapse discourse-relative truth into a feature of individuals' beliefs, into something attributed absolutely to individuals' mental states, as that would be to turn Foucauldian discourse-relativism into subjective relativism. We cannot explain the appropriation of the truths of a discourse with an account that takes truth out of discourse, relocates it entirely in states-of-mind, and thus presents power as causing beliefs. In order to clarify the appropriation of discourse-relative and power-constructed truth, without distorting anything in the process, we must consider the perspectivist notion of truth, which is illuminating as it is exegetically convenient. That this is so indicates not only the importance of the differences among Foucault's various notions of truth, but also that there is integration beneath the appearance of miscellany in his uses of "true" and "truth."

The Perspectivist Notion of Truth

Perhaps the most difficult notion of truth in Foucault's work is the Nietzschean perspectivism that makes truth always a function of interpretation and denies that there is anything *but* interpretations. This is a notion in which truth is "not something there, that might be found or discovered—but something that must be created" (Nietzsche 1968:298a). Truth is not the linguistic capturing of facts because "facts [are] precisely what there is not"; there are no facts to be articulated, there are "*only interpretations*" (Nietzsche 1968a:267; my emphasis). The idea of "the world" as a determinate disposition of what there is and which might be mirrored in thought and language "is not a fact but a fable" (Nietzsche 1968a:330). The idea of a single meaning that might be discerned with enough effort is a philosophical myth; there is no "meaning … but countless meanings" (Nietzsche 1968a:267).

Understanding Foucault's perspectivist notion of truth first requires appreciating how perspectivism differs from the facile relativism usually attributed to him. To most analytic philosophers, "relativism" is what Michael Krausz calls "extreme relativism," or the view, most briefly articulated, as holding that "all claims involving truth … are on a par" (Krausz 1989:1). Contrary to the common assimilation of perspectivism to this sort of relativism, perspectivism is different in conception and not a simple, egalitarian leveling of all truth-claims to the same status consequent on the abandonment of objectivity. Instead, perspectivism is the denial of the possibility of descriptive completeness. Rather than denying that any truth-claim can be proven, and so making them all equal, perspectivism denies the possibility of a global and correct understanding or description of the world within which diverse individual interpretations could be integrated as so many true but incomplete points of view on "the same thing." As Alexander Nehamas puts it, Nietzschean perspectivism denies that "there could ever be a complete theory or interpretation of anything, a view that accounts for 'all' the facts" (Nehamas 1985:64). This is what both traditional philosophy and science desire and assume possible: achievement of a description of the world so complete and objective that all perspectival differences would be accounted for and rationalized within it.

Perspectivism is, of course, relativistic. Krausz describes it as holding that "cognitive, moral, or aesthetic claims involving such values as truth, meaningfulness, rightness, reasonableness, appropriateness, aptness, or the like are relative to the contexts in which they appear" (Krausz

1989:1). Because it is relativistic, perspectivism is plagued by the same possibility of self-referential inconsistency that plagues simpler forms of relativism generally and Foucault's historicism in particular. The trouble is that, as with some of Foucault's genealogical claims, it is difficult to accept that the assertion of perspectivism is proffered as just one more perspective among others. This persistent threat of self-referential inconsistency inclines many to think that, in order to work, Foucault's relativization of truth to discourse and his constructivism regarding the production of truth by power must finally be read as about what passes for true as opposed to what *is* true. However, Foucault's own rejection of this reading bars us from resolving the matter of possible inconsistency in this way. It seems, then, that there is no easy resolution, and that we must map out Foucault's faces of truth in the hope that his relativism will emerge as viable.

Though it is important to distinguish Foucault's Nietzschean perspectivism from extreme relativism, perspectivism per se must not be distorted in the process. The likeliest distortion is an ontological version of the epistemic construal of relativism as holding truth relative to conceptual schemes. The distortion occurs when bafflement at how there can be only interpretations leads to introduction of a noumenal or "thing-in-itself" world as what interpretations are interpretations of. Blending Davidsonian and Foucauldian terms, we can say the error is in thinking that discourses have different regimes of truth in being different conceptual schemes that differently organize a unitary but directly unknowable reality.

An example of this misconstrual of perspectivism occurs in May's otherwise excellent treatment of Foucault's genealogical analytics. May err's in his discussion of Foucault's appropriation of Nietzschean perspectivism. Following Nehamas, and correctly describing perspectivism as not vulnerable to arguments against (extreme) relativism, May also correctly argues that perspectivism does not claim "that the world contains many meanings but, rather, that every view upon the world is an interpretation, a limited and revisable perspective" (May 1993:80). He adds that it is "perspectives which are plural, not the world" and expands on Nehamas by saying that, in claiming that the world has countless meanings, Nietzsche meant that "the world is ontologically indeterminate" and supports an unlimited number of interpretations (May 1993:79). May goes on to say that what "interpretations are interpreting cannot [itself] be rendered in any interesting sense" (May 1993:79). By speaking of something that cannot be "rendered," that cannot be described or discussed, he strongly suggests that there must be a noumenal something that interpretations mediate, a Davidsonian "content" that our conceptual schemes organize.

Nietzsche explicitly claimed that "[t]he antithesis 'thing-in-itself' and 'appearance' is untenable," so clearly his perspectivism is not one in which interpretations are phenomenal structurings or organizations of a noumenal world not knowable in itself (Nietzsche 1968a:298). Nietzsche is clear that there are only interpretations. However hard this claim may be to make out, it should not be made more readily intelligible by supplying a noumenal world to bear interpretations. May seems to do just that in failing to resist the linguistic and conceptual pressures to complete the idea of a perspective or interpretation by providing the seemingly required object that is interpreted or on which one takes a perspective. Certainly Foucault should not be read as qualifying Nietzsche's perspectivism in this manner. Positing a noumenal world to "support" perspectives or discourses is positing an unknowable absolute or precisely the sort of essence genealogy expressly forbids and opposes. Foucault is adamant in rejecting posited "conditional" transcendencies. He says of genealogy that it works "without ... reference to a subject which is either transcendental in relation to the field of events or runs in its empty sameness throughout the course of history" (Foucault 1980b:117).

Once we appreciate how perspectivism makes truth internal to interpretations and do not attempt to anchor interpretations in something that supports those interpretations while forever eluding them, we are able to better understand Foucault's agreement with Nietzsche that we should press the question: "After all, why truth? ... Why are we concerned with truth?" (Bernauer, J. and Rasmussen 1988:15). Most traditional philosophers would reject this question out of hand, taking it as frivolous or perverse. However, the question is a serious one if the interpretation-rationalizing totality that perspectivism denies is thought to be impossible. The question then arises as to why we have "the will to truth," why we are concerned—even driven—to establish a single actual or possible perspective as the uniquely correct one.

There is no doubt that Foucault takes this question of truth's value as critical, considering it his most important single intellectual debt to Nietzsche (Allen 1991). Foucault contends that "devotion to truth ... arose from the passion of scholars" and asks, "Why, in fact, are we attached to the truth? Why the truth rather than lies? Why the truth rather than myth? Why the truth rather than illusion?" (Foucault 1971:78; 1988b:107). He describes this as "one of the fundamental problems of western philosophy," adding that instead of theorizing about the nature of truth, "instead of trying to find out what truth ... is," we would be better advised to try to answer Nietzsche's question of how it is that " 'the truth' has been given this value" and why we have placed ourselves "absolutely under its thrall" (Foucault 1988b:107).

Foucault's question about the value of truth must not be interpreted superficially as asking why we value the truth in cases where an illusion or an evasion would prove more productive. This interpretation misses the point, because if we take the question "why truth?" and its variants in this way, we leave untouched the deeper issue by assuming that there is truth in contrast to what are taken or known to be illusions and evasions. The truly Nietzschean interpretation has to do with why we think there is truth, or only one way things are, and why we then give total priority to *that*, to the one way we think things are or must be. The Nietzschean interpretation does not merely contest the value of truth over lies, myths, and illusions; it impugns the distinction between "the truth" and what passes for true.

When we understand that the Nietzschean question Foucault poses about truth's value is about why we take the world to be a certain way regardless of our perceptions, it emerges that perspectivism denies that the world *is* a certain way independently of how we take it to be. In other words (and in line with Nehamas's account), we see that perspectivism is not a positive thesis about the nature of truth, but rather rejection of the need or possibility of positing a way things are, a determinate state of being, beyond our perspectives. That is how perspectivism is a denial of "a complete theory or interpretation of anything," a denial of the possibility of "a view that accounts for 'all' the facts" (Nehamas 1985:64). Perspectivism does not relativize truth to subjects' beliefs or conceptual schemes, incoherently holding each such relativized truth as absolute for a subject or scheme. Perspectivism acknowledges a multiplicity of diverse interpretations and denies that there is a way the world is that encompasses and therefore (at least in principle) rationalizes those interpretations.

With a better understanding of Foucault's perspectivist notion of truth, we can return to the question of the appropriation of discourse-relative and power-produced truth by participants in discourses. We need to see how what is appropriated as truth is not merely so many caused beliefs but is sustained in discourse and presented to participants in a discourse for appropriation. Writing about Leibniz, Nietzsche, Whitehead, William James, and Henry James, Deleuze says that for all of them "perspectivism amounts to a relativism." But Deleuze adds that theirs' was not the familiar sort of relativism, which some "take for granted" and others vigorously contest in philosophical debate. What Deleuze sees in the work of these perspectivist thinkers is a form of relativism that, rather than being "a variation of truth according to the subject"—that is, a relativization of truth to individuals' beliefs—is instead an understanding of "the condition in which the truth of a variation appears to the subject" (Deleuze 1993:20). Deleuze goes on to say that

perspectivism "is clearly a pluralism" but maintains that it is not a pluralism in virtue of what he calls "discontinuity" and is not the fragmentation of truth into so many instances of holding something true
(Deleuze 1993:20).

Deleuze is in part making the point that simple or "extreme" relativism
attributes truth absolutely to the belief-bearers who hold things true,
self-destructively retaining and only fragmenting the idea of absolute
truth that it supposedly repudiates. If read as this sort of relativist, Foucault's views are made vulnerable to a long series of traditional
antirelativist arguments. In particular, Foucault may be charged with
tacitly but inconsistently employing "principles ... that have nothing to
do with power relations" in presenting his genealogical analyses as possessed of greater authority than they could have if they were about beliefs (Nola 1994:37).

I take Deleuze to mean that, when interpretations held by two or more
subjects conform to one another, they do not do so by sheer coincidence
of numerically distinct beliefs. Similarity among interpretations is not
just coincidental in the sense of two or more subjects happening to form
closely similar or even identical interpretations. Deleuze is trying to say
how interpretations may be intersubjective without positing a thing-in-
itself world that underlies interpretations and explains interpretive similarity. Deleuze seems to want to articulate how there may be objects of
interpretation that are similarly presented to different subjects for appropriation, without themselves being anything more than parts or elements of a discourse. If this can be done, then Foucault's genealogical
analyses would be the mapping of the development of those interpretive
objects and not be only about the formation of beliefs. Those analyses
might then have a measure of authority not deriving from the disciplinary principles Foucault is impugning and to which he could not have recourse without inconsistency.

In considering the perspectivism of thinkers as different as Nietzsche
and Henry James, Deleuze makes the suggestive comment that "every
point of view is a point of view on variation" (Deleuze 1993:20). It is not
my intention to explain Deleuze, so whatever else Deleuze means by
"variation," his use of the term suggests that points of view may be interpretations not only of things and events, but also of ideas that gain a
measure of self-sufficiency through frequent use and explicit and implicit references to them in sustaining discourse. Through constant employment, certain ideas do gain a measure of autonomy in a discourse
and come to constitute intersubjective objects of beliefs and attitudes.
For example, stereotypes are "variations" that, though not objects, are
not reducible to so many held points of view or features of so many beliefs. A given racial stereotype, for instance, has a certain autonomy in

that even though it is an interpretation of something (a perspective on the members of a race), it is a complex ideational construct capable of eliciting different interpretive responses from different individuals: amused contempt or virulent antipathy. The stereotype, then, is not identical with the contempt felt by one individual and the antipathy felt by another. The stereotype is an intersubjective object of diverse attitudes, but without being a thing.

Deleuze's treatment of perspectivism and his attempt to describe the "variations" that are the objects of perspectives very likely have roots in Foucault's own work. In *The Order of Things* and particularly in *The Archaeology of Knowledge*, Foucault primarily addresses how concepts come to be constituted within discursive formations (Foucault 1972, 1973). If archaeology was our main concern, we would now consider how Foucault traces the formation of concepts in discourse. However, our main concern is genealogy, and pursuing Foucault's earlier thinking on concept-production would require too much explaining to practically accomplish here. Moreover, considering Foucault's treatment of concept-formation requires discussing his development of the work of Georges Canguilhem, which I save for Chapter 7 as a way to relate genealogy to archaeology and ethics. Thus I will expand on Deleuze's "variations" within a briefer theoretical treatment (one that Rorty avails himself of and may well be familiar to readers).

The theoretical treatment of the objects of perspectives I want to discuss is Richard Dawkins's attempt to facilitate a Darwinian account of culture by introducing the concept of "a new kind of replicator" capable of cultural transmission comparable to genetic transmission. Dawkins posits there are ideational gene-like items that are determinative factors in the development of a culture and are capable of survival independently of individuals' beliefs and attitudes. He calls these cultural genes "memes," playing on the Greek *mimesis* (imitation). Examples of memes are "ideas, catch-phrases, [and] fashions," as well as practices such as "ways of making pots or of building arches" (Dawkins 1976:206). The point is that "as genes propagate themselves ... via sperm or eggs, so memes propagate themselves ... via a process which, in the broad sense, can be called imitation" (Dawkins 1976:206).

As an example Dawkins offers that when a scientist has or hears a good idea, he or she passes the idea on to colleagues and students, and the idea is then used in articles and lectures by that scientist and others. "If the idea catches on, it can be said to propagate itself" (Dawkins 1976:206). This "catching on," which seems to be Rorty's notion of "uptake" captured in a new metaphor, is the analogue to natural selection. Some new ideas will catch on while others will not. Ideas that do become cultural artifacts and, as such, are sustained in discourse independently of any given subject's interpretations. They then serve as inter-subjective objects of interpretation for participants in the sustaining discourse.

Philosophers other than Rorty have availed themselves of Dawkins's memes, notably Dennett. Unlike Rorty, Dennett's is a reductivist project that focuses on the nature of mind and privileges the physical sciences. Rorty's nonreductivist project is closer to Dawkins's and is to give a Darwinian account of the development of whole "vocabularies" or discourses. Rorty maintains, "Memes are things like turns of speech, terms of aesthetic or moral praise, political slogans, proverbs, ... stereotypical icons, and the like." Additionally, memes "compete with one another ... as genes compete" with one another, and different "batches of both genes and memes are carried by different human social groups" (Rorty 1991c:4). Because of this, a particular group's memes are presented to its members in the process of enculturation and thereafter as so many givens on a par with items in the physical environment. Thus individual members of societal groups not only form perspectives on their physical environment, but on a cultural environment as well. The elements of that cultural environment will be a range of cultural artifacts, such as judgment-generating terms of aesthetic or moral praise and stereotypes, and each of these elements will be an object of interpretation by group members.

By positing cultural items like Dawkins's memes, or perhaps Deleuze's variations, we are able to see more clearly how something can be an object of a perspective or an interpretation—and a product of power—yet not be either a thing nor only a feature of individuals' beliefs. Of course, without individuals who hold things true there would be no memes or variations, as there would be no discourses. But the point is that memes or variations are not simply reducible to the particular beliefs and attitudes that constitute individuals' perspectives, much less to the specific behavior of those individuals. The concept of an objective sexual nature serves as an example. According to Foucault, this concept is an element in the deployment of sexuality and a product of power; it is a cultural construct that is erroneously taken as an objective nature. The successful deployment of our present sexuality requires an underlying absolute, the manifestations of which can then be construed as suppressed or distorted. Learned discourse propagates the idea that underlying our sexual desires and activity there is a sexual nature or essence that explains them. Members of society are taught about that underlying nature and so form interpretations of what is presented to them as fact, but which is actually a construct created and sustained in discourse.

With the idea of culturally or discourse-sustained intersubjective objects of interpretation in place, we can describe how individuals participating in a discourse appropriate that discourse's truths. The truths that are relative to and sustained in a discourse, and as such are the products of power, are appropriated by individual subjects when those subjects come to have beliefs about and attitudes toward those (discourse-sustained and discourse-determined) truths as matters of fact. This occurs when subjects individually come to hold true the truths of their shared discourse.

This account of how subjects appropriate truths does not reveal simply that subjects come to have certain beliefs. It says that, just as subjects form beliefs and attitudes about and toward things and events, they form beliefs and attitudes about and toward cultural constructs or memes. A subject is surrounded not only by the physical components of her or his world, but also by cultural "objects" presented to the subject in myriad ways, ranging from explicit descriptions by experts to the unreflective impact of casual remarks. The subject is inundated by the multifarious presentation of "scientific fact" and "common knowledge" not only through formal and informal schooling, but more indirectly through implication, innuendo, and adverse reactions to things said and done (for instance, surprise shown at ignorance or doubt or assumptions evident in comments and questions). The bombardment of the subject's senses by the physical world is at least equaled by the barrage of cultural data that assails his or her awareness in the form of cultural objects. The subject needs to deal with these cultural objects as much as with any physical thing or event that he or she encounters and must manipulate, navigate around, be present at, or avoid. It is in dealing with these cultural objects as unproblematic givens that a subject appropriates the truths of discourse, because in dealing with them as with things and events, the subject treats these cultural objects as so many more bits of reality. To the extent this is the case, Foucauldian tracings of the production of cultural objects assume an importance greater than psychological accounts of belief-formation.

We should note this account may well be resisted because of the weight of our epistemological tradition. When some readers first consider Foucault's discourse-sustained, power-produced truths, those truths seem not to be different from beliefs or features of beliefs. Some find it hard to see how truths could be relative to discourse or the products of power other than as the beliefs formed by particular discourse-using individuals. They also find it difficult to see how truths could be present in a discourse without simply being so many beliefs held by participants. Consequently some find it hard not to construe power as overt or covert manipulation, as only a kind of pervasive imposition of beliefs. It takes a short step to construe Foucault's relativism and constructivism as only about the ideological shaping or distortion of truth. But once it is clear that discourse-relative and power-produced truths are separable from beliefs in being intersubjective objects of beliefs very much as are things and events, a space opens up between what the subject believes and the objects of (some of) those beliefs. We are then able to separate truths as discourse-relative and as products of power, on the one hand, and what subjects believe on the other. Once we understand that there is something "there" to be appropriated, to have beliefs about, we understand how coming to have beliefs about a discourse's truths is the appropriation of something and is the forging of a perspective and so of a particular Foucauldian subjectivity.

Once we answer the question of how a discourse's truths are appropriated, we understand better that Foucault's relativism has to do with how truth is generated in and sustained by discourse. We understand better that his constructivism has to do with the way power produces truth in discourse and how power-relations determine its appropriation. We also understand better that his perspectivism has to do with the way truths are appropriated by individual participants in a discourse, and so shape the subjectivities of those individuals by constituting their perspectives. This enhanced understanding enables fuller appreciation of the integration of the relativist, constructivist, and perspectivist notions of truth and counters the initial appearance of diversity and even of incompatibility among the uses Foucault makes of them. Having tackled the three most philosophically important notions of truth, we now turn to two other faces of truth that Foucault employs to investigate how they fit within the whole.

The Experiential Notion of Truth

Lawrence Kritzman observes: "Foucault was concerned, above all else, with the idea of experience" (Kritzman 1988:xviii). Aside from the relativist, constructivist, and perspectivist notions of truth, Foucault employs a fourth notion he characterizes by distinguishing between truth consequent on inquiry (*l'enquête*) and truth consequent on a test or trial (*l'épreuve*). The contrast is between truth gained as the result of investigation and truth gained as the realizational outcome of an acutely challenging experience. So long as we do not read "insight" to mean the discernment of objective truth, we can understand the latter (realizational) outcome as an insight resulting from great cognitive dissonance and consequent intense reflection forced by some crisis. Truth so won is a truth that "does not belong to the order of that which is, but rather of that which happens: it is an event" (Foucault 1974, in Miller 1993:271). An example is someone who sustains torture to establish their innocence or undergoes trial by combat to establish the rightness of their actions. A less dramatic but more useful example is someone who experiences the pressing need to understand or interpret an occurrence that impugns a large part of their belief-structure and value-set—a loss of religious or political faith.

The experiential notion of truth will seem very odd to traditional philosophers, because it looks as if it is about the sort of realizations people sometimes have as a consequence of a forceful compilation of cognitive and emotional factors, but not through reasoned reflection and consideration. As such, experiential truths appear to be personal revelatory understanding, which philosophy does not really address. Foucault himself speaks of experiential truth as "repugnant to both science and philosophy" (Foucault 1974, in Miller 1993:270). But the notion is not as odd as it first appears or perhaps as odd as Foucault would like. Examples of experiential truth can be strongly reminiscent of Alisdair MacIntyre's account of "epistemological crises"—circumstances where individuals find themselves forced to question what they have till now accepted as how things are. Characteristic of these perplexing situations is that the evidential criteria previously used to resolve doubt are themselves impugned by whatever prompts the epistemological crisis (MacIntyre 1977). Resolution of pressing perplexities thus requires deciding what to use as criteria for counting something as evidence. This procedure—forging evidential criteria in the process of resolving a pressing perplexity—is something akin to what Foucault was after in discussing a kind of truth that is not discerned after investigation but rather established in confronting and dealing with an intense cognitive challenge.

John Wisdom also considers a kind of achievement of truth that bears striking resemblance to Foucault's experiential notion of truth. Wisdom explores the difference between "vertical" and "horizontal" reasoning, emphasizing that in some cases, paradigmatically judicial ones, what is deemed to be "the truth" is not something that is finally discovered but is a function of decision. As Wisdom puts it, in these cases the process "is not a *chain* of demonstrative reasoning. It is a presenting and representing of those features of the case which *severally co-operate* in favour of the conclusion." Wisdom adds that in these cases deciding the matter at issue is a process of "weighing the cumulative effect of one group of … items against … another group" (Wisdom 1955:195).

The initial oddness of Foucault's notion of a sort of truth that arises in the heat of dealing with compelling perplexity, or in a so-called "limit-experience," is dispelled by considering that sometimes truth is how things "come together" after a process that is more one of decision than inquiry. The experiential notion of truth, which otherwise looks hopelessly romantic and recalls Foucault's early obsession with the purity of madness, is demystified by Foucault's acknowledgment that a limit-experience is not a "sudden illumination which makes 'the scales fall from the eyes'" (Foucault 1989:304). Achieving experiential truth may be an arduous process of reflection, extending over a considerable period of time and involving familiar investigatory procedures to complement the deep rethinking of something that suddenly or gradually comes to appear problematic.

Though not explicitly claimed, there is little doubt that Foucault thinks of his own achievements in rethinking madness, penality, and sexuality as the gaining of experiential truth in limit-experiences. Speaking of the truth conveyed in his books, Foucault claims that truth "is not found in a series of historically verifiable proofs; it lies rather in the experience which [a] book permits us to have" (Foucault 1991a:36). Clearly he takes himself to have had and to be providing the opportunity for experiential truth, the opportunity of redefining perspectives and so subjectivity. Importantly, this bears on the persistent puzzlement over the ahistoricist tenor of Foucault's genealogical pronouncements. If we put the notion of truth aside for the moment and borrow the idea of epistemological crisis-resolution from MacIntyre, we can describe Foucault as working out such resolutions in *Discipline and Punish* and *The History of Sexuality*. In the former, we can imagine the catalyst to be Foucault's own work towards penal reform; in the latter we can imagine the catalyst to be his own marginalization on the basis of homosexual orientation (Miller 1993:185–98, 56, 255–57; Macey 1993:256–89; 14–15, 86–87). In both cases the things developed are resolutions because genealogical analysis enables and effects restructuring of perspectives and subjectivity. In permitting us to have experiences resulting in the appropriation of Foucault's epistemological–crisis-resolving interpretations, and so the reshaping of our subjectivities, the books occasion truth in the experiential-truth sense.

As this suggests, the experiential notion of truth has more to do with the mode of appropriation of truth than with truth as such. It is in this respect that the notion of truth as something wrested from challenging situations is of greatest interest to us. Individuals accept or appropriate a large number of discourse-dependent, power-produced truths in the process of being reared and enculturated and as participants in a discourse. But unless lives are wholly placid and unremarkable, there will be times when encounters with discourse-dependent truths that are new will generate serious intellectual turmoil. As a case in point, take the young adult whose religious beliefs clash with some newly encountered idea or situation: a woman raised as a conservative Catholic may have her moral condemnation of abortion challenged by an unwanted pregnancy; a man raised as a fundamentalist Baptist may have his creationism challenged by exposure to Darwinian evolutionary theory. These are instances of major cognitive clashes and consequent changes in beliefs and attitudes perceived by subjects as hard-won achievements of insight occasioned by deeply disruptive intellectual trials. In these cases, individuals would embrace new truths after great agitation, indecision, and anguished reflection. And because the new truths are so hard-won, they are considered epiphanies or deliverances by their subjects and exert a powerful grip over them.

The wresting of a significant new truth from deeply challenging bewilderment can be described in MacIntyre's terms as the resolution of epistemological crises and the adoption of new correctness-criteria and the consequent acceptance of new descriptions of how things stand. In Wisdom's terms, a profound decision is made about how something is to be construed. In Rorty's terms, it is the abandonment of one vocabulary, with its attendant truths, and the adoption of another, with its attendant truths. In terms favored by Gadamer and Ricoeur, it is a narrational change, a change in which a subject's life- and identity-defining narrative is altered by incorporation of a new perception, with all the large and small adjustments that entails. Given the complexity of our belief-structures, the amplitude of the discourses in which we participate, and the inertia of intellectual habits built up over years, it does seem plausible to hold that it is only in the context of drastic confrontations between old and new ideas that we are able to genuinely adopt new perspectives (as opposed to only changing particular beliefs or making small adjustments to beliefs that remain substantially unchanged).

Notable about these perspectival changes in the context of explaining Foucault is that the occasions for experience-emergent truth almost always *happen* to people. Epistemological crises normally befall individuals who are unprepared for them. It seems to be integral to Foucault's experiential view of truth that one should actively try to provoke such occasions. Some of his attempts to do so are intellectual in nature, as in rethinking penality and sexuality, his treatment of madness, and his exploration of Greek and Roman sexuality (Foucault 1965; 1986; 1988a). A sort of methodological effort is his practice of taking the most extreme stand on an issue for the sake of argument (witness his infamous 1971 debate with Noam Chomsky [Miller 1993:201–03]). More problematic efforts include experimentation with sex, sadomasochism, and drugs. By whatever means, Foucault seeks to deliberately produce occasions for perspectival change by trying to induce limit-experiences. He seeks, often daringly and sometimes with a hint of desperation, to achieve novelty of thought, taking it as axiomatic that a worthwhile intellectual life demands constant change: "Modifying one's own thought and that of others seems to me to be the intellectual's reason for being" (Foucault

1989:303). He adds that the work of the intellectual is "to shake up habitual ways of working and thinking, to dissipate conventional familiarities, to re-evaluate rules and institutions" (Foucault 1989:305). Of his own work, he says: "When I write, I do it above all to change myself and not to think the same thing as before" (Foucault 1991a:27).

The importance of the value Foucault places on experiential truth most relates to its being the sole avenue open to individuals to escape from crippling subjectivities imposed by unfortunate power-relations. If power cannot be escaped, achievable liberation can only be a change of subjectivity attained by reconstrual of how one is defined as a person. Novelty of perspective or construal is all that can bring this about, and the occasion for such change is the limit experience or the wresting from experience of a new truth. This is how *Discipline and Punish* and *The History of Sexuality* offer truth "not found in a series of historically verifiable proofs" but rather found "in the experience which [a] book permits us to have" (Foucault 1991a:36). Consider the convict released from a penitentiary, or the person seeking release from a psychologically debilitating gender-role. Each needs the sort of change of subjectivity achievable only through the cognitive disruption of a limit-experience and the resulting gain of new truths about themselves, others, and their interrelations. On the academic level, escape from a stultifying orthodoxy may be possible only through experiential truth gained in the limit-experience of wholly rethinking a subject matter.

It would appear that the relation of the experiential notion of truth to the relativist, constructivist, and perspectivist notions is one of opposition; it offers the only counter to the machinations of power. And if the main job of the intellectual is "to shake up habitual ways of ... thinking, to dissipate conventional familiarities," then the intellectual must pursue experiential truth and provide occasions for it to others by doing genealogy. Deleuze's comment that Foucault offers "counterphilosophy" not only characterizes Foucault's own projects, but also what Foucault sees as the proper occupation for intellectuals (Deleuze 1984:149).

The Semi-Objectivist Notion of Truth

The fifth and final Foucauldian notion of truth we consider looks to many philosophers to be one that Foucault has no right to use on pain of inconsistency. Given Foucault's relativism, philosophers are unprepared to have truth treated as discourse-relative at one point, as power-produced at another, and still allow him to use "true" and "truth" in ordinary ways. The latter uses appear inconsistent with the former two. The appearance of inconsistency, however, is due less to Foucault than to his critics' theory-biased expectations. As discussed in Chapter 3, Foucault, like Dewey and Rorty, does not offer a theory of truth. Moreover, if we read him and them as doing so, "we shall get them wrong," because the point of their work is not to offer competing theories but to show how all such theories are themselves historical products pretending to ahistorical discernment (Rorty 1982:161). Critics err if they think Foucault's relativist and constructivist accounts of truth are *theories* about the nature of truth, and so that when he uses it in the ordinary way, he is inconsistently ignoring or violating his own theoretical claims.

We can clarify the alleged inconsistency by noting that the five faces of truth are contextual. They deal with the ways "true" and "truth" are used and work in various sorts of discussions. Apparently inconsistent uses of "true" and "truth" are a result of making ill-conceived cross-contextual comparisons. Theory-driven cross-contextual comparisons wrongly assume that since "true" and "truth" have the same *force* in various contexts, whatever is said to be true in those contexts must be true in the same way (for instance, by corresponding to the facts). The pragmatic point to be made is James's: Truth is "the name of whatever proves itself to be good in the way of belief" (James 1978:42). Rorty amplifies, saying, "On James's view, 'true' resembles 'good' ... in being a normative notion, a compliment paid to sentences that seem to be paying their way" and adds that, for James, "true" is "a term of praise" (Rorty 1982:xxv, 1991d:127). The commendatory force of "true" and "truth" may be acknowledged as the same across different contexts, as is that of "good" or "desirable," without postulation of an "essence" that explains that force. Foucault's various uses of "true" and "truth" need not have any more in common than the commendatory force James thought was the whole of truth-ascription. Their uses are contextual, and Foucault is hardly likely to forget James's force, since his Nietzschean concern about the value of truth has to do with why uses of "true" and "truth" do in fact have commendatory force.

It may be thought that Foucault's critics—as well as this discussion—simply make too much of his occasional objectivist-sounding uses of "true" and "truth." After all, Foucault has as much right as anyone to use "true" and "truth" in an ordinary or prephilosophical way. But it would be disingenuous to allow him to claim that truth is a product of power without wondering just what he has in mind when he purportedly uses "true" and "truth" in ordinary ways. The whole point is whether the apparently ordinary uses in question are ordinary; in fact many would argue that ordinary or prephilosophic uses of "true" and "truth" do entail that the sentences we deem to be true are true because they accurately portray the world. Many would argue further that this objectivist entailment is not a theoretical one at all, but part of what it *means* to say something is true, so that it is really Foucault who is introducing theory by trying to detach truth from accurate portrayal. Thus it seems that however innocent, Foucault's apparently ordinary uses of "true" and "truth" do warrant further scrutiny.

Perhaps the most troubling use of truth occurs when Foucault sounds as if the truth of his genealogical claims is not power-produced. To dispel this apparent inconsistency, we need to describe the difference between, on the one hand, Foucault's speaking of truth as discourse-relative, power-produced, perspectival, and experiential and, on the other, his putatively ordinary uses of "true" and "truth." The difference is one between his speaking as a genealogical critic of a discourse and his speaking as a full participant in a discourse. We can then describe the reservations that Hoy and Habermas have regarding Foucault's apparently ahistoric pronouncements about historical developments as a concern that while speaking as a genealogical critic of a particular discourse Foucault sometimes sounds like a full participant in ordinary discourse (Hoy 1986; Habermas 1987b:273–74). If we ask why it is problematic that Foucault sounds like a full participant in ordinary discourse, we realize that Hoy, Habermas, and others conceive of ordinary discourse as presupposing that truth is accurate portrayal and not commendation. Those who take Foucault as inconsistent in his uses of truth assume that it is part of the meaning of ordinary uses of "true" and "truth" that what is described as true is independent of construal, is "objective," and is neither relative to discourse nor produced by power. Foucault's use of "true" and "truth" in apparently ordinary ways, then, makes it appear "that he intends to distinguish ... objective, i.e. discovered, truth from his own use of the term" (Nola 1994:39).

Despite these clarifications, ambiguities remain. In particular, it is difficult not to read Foucault's contentions about penal reform and the suppression of sexuality as discernment of what was "really" going on, and so as corrections of historical distortions rather than merely interesting new interpretations. Foucault himself acknowledges the problem in a more abstract way, noting it is necessary to ask: "What historical knowledge is possible of a history which itself produces the true/false distinction on which such knowledge depends?" (Foucault 1991b:82). Unfortunately, Foucault offers little answer. In a somewhat different context he remarks that sorting out "the difficult relation with truth" must begin with "the way in which truth is found used inside an experience" (Foucault 1991a:36). But if resolution of questions about historical truth is to begin with what we find "inside an experience," it would begin with the experiential impact of his genealogical ideas and analyses *on Foucault*. The question about historical knowledge thus becomes one about why Foucault expects us to find his perspectives compelling. May raises this very question when he notes that, given the scope of genealogical impeachment of established principles and histories, Foucault owes us "an account of how it is that we can accept his inquiries as justified, and possibly as true" (May 1993:71). The question also prompts Rorty to complain that, in not respecting the distinction Rorty draws between the public and private, Foucault misguidedly proceeds as if his philosophical project should be *our* philosophical project (Rorty 1991a:198). As will be obvious, we are back to the question of the cogency of Foucault's claims; we will again postpone giving an answer until Chapter 7.

Aside from ambiguities regarding the nature and presentation of his analyses, there is textual evidence that Foucault on occasion slips into an objectivist use of "true" and "truth." There are passages that support interpretation either as explicitly distinguishing between power-produced truth and objective truth, or as implying that difference. In one, Foucault seems to explicitly differentiate between these two sorts of truth by dismissing one. He remarks that "by truth" he does not mean "the ensemble of truths which are to be discovered and accepted," but instead "the ensemble of rules according to which the true and the false are separated and specific effects of power attached to the true" (Foucault 1980b:132). Dreyfus and Rabinow treat this passage somewhat differently, interpreting Foucault to say that by truth he does not mean "those true things which are waiting to be discovered" (Dreyfus and Rabinow 1983:117). Either way, passages like these do not only enable critics to conclude that Foucault distinguishes objective truth from power-produced truth and thereby concedes the coherency of the former. By suggesting that he is, after all, concerned only with apparent or ideology-distorted truth, these passages also enable critics to conclude that Foucault must distinguish real and apparent truth because he "needs the distinction between what is true and what we take to be true" in order to unmask the power relations "he alleges determine our discourses about what we believe to be true or false" (Nola 1994:39).

In another passage Foucault draws a somewhat different distinction, one still suggestive of a notion of truth that is unproblematic because outside the domain of power. Foucault says that it is "perhaps a little risky to speak of the opposition between true and false as a ... system of exclusion" and contrasts "the constraints of truth" with prohibitions that are "arbitrary in origin" or that develop "out of historical contingency." He then characterizes only the latter prohibitions or historically contingent constraints in almost exactly the way he describes the production of truth by power. This strongly suggests there is, after all, a difference between power-produced truth and some sort of truth that constrains us in ways different from how power-produced truth does so (Foucault 1972:217–18).

In other relevant passages Foucault does not so much distinguish sorts of truth or only present his analyses and accounts as correct, but more or less explicitly refers to those analyses and accounts as true. For instance, at one point Foucault challenges his critics, demanding to know whether any of them has shown that his genealogical accounts are "false [or] ill-founded" (Foucault 1980b:87). The clear implication is that he thinks his genealogical accounts are true and well-founded. This passage could be understood as meaning Foucault is confident he has provided meticulously researched support for his reconstruals of the histories of penality and sexuality. However, not only does the reference to proper research raise the same question about objectivity, he makes things worse by going on to describe genealogy as "a form of history which can account for the constitution of knowledges, discourses, domains of objects, etc." (Foucault 1980b:117). This could, again, mean that genealogy offers alternative accounts of the constitution of knowledges and so on, but though individually explicable, such remarks have a cumulative force that is difficult to explain away.

Still other examples are apparently straightforward references to unconditioned truth. In the context of discussing a number of political questions (responding to the claim that whoever has the power to shape or "formulate" truth also has the power "to express it as he wishes"), Foucault remarks that doing so—that is, expressing the truth in some self-serving way—"does not mean however that what he says is not true" (Bernauer, J. and Rasmussen 1988:17). The implication is that power-produced truth, at least in cases of domination or ideological indoctrination, may nonetheless coincide with what really is true (compare Nola 1994:39–41). Again in a political context, speaking in particular of censorship and propaganda, Foucault says, "Nothing is more inconsistent than a political regime that is indifferent to truth" and adds that the "task of telling the truth is an endless labour" (Foucault 1988b:267). There are also some references to truth "about oneself" that can be construed in an objectivist manner, as if there is, after all, something about oneself that is not a product of power-relations (Foucault 1988b:240; 1983a:212, 214).

Foucault is not unique in seeming ambiguous about truth and puzzling us with pronouncements and modes of presentation apparently at odds with his perspectivism, constructivism, and discourse-relativism. For instance, there is a similar ambiguity in Gadamer's hermeneutical work, where one finds uses of "true" and "truth" that sound objectivist in nature and at odds with Gadamer's hermeneutical principles (Gadamer 1975:267; Bernstein 1983:168; one might speculate about Foucault's and Gadamer's common Heideggerian background, but that is beyond the scope of this book). The point is that the complexity of contemporary relativist positions, in Krausz's contextualist sense, ensures there will be problems regarding their articulation and implementation. Unfortunately, the diversity of these problems has led to something approaching an established practice for dealing with relativist contentions. The regrettably simplistic maneuver is to construe any ambiguity regarding truth as indicating that the relativism in question has to do with the "soft" truths of the social sciences and politics and not the "hard" truths of the physical sciences and the material world. In the case of Foucault, he is taken as sharing the common view that, though physics and chemistry discern hard truths about reality, sociology and political science map current culturally and ideologically determined belief-structures. His otherwise highly disruptive views then can be understood as about what most are willing to consider problematic (how things appear) and not about what they take as sacrosanct (how things are).

This interpretation distorts Foucault's views by undermining the radicalness of his relativism, constructivism, and perspectivism. But it is one not easily ruled out if he is held to the implications contained in the passages noted. We can make some headway by again comparing Foucault with Rorty, who is unambiguous about how "true" and "truth" only commend sentences that "seem to be paying their way," but acknowledges that, regardless of our beliefs, cultural constructs, and any amount of pragmatic consensus, "there is such a thing as brute physical resistance" (Rorty 1982:xxv; 1991d:81). Acknowledging that resistance is not a concession in the realist/irrealist debate, which Rorty sees as only an unfortunate legacy of Cartesian epistemology (Rorty 1991a:21–172). The concession amounts to very little, because it does not qualify Rorty's total rejection of the idea that what is true is true in virtue of some way the world is. Rorty claims that the idea of "the world," which makes our thoughts and sentences true or false, is either just the "vacuous notion of the ineffable cause of sense" or simply everything that "inquiry at the moment is leaving alone" (Rorty 1982:15). As indicated earlier, the brute reality Rorty acknowledges has no epistemic role to play with respect to truth-claims. He insists on the purely linguistic nature of truth and is thoroughly Davidsonian in denying that any *thing* makes sentences true (Davidson, D. 1984:194). However real the world, it plays no role in the justification of the truth of sentences. As Sellars stressed decades ago, all that can justify or confirm one description or proposition as true is another description or proposition: "Semantical statements ... do not assert relations between linguistic and extra-linguistic items" (Sellars 1968:82).

Foucault's semi-objectivist notion of truth poses problems because it appears or is taken to imply that some things are true, not because of power, but because of how the world is. It seems, therefore, that by saying there are truths "to be discovered and accepted" he means that some truths are independent of power (Foucault 1980b:132). But if we accept the view of Rorty, Davidson, and Sellars—that truth is wholly linguistic and that what establishes some sentences as true is not the world but other sentences—then we can see how Foucault's semi-objectivist uses of "true" and "truth" do not imply a distinction between hard truths about the world and more elastic truths about ourselves and our activities. Instead, those semi-objectivist uses embody a distinction between the world and truth. Thus it emerges that Foucault's various notions of truth are not so many stages or levels on a spectrum running from the hardest truths of physics through the softer truths of convention and ideology to the softest truths of personal interpretation. The faces of truth simply mark differences among the many sorts of things we *say*. In short, "there are different truths and different ways of saying [the truth]" (Foucault 1989:314).

If we keep in mind the wholly linguistic nature of truth and that Foucault does not offer a theory of truth, we can argue with May that passages suggesting a distinction between power-produced and objective truth merely indicate that Foucault focuses only on some truths at any given point in his analyses and remarks, leaving aside those not immediately at issue (May 1993:85–109). Under this interpretation, truths Foucault dismisses as unproblematic are jointly "the world," in the harmless sense Rorty describes as all those things "inquiry at the moment is leaving alone" (Rorty 1982:15). This interpretation accords well with the focused, local nature of genealogical analysis. It also accords well with Foucault's rejection of construing power-produced truth to be merely ideology's distortions and suppression of underlying truth because "like it or not, [ideology] always stands in virtual opposition to something else which is supposed to count as truth" and requires postulation of underlying truth as precisely the sort of essence genealogy opposes (Foucault 1980b:118). Because of his earlier philosophical inclinations, Foucault explicitly repudiates underlying truths. Speaking of his abandonment of "naturalism," he says he jettisoned the idea that we might "rediscover the things themselves" and discern "behind the asylum walls, the spontaneity of madness; through the penal system, the generous fever of delinquency; under the sexual interdict, the freshness of desire" (Foucault 1988b:119–20). The culmination of this repudiation is the generalized version of the repressive hypothesis in *The History of Sexuality*.

It seems, then, that the semi-objectivist notion of truth is best understood in terms of four interwoven factors: that "true" and "truth" have commendatory roles irrespective of what might be said about how things are true; that Foucault does not always speak as a genealogical critic; that truth is wholly linguistic; and that genealogical analysis is limited to particular sets of truth-claims. Nonetheless, as the reader should expect by now, problems remain. Consider a passage quoted earlier. Foucault says that by truth he does not mean "truths which are to be *discovered* and accepted" and he appears to contrast those truths with power-produced truths (Foucault 1980b:132, my emphasis; compare Nola 1994:39–41). This is perhaps the toughest passage to interpret. For instance, it does not sound as if there is always an indeterminate number of truths that are not at issue at any given time, but as if there is a determinate number of truths that are never at issue. Yet as Wisdom would point out, we face something that cannot be decided by "a chain of demonstrative reasoning." I can only present Foucault's complex view of truth so that its various aspects may "severally co-operate in favour of the conclusion" that his is not a view vitiated by inconsistency (Wisdom 1955:195).

Summing Up

Foucault employs "true" and "truth" in at least five distinct (though certainly overlapping), complementary, and interrelated ways. His relativist, constructivist, and perspectivist uses of truth depend primarily on whether his concern is with the defining practices of discourses, the role of power-relations, or the value placed on truth by the philosophical establishment. Foucault's use of the experiential notion of truth has more to do with the possibility of radical perspectival change and the mode of appropriation of some beliefs. As for the semi-objectivist notion, questions are bound to persist, but given that he is not offering an account of the nature of truth, Foucault has every right to avail himself of the commendatory force of "true" and "truth" and to put aside as unproblematic any number of truths with which he is not immediately concerned. More worrisome is Foucault's presentation of some genealogical claims as having the cogency of ahistorical truths. Nor is this a problem limited to what Foucault actually says. Rorty fears that in the final analysis genealogy cannot claim to expose the deployed nature of dominant truths, such as those about penality and sexuality, without implying that it reveals hidden realities and suppressed truths (Rorty 1986; 1991c).

Foucault's five notions of truth do not constitute one theory of truth; instead they constitute acknowledgement and exploration of the wholly linguistic nature of truth. And though Foucault is not offering a theory of truth, he is saying something new about truth. The Foucauldian faces of truth need not separately nor collectively constitute a theoretical account to provide a new perspective on truth. Together they may constitute a pluralistic perspective that counters the traditional view that truth is monolithic and is the sort of thing that supports productive theorizing. For Foucault, truth does not support theorizing because it is neither diachronically nor synchronically monolithic; rather it is historical and heterogeneous. In being what is true in temporally and internally disparate and diverse discourses, truth has been different things at different times and is different things at the same time. Up to this point, it might be argued (as Rorty does) that Foucault offers nothing more than Dewey (Rorty 1982:xviii; 1991c:3, 1991b). But the role of *power* is new. Foucault offers a persuasive account of the mechanics of truth's production and of its subtle or radical redefinition in disparate discourses and epochs. For Foucault, perhaps like for others, truth is relative to discourse, is perspectival, is found in subjectivity-defining experiences, and may often be accepted as unproblematic. But for him truth is also a product of nonsubjective, impersonal power, and that is a novel idea.

In spite of Foucault's resistance to holistic interpretation, something needs to be said in closing about how one might pull together the five notions of truth in order to best understand Foucauldian relativism. Though not an extreme relativist in thinking that all views or claims are equally valid, Foucault is in some sense a relativist. But as Krausz remarks, the "range of positions characterizable as relativistic is varied and heterogeneous"; there is also the question of which "opposing concept" to use in contrasting relativism to that which it counters in its various incarnations (Krausz 1989:2,3). We can clarify Foucault's relativism by focusing on that "opposing concept" and positing that his various uses of "true" and "truth" most directly counter what Barry Allen describes as the "classical" conception of truth. Allen defines this conception in terms of four elements: "the priority of nature over language, culture, or [history]"; "the idea that truth is a kind of sameness ... between what is said and what there is"; the "derivative character of the signs by which truth is symbolized"; and the unquestioned value of truth (Allen 1993:9–10). For Foucault, nature has no priority over language; discourse determines what nature *is*. Truth does not mirror anything; truth is wholly linguistic and a product of power. Signs are not derivative but primary; their uses constitute what they supposedly symbolize. Far from being sacrosanct, the value of truth poses "one of the fundamental problems of western philosophy" (Foucault 1988b:107).

Perhaps surprisingly, it is not power, nor even truth as a product of power, that lies at the heart of Foucault's opposition to the "classical" conception of truth and so of his relativism. Despite the glamorous aura of power, and the priority given to it by admirers and critics alike, only when nature is subordinated to language, culture, and history, and truth ceases to be a sameness of what is said and what there is, does the question arise as to how truth occurs and plays the role it does. That is when the concept of power is proffered in answer. It is when Foucault "thematizes" the reciprocal influence of practice on discourse, something he neglected during his structuralist phase, that he needs power as the mechanism that manufactures truths and so shapes the discourses to which truths are relative (Foucault 1980b:105; Dreyfus and Rabinow 1983:104). To the extent that we can mark off earlier and later stages in Foucault's thought, his relativism antedates his conception of power because even his earliest works oppose the four elements Allen enumerates.

Foucault's claims about power producing truth are not the most central part of his relativism. Most central is his critical rejection of the dominant conception of truth and not claims about discourse, power, perspectives, or experience. Prior to polemical opposition to specific claims by Foucault about truth (for instance, that it is a product of power), there is a basic interpretive resistance to his negative stance regarding truth, to his rejection of truth as the ideational and linguistic mirroring of autonomous reality (compare Fodor 1987). As Rorty remarks about metaphors that have yet to be taken up, Foucault's rejection of traditionally conceived truth "initially sound[s] crazy" (Rorty 1991c:3). The unwillingness to take seriously his rejection of the dominant conception of truth becomes clear when we engage in a little genealogy ourselves and probe beyond the claims and counterclaims to uncover what Foucault's critics evade or surreptitiously qualify.

The most common critical ploy is to read Foucault as concerned with ideology-distorted truth and as silent on underlying, suppressed truth. A philosophically significant example is May's sympathetic attempt to reconcile Foucault's apparent claims to correctness in genealogical analysis with his avowed historicism. May argues that we have to draw a distinction that "Foucault neglected in his epistemic inquiries: the distinction between justification and *truth in an ultimate sense*" (May 1993:71, my emphasis). This is a philosophical standby device—draw a distinction when faced with an insurmountable problem. But, we have to ask, What is the insurmountable problem? If it is the appearance of inconsistency, then the cure is worse than the disease, for May's distinction introduces a considerably more serious inconsistency into Foucault's thought than his ahistoricist-sounding claims and objectivist-sounding uses of "true" and "truth." To attribute to Foucault a distinction between discourse-relative or power-produced truths and some sort of ultimate truth is to attribute something his perspectivism specifically denies: that there is one way the world is behind our interpretations. In doing so, May also, quite wrongly in my opinion, claims that Nietzsche's perspectivism is not integral to Foucault's thought (May 1993:79).

The initial resistance to Foucault, then, is not to his brand of relativism as such; it is to how his work, especially his genealogical analytics, is predicated on the possibility of relativizing truth in the historicization of rationality and knowledge. There is a great critical unwillingness to even begrudge that this is a viable project or that it can be done without proffering a competing theoretical account of truth (or the tacit and inconsistent presupposition of the traditional account). But like Rorty, Foucault criticizes, disputes, thwarts, and ridicules truth conceived in terms of Allen's four elements without trying to offer an alternative theoretical account of truth. Foucault's five faces of truth are genealogical mappings of uses of "true" and "truth." He understands that efforts to give analyses or definitions of truth are doomed to fail because if truth is equated with any other property it still always makes sense to ask if a belief or sentence having that property is true (Putnam 1978:107–09; White 1970:125–126; Rorty 1991d:127; Prado 1987:54). Foucault would endorse Rorty's characterization of pragmatism as antiessentialism regarding truth (Rorty 1982:162). As we have seen, Foucault has a good deal to say about truth, but it is all about *truths*, not about something unitary lending itself to theoretical exploration and discernment. In this way, in spite of how much he does say about truth, Foucault's is a Rortyan change of subject regarding truth (Rorty 1982:xiv). The difference is that in Foucault's case the change of subject is not from truth to something else, but a change from theorizing about the nature of truth to investigating how "true" and "truth" work in diverse contexts, exploring how "true" and "truth" come to work as they do in those contexts, and trying to understand why we value truth "instead of trying to find out what truth ... is" (Foucault 1988b:107).

Given the Foucault-Rorty opposition to essentialist conception of truth, it is tempting to pursue my running comparison of the two and try to deal with Foucault's relativism by reading him as a pragmatist. However, three points block this move: First, there is a real question about how close Rorty's neopragmatism is to that of his avowed hero, Dewey; Rorty is quite distant from C. S. Peirce. Thus, similarities between Foucault and Rorty are not necessarily similarities between Foucault and two of the three classical pragmatists (see Prado 1987:41–47). Second, the classical pragmatists try to rearticulate truth in terms of effectiveness and utility and oppose the traditional conception of truth primarily because of its metaphysical implications. They are "suspicious of the notion of *truth* because of its association with metaphysical absolutes outside experience" (Matson 1987:454). Foucault would concur, but he cannot accept what fuels the classical pragmatists' efforts to rearticulate truth, which is agreement on the value of truth. For Peirce, truth is "a phase of the *summum bonum*" and James is indignant at the charge that pragmatists deny truth, insisting they want only "to trace exactly why people ... *always ought to follow it*" (Peirce 1931:para. #575; James 1907 in Thayer 1982:220, my emphasis). Third, Foucault cannot accept Peirce and Dewey's faith in scientific method. Dewey endorses Peirce's notion of "concordance" at the end of inquiry, saying that "scientific methods ... exhibit free intelligence operating in the best manner" and that failure to use these methods results in "waste, confusion and distortion" (Dewey 1938:345n,535).

But if we cannot read Foucault as a pragmatist, we can interpret his five notions of truth along pragmatic lines by emphasizing what is common to Peirce, James, Dewey, and Rorty: the idea that "true" and "truth" have a common commendatory force that is detachable from theoretical claims about a property or relation to which that force is attributable. Given this idea, we can integrate the five faces by construing the different Foucauldian uses of "true" and "truth" as held together, as being about "the same thing," not by virtue of being disparate elements of a unitary view (much less of a theory of truth) but by virtue of their shared *inter*-discursive commendatory force. As for the dissimilarities among them—what makes them five distinct notions—they are differentiated not by being mutually inconsistent theory-laden views, but by the contextual peculiarities of their *intra*-discursive justificatory roles.

Though Foucault explicitly says that "there are different truths" and different ways of saying the truth, I have not found explicit acknowledgment that these different truths and ways have a common commendatory force (Foucault 1989:314). Yet there is implicit acknowledgement of this common force in Foucault's concern with the Nietzschean question of the value of truth. The Nietzschean question, in asking for the value of truth, queries and so acknowledges and highlights the common commendatory force at issue. The trouble is that we take truth's commendatory force for granted, immediately focusing on *why* divergent uses of "true" and "truth" all have commendatory force. Therefore this is what Foucault concentrates on, since he is most concerned to oppose the tacit claim that truth's putatively unquestionable value—hence its commendatory force—is a consequence of mirroring nature. Thus pragmatic interpretation of Foucault's notions of truth (that is, stressing inter-discursive commendatory force and intra-discursive justificatory force) is a viable way to better understand how the notions hang together. Additionally, this interpretation affords newcomers to Foucault a productive—but revisable—way to approach a series of claims and implications about truth that may otherwise appear too disjointed.

I want to end with a Foucauldian adaptation of Nietzsche's aphoristic summation of what he calls "the history of knowledge," a summation that Rorty echoes in locating traditional epistemology's genesis in the representationalism that casts the mind and language as mirrors of nature (Rorty 1979a). Nietzsche tells us, "When we try to examine the mirror itself we discover … nothing but things upon it. If we want to grasp the things we … get hold of nothing but the mirror" (Nietzsche 1982:141). It seems that when we try to examine truth, we discover nothing but true sentences. When we try to grasp what it is that makes those sentences true, we get hold of discourses, power, and subjectivity-defining experiences.

7 Archaeology, Genealogy, Ethics

Novelty always comes hard in philosophy, given its pretensions to discern timeless truth. Established ideas are taken to represent hard-won truths, and so are ardently defended with righteous vigor and all the resources afforded by incumbency. Challenges to established principles and methods are met by precisely those procedural canons and assessment-criteria that the challenges directly or indirectly impugn. The ironic but nonetheless inescapable result of the nature of philosophical conviction is that when new ideas, principles, and methods do succeed in displacing previously established ones, the new ones are heralded as representing deeper truths, or truths somehow formerly obscured or missed, which then become as entrenched as what they displace. Wittgenstein predicts the success of his project means that arguments he used would no longer be understood because people would not appreciate "why all this needed saying" (Wittgenstein 1980:43e).

Despite all the talk about postmodernism and the actual adoption of Foucauldian views by many contemporaries, ours is not a postmodern age; what Foucault has to say still needs saying. That is why his work continues to prompt deep resistance and why much of what he says looks to many as if it inadvertently violates or deliberately flouts the rules of reasoned inquiry. As with rejection of Derrida's work on the authority of precisely those whose authority Derrida contests, Foucault's genealogical accounts and analyses are met with reiteration of what they oppose or differently explain. His historicization of rationality is met with charges of irrationality on the grounds that rationality can only be ahistorical; and his relativization of truth is met with charges that he cannot mean "real" truth on the grounds that he presupposes objective truth in making any claims at all and denies it at the cost of intelligibility. Even though odd to say so, this is all as it should be. Genealogy would fail if it succeeded in displacing established philosophical principles and methods and became codified and itself established as the dominant truth of an era. Genealogy cannot cease to be marginal and oppositional and still be genealogy. What genealogy offers must always need saying; its analyses must always strike the orthodox as counterintuitive and its arguments must at first seem to not be arguments at all in appearing to violate proper—read "accepted"—intellectual procedures.

Nor can genealogy become the established truth, because it has no content in the sense of principles or canons to replace those its analyses render suspect in showing them not to be inevitable. To the extent it has one, genealogy's methodology consists of admonitory directives regarding the futility of searching for origins or essences and the need to pursue the marginal, the obscured, the forgotten, the overlooked. Genealogy is not a position; it is at base a problematizing *attitude*, and as such it draws its life from what it investigates and opposes. In being mainly attitudinal, genealogy is like pragmatism. Rorty notes that pragmatism does not try to replace foundationalist epistemology, the philosophy of language, or any other sort of Capital-P Philosophy; it does not aspire to itself become the established philosophy but rather to usher in a "post–philosophical culture" (Rorty 1982:xxxvii–xliv). Underlying the attitudinal character of both genealogy and pragmatism is a realization that Rorty claims "ties Dewey and Foucault, James and Nietzsche, together"; this realization was referenced in Chapter 1: "There is no ... criterion that we have not created in ... creating a practice, no standard of rationality that is not an appeal to such a criterion, no rigorous argumentation that is not obedience to our own conventions" (Rorty 1982:xlii).

This realization is the gist of our review in Chapter 6, that "[t]ruth is a thing of this world" (Foucault 1980b:131). It holds that one must be prepared to consider problematic whatever presents itself as evident, manifest, or inescapable. What is so taken must be recognized as always being products of "multiple forms of constraint" and not mirrorings of reality (Foucault 1980b:131). Genealogy, then, is essentially a readiness to continually problematize established truths through development of alternative accounts and critical analyses of targeted facts, concepts, principles, canons, natures, institutions, methodological truisms, and established practices. Genealogy cannot become the dominant truth of an age for it can only exist as opposition cashed out in table-turning construals bolstered by convincing historical detail and seasoned with startling, perspective-altering reversals and inversions of the familiar. That is how it enables us to resist power's otherwise inexorable tendency to become ever more restrictive and confining.

Archaeology and Foucauldian ethics are modes of analysis like genealogy; they are not philosophies in the traditional sense of offering a *Weltanschauung*, a worldview. But there are differences. Unlike genealogy, neither archaeology nor ethics is primarily attitudinal and problematizing. This is likely why so many traditional philosophers see both, especially the former, as more philosophical. Unlike genealogy, archaeology at least appears to aspire to replace epistemology, as we saw earlier, and Foucauldian ethics seem to serve a rather more substantive self than one finds in *Discipline and Punish* (compare Rorty 1986). However, my objective is to introduce the reader to genealogy, so this is not the place to pursue archaeology and Foucauldian ethics. It will prove more useful to consider, even if briefly, what unifies Foucault's archaeological, genealogical, and ethical analytics. A reader armed with a good understanding of genealogy will be able to productively pursue Foucault's earlier and later works, but doing so will be greatly facilitated by some understanding of how that which is most central to the three modes or domains of analysis operates in each.

The most important unifying element in Foucault's archaeological, genealogical, and ethical work (and what prevents the three modes of analysis from dividing into distinct early, middle, and late periods, as we divide the work of the "Tractarian" and "later" Wittgenstein), is the basically historical approach in each (compare Dreyfus and Rabinow 1983:104, O'Farrell 1989). Thomas Flynn tells us, "All of Foucault's major works are histories of a sort" (Flynn 1994:28). Foucault himself describes his books as "work on the history of thought" (Foucault 1989:294). But as Flynn carefully notes, the "challenge is to determine what sort of history [Foucault] does" (Flynn 1994:28).

Foucault is not, as many think, a familiar sort of intellectual historian. He contends that the history of thought is "not simply a history of ideas or of representations, but also the attempt to respond to this question: How is it that thought ... can also have a history?" (Foucault 1989:294). This question encompasses important issues, such as how representation became problematic and how we made thought—and thus ourselves as thinkers—objects of scientific inquiry. These are not answered by intellectual history because they undercut that history in querying its possibility. Speaking of his archaeological mode of analysis, Foucault remarks that "such an analysis does not belong to the history of ideas" but is instead "an inquiry whose aim is to rediscover on what basis knowledge and theory became possible; within what space of order knowledge was constituted" (Foucault 1973:xxi). He describes genealogy as the attempt to "emancipate" obscured knowledges from "subjugation," and so to make those knowledges "capable of opposition ... against the coercion of a theoretical, unitary, formal and scientific discourse" (Foucault 1976:85). The sort of history being done, then, is of a special sort.

As should be clear to readers at this point, genealogies are histories in the sense of being tracings of descent and emergence concentrated on the marginal and subjugated. But it should also be clear that genealogies are not passive tracings of the historically contingent development of knowledges, institutions, and practices. Rather, they are actively competing histories in the sense that in constituting alternative accounts by unearthing the obscured and ignored, they impugn and prompt rethinking of established accounts. Foucault puts the point quite clearly in telling us that whereas archaeology is the "analysis of local discursivities," genealogy consists of "the tactics whereby, on the basis of the descriptions of these local discursivities," the newly emancipated knowledges are "brought into play" (Foucault 1976:85). Genealogy, and in a more qualified way Foucauldian ethics, are "guerilla history"; the objective is not merely to unearth and trace, but to provide alternity in an intellectually competitive way. Given the essentialism and objectivism that characterize contemporary disciplinary inquiry, the very existence of an alternative account poses a challenge; if our various disciplines claim to discern *truth*, presented redescriptions must be disproven, assimilated, or dangerously ignored. This is the force of Arac's point about how defense of a subject against Foucault requires "redefining the subject" (Arac 1991:vii).

Archaeology is less concerned with providing alternity than to delineate and understand it. Describing genealogy as having to do with the "antecedents of a socio-intellectual reality," Gary Gutting describes archaeology as primarily "concerned ... with the conceptual structures subtending the reality" (Gutting 1994:12). Archaeology traces and charts the conceptual structures that make possible, support, and define a socio-intellectual reality. By identifying and grasping the conceptual structure that subtends a socio-intellectual reality, we understand an *episteme* or conceptual framework or what Wittgenstein might have called "a form of life." However, as noted in Chapter 2, the enabling and supporting conceptual structures are not unidirectional determinants of practices. Recall that Foucault is a post–structuralist in that he understands the structures that subtend a socio-intellectual reality to be themselves historical and reciprocally affected by practice. In tracking and mapping an *episteme*, in investigating how disciplinary fields of inquiry became possible (including fields like "general grammar, ... natural history and ... analysis of wealth" and their modern counterparts, linguistics, biology, and economics), Foucault is doing history because he is concerned with contingent "conditions ... established in time" (Foucault 1973:208).

Of greatest interest here is that the historical factors most central to the support and definition of a socio-intellectual reality, and so what archaeology most directly maps, are not ideas or events but *concepts*. Witness the priority Foucault gives to concepts in defining disciplinary knowledge, the main subject of archaeology, as in part a dynamic discursive context or "field of coordination and subordination of statements in which concepts ... are defined, applied, and transformed" (Foucault 1972:182–83). Gutting concurs that much of Foucault's work "falls in the genre of 'the history of concepts'" but points out that these are concepts as "understood by ... Georges Canguilhem" (Gutting

1994:7). These are not concepts as mere recognitional capacities but scientific concepts or basic interpretive ideas; the key difference has to do with their derivation or inception. For Canguilhem, scientific concepts operant in theories are not generated by theories. Canguilhem, contrary to the familiar positivistic understanding that scientific concepts are generated in the process of theoretically interpreting data, thinks scientific concepts precede theories and are diversely developed in disparate and even contradictory theoretical ways. A simple example is the concept of temperature arising as an understanding of hot and cold as a variable property rather than as, say, disparate intrinsic states of things or purely subjective reactions. Once the concept arises of temperature as a property that might be increased or diminished, gained or lost, the concept admits of varying theoretical interpretation; for instance, it may be interpreted as addition, depletion, or loss of caloric fluid, or as intensification or abatement of mean kinetic energy.

In Canguilhem's view, a given concept will be longer-lived than the theories in which it is developed, which means that its history will be neither encompassed by nor the same as the history of any given theory. The history of a concept may be studied with reference to various contemporaneous and succeeding theories in which that concept is employed and developed. Foucault takes up Canguilhem's view of concepts, but as with everything else, he rethinks the view in appropriating it. Foucault broadens the notion of a concept well beyond its scientific sense; whereas Canguilhem considers concepts specific to disciplines, Foucault sees concepts as not only prior to theories, but also as prior to the disciplines within which theories are developed. This modification enables a more radical approach to the sort of conceptual history at the heart of archaeology, because it allows Foucault to link and compare "apparently very different disciplines by showing similarities in their basic concepts" (Gutting 1994:9). The fruits of archaeological investigations are then not only the chroniclings of theory development or even of discipline development, but histories of the *epistemes* or conceptual frameworks that define whole eras.

The Order of Things, the prototypical archaeological treatment of the human sciences, illustrates the conceptual history at issue in being primarily the history of the concept of *man* (compare Gutting 1994:11–12). (In this discussion "man" does not admit of replacement with an inclusive term like "human" or "person," not only because it is the term Foucault employs, but more importantly because the term essentially *is* exclusive in denotation and connotation, as is evident from much of the history of the human sciences.) Foucault construes social-scientific disciplinary knowledges as turning on the advent and diverse development of the concept of man as something that is at once in the world and aware of the world. Man is "that entity for which representations of objects exist"; man is that which "is both an object in the world and an experiencing subject" (Gutting 1994:11). But whereas the human sciences that Foucault investigates take this concept as definitive of what it is to be human, he takes it as one among several possibilities. Whereas sciences take the concept of man as historical, only in being a temporal articulation of an ahistorical truth, Foucault takes it as being created at the end of the eighteenth century. And whereas sciences take the concept as gradually being more and more fully comprehended and corroborated through widely varying research, Foucault takes it as in the process of decline. He tells us that "man is an invention of recent date. And one perhaps nearing its end." The "man" of the concept of man is about to disappear "like a face drawn in sand at the edge of the sea" (Foucault 1973:387). This is mainly because men like Hegel, Freud, and Saussure raised anew "the great problem of the sign and meaning" and so problematized representation. The consequence is that "man is disappearing" (Foucault 1989:6).

According to Foucault, the key factor in this concept was Kant's investigation into the conditions of representation. For Descartes, representation is identical with thought; representation or thought just is ideas being before the mind. With Kant our capacity to entertain representations of objects becomes problematic because his Copernican revolution recasts representation as an *active* operation, not just a passive receptivity. It then becomes important to understand how representation operates, what rules govern it, and the limits it may have. These questions soon overflow the boundaries of epistemology, where these questions arise, and spawn a host of disciplines concerned with investigating the multitudinous aspects of how we represent the world, how we represent ourselves, and how it is that we are, as things in the world, representers of the world. Thus, in archaeology's excavation of what shaped the present *episteme* or conceptual framework, it seeks and investigates what concepts arose, were developed, and came to function so that modern disciplinary inquiry "orders all these questions around the question of man's being"; that is, that modern disciplinary inquiry conceives the project of understanding ourselves to be the fathoming of a given nature and thereby "allows us to avoid an analysis of practice" (Foucault 1972:204).

What, then, of Foucauldian ethics? What role does conceptual history play in Foucault's ethics? In a typically revisionist manner, sounding rather more as if he is describing archaeology, genealogy, and ethics, Foucault offers a characterization of genealogy as having three "domains," which are "an historical ontology of ourselves in relation to truth ... an historical ontology of ourselves in relation to a field of power

[and] an historical ontology in relation to ethics" (Foucault 1983b:237). In the first domain the concern is with how "we constitute ourselves as subjects of knowledge"; in the second the concern is with how "we constitute ourselves as subjects acting on others"; in the third the concern is with how "we constitute ourselves as moral agents" (Foucault 1983b:237). This third domain of genealogy, or the historical ontology having to do with how we become moral agents, is what Arnold Davidson also describes as a domain, though Davidson considers it in its own right as Foucault's ethics and not as a part of genealogy (Davidson, A. 1986:221). But there is no conflict here. As Dreyfus and Rabinow correctly and emphatically point out, " *There is no pre– and post–archaeology or genealogy in Foucault*" (Dreyfus and Rabinow 1983:104). Gutting, more dubious than Dreyfus and Rabinow about Foucault's methodological consistency, suggests that terms like "genealogy" are in any case best understood as "retrospective (and usually idealized) descriptions of Foucault's complex efforts to come to terms with his historical material" (Gutting 1994:6). Nothing turns on whether Foucauldian ethics constitute a domain within genealogy or in its own right. What matters is that Foucault answers the question of how we constitute ourselves as moral agents by providing an historical ontology and proceeds in basically the same way he does in his archaeological and genealogical projects (in this case by investigating Greek and Roman ethical concepts and contrasting them with current ethical concepts).

The contrast problematizes our current rule- or law-centered conception of ethics, which Foucault calls "Christian" and MacIntyre characterizes as an unworkable mix of Enlightenment moral autonomy and a categorical morality ultimately based on divine law (MacIntyre 1981:60; compare 2, 135, 201, 225, 239, 244). The problematization is achieved, in proper genealogical fashion, by providing an alternative: the largely forgotten Greek conception of ethics as having to do not with conformity to law but with how best to live. Foucault tells us that for the Greeks *ethos* was "deportment and the way to behave. It was the subject's mode of being and a certain manner of acting visible to others" (Foucault 1984b:6). The ethical project was the creation of not only a moral agent but of an admirable moral life. Significantly, in this sense being ethical is reserved for a relative few, "the bearers of culture," those with the ability, education, and means to appreciate, plan, and "live a beautiful life, and to leave to others memories of a beautiful existence" (Foucault 1988a:45; 1983b:230). Ethics in this sense is not normalization of the many. There is an evident Nietzschean cast to this understanding of ethics, and what it captures might better be described from today's perspective as the *aesthetics* of self-development and life-management rather than as the ethics of the self.

The history of concepts comes into Foucauldian ethics in the attempt to bring to light, investigate, and build on what Foucault calls "techniques of the self," which the Greeks developed and applied in the noble project of creating a moral self and life. The historical unearthing prompted by ancient but evocative works, passages, and allusions reveals techniques that had to do with "the freedom of the subject and the relationship to others, i.e., that which constitutes the very matter of ethics" (Foucault 1984b:20). Foucault maintains that the Greeks considered "the freedom of the individual as an ethical problem"; in his view "in Antiquity the will to be a moral subject, the search for an ethics of existence, was principally an effort to affirm one's liberty and to give one's own life a certain form" (Foucault 1984b:6; 1989:311). The ancient moral quest, therefore, was "essentially a search for a personal ethics" in contrast to the Christian conception of ethics "as obedience to a system of rules" (Foucault 1989:311). With Christianity the will to be a moral agent and live a moral life was transformed into the will to be a moral *subject:* one living in accordance with the law. The crucial question for the Christian is: What is the Law? This is a point often missed because Christian conformity to the law differs from antecedent Judaic conformity to explicit (putatively divine) decrees and their intricate interpretations. Christian conformity is to the embodiment of the law in the figure of Christ. Being moral is still a matter of conforming, but to a paradigm made available through parables, admonitions, and examples rather than to edicts and ordinances. This new understanding of ethical obedience is what Thomas à Kempis summarizes in his aptly titled *The Imitation of Christ;* he informs the faithful that anyone seeking to achieve moral perfection and enlightenment "must endeavour to conform his life wholly to the life of Christ" (Kempis 1894:1).

Contrary to Judeo–Christian conception of being ethical by conforming to law or example, the Greco–Roman conception was more fundamental. The basic question asked by Socrates, Plato, Epictetus, Aristotle, Epicurus, Seneca, and Marcus Aurelius presupposes less; their question is How ought I to live? But if the ancient philosophers did not answer in terms of conformity to law or example, they shared a commitment to truth in the sense that each proffered answer is a claim that the best way to live is in accordance with a given nature: for instance Plato's tripartite soul, Aristotle's rational essence, or Epictetus's wholly determined moral agent capable of choice only in attitude taken toward physical necessity. This is not the sort of answer Foucault seeks, which is why his ethics are not merely glorification of Antiquity's ethical views. Our immersion in power-relations means that he needs "techniques of management," ethics in the sense of a "practice of self," which will enable us to best order our lives and recreate ourselves, always within power-relations but "with a minimum of domination" (Foucault 1984b:18). We cannot hope to escape power, but we can hope to follow the Nietzschean admonition to recreate ourselves and do it to the greatest degree allowed us within power-relations. To do that, we have to understand and resist what we find detailed in *Discipline and Punish* and *The History of Sexuality,* namely, how in our social order "the individual is carefully fabricated ... according to a whole technique of forces and bodies" (Foucault 1979:217).

What we find in *The Use of Pleasure* and particularly in *The Care of the Self,* then, is an historical investigation, which could be described as archaeological or genealogical, into Greek and Roman techniques of the self. The objective, unlike archaeology's attempt to trace and grasp a conceptual framework or genealogy's attempt to map power-relations, is primarily to recapture productive techniques of self-management that we can adapt and develop in order to avoid being entirely fabricated as subjects and moral agents. The aim of the conceptual history of Foucauldian ethics, of the attempt to "rethink the Greeks today," is not, as noted, a matter of casting Greek ethics as an ideal to be emulated. Rather, it is a matter of "seeing to it that European thought can get started again on Greek thought as an experience given once and in regard to which one can be ... free" (Foucault 1989:325). The specifics of the investigation center on "how the experience of sexuality as desire had been constituted for the subject"; on the techniques by which desire and pleasure were molded and delineated (Foucault 1989:310). It should be noted, though, that sex and sexuality are purportedly only the means to understanding how the subject was shaped as a moral agent in Antiquity; Foucault does not consider *The Care of the Self,* his book most centrally concerned with ethics, to be a book about sex or sexuality (Foucault 1983b:231).

Having stressed that it is the historical character of archaeology, genealogy, and Foucauldian ethics that unifies them as domains of analysis, it is necessary to reiterate and clarify that Foucault eschews totalizing or essence-seeking history and disavows an interest in the past as such. He tells us his interest in the past is not a matter of "writing a history of the past in terms of the present" but rather is a matter of "writing the history of the present" (Foucault 1979:31). He describes his work as beginning "from a question posed in the present" (Foucault 1988b:262). With respect to archaeology, the basic idea is less to trace the chronological development of something than to unearth, articulate, and grasp a totality, namely, the "deep structures that determine the limits and possibilities of knowledge for any given period" (Ingram 1994:232). As noted earlier, archaeology carries something of the structuralist project of discerning determinants of practices, and it also contains hints of Foucault's earliest ambitions about discerning pure forms such as the "spontaneity of madness" prior to the institutionalization of mental illness (Foucault 1988b:119–20). But as we saw in Chapter 2 (in considering the shift from conceiving of signs as naturally and individually resembling what they represent to a system of arbitrary symbols), archaeology is primarily designed and intended to enable comprehension of a temporally or culturally distant conceptual framework and to facilitate comparison of it with another or our own. The similarities between Foucault and Gadamer are very close in this respect. Philosophical hermeneutics, as the theory of interpretation, shares with archaeology the cardinal concern with understanding alien interpretive schemes. But unlike Foucault's oppositional objective, Gadamer seeks a "fusing of horizons," a consolidation of a remote perspective on the world with our own (Gadamer 1976).

With respect to genealogy and ethics—in their own right or as a domain of genealogy—the basic idea is that, if we feel there is something seriously amiss (say with how penal reform has failed or how widespread talk about sexuality has restricted rather than freed us), we have to look hard at the sources and development of the key notions and ideas we take to be central to and definitive of what concerns us; this means doing not totalizing but "effective" history. In Foucault's words, we have to investigate "the historical conditions which motivate our conceptualization. We need a historical awareness of our present circumstance" (Foucault 1983a:209). That awareness problematizes current truths both by tracing their descent and emergence and by uncovering alternatives. We gain this awareness by asking questions like Foucault's—whether "the critical discourse that addresses itself to repression" of sexuality really does "act as a roadblock to a power mechanism" or rather is in fact a mechanism integral to what it supposedly opposes (Foucault 1980a:10). We problematize the accepted, the obvious, the supposedly fundamental; we also pursue what has been obscured or suppressed; we pay close attention to enabling accidents and coincidences and discount established essentialist histories. In short, we trace the inception and development of concepts that were employed, became established, and so became the dominant truth.

Concluding Observations

To close this introduction to Foucault's genealogy, I return as promised to the question of the cogency of his claims. In my experience, many of those who are initially intrigued by Foucault falter in their pursuit of his work when they begin to understand the extent of his relativism. They puzzle as to why they might consider Foucault's accounts, analyses, and histories preferable to the established ones he rejects. Underlying their puzzlement is the conviction considered in Chapter 5, that philosophical writing is always truth-establishing and polemical (Moulton 1983). Foucault offered novel construals of the institutionalization of madness, of the development of the human sciences, of the evolution of penality, and of the deployment of sexuality. Many believe that to merit consideration for possible adoption over those construals Foucault opposes, his construals must be rationally compelling and not merely tenable and interesting. When Foucault's discourse-relativism, constructivism, and perspectivism are acknowledged, concern is generated that if his archaeological, genealogical, and ethical construals cannot be assessed for truth-value, they can only be rhetorically persuasive and therefore only emotively or arationally and even irrationally compelling (compare Prado 1984, esp. 61–63). If choosing between Foucault's construals and established ones is a matter of being persuaded by artful presentation, as opposed to being rationally convinced by sound arguments, many are inclined to agree with Armstrong's views on intellectual hygiene and to think that Foucault's work should be avoided as we would avoid exposing ourselves to any possibly irresistible and mesmerizing siren-song.

The question of the cogency of Foucault's claims poses a particularly serious problem for philosophers in the analytic tradition, because for them the question is rooted in their rejection of relativism. That question is thus usually posed in terms of whether Foucault's accounts, analyses, and histories are themselves true. Taylor characterizes Foucault as a "neo-Nietzschean" and demands to know where the argument is "that will show the ... Nietzschean claim to be true"; he insists that subordination of truth to power is a position that "has to show itself to be a superior construal" and that the debate must be conducted in the language and according to the standards of those he calls the "defenders of critical reason" (Taylor 1987:484, 483). Focusing on remarks that Foucault makes in *Power/Knowledge* about his analyses and Marxian and psychoanalytic theories, Nola asks on what grounds Foucault claims "that theories which rival his own are false" (Nola 1994:37). May is more sympathetic but still poses the question in terms of truth and falsity, contending that because of "the radical questioning" that genealogy fosters, Foucault owes us, but fails to provide, an account of why we should "accept his inquiries as justified and possibly true" (May 1993:71). There is more than a little foundationalist thinking in all this, because the idea is that the only justification for a philosophical claim is its putative truth. If justification is not only forthcoming but even precluded, it is assumed that one is dealing not with reasoned arguments but with rhetorical beguilement.

In this regard, defenders of Foucault usually focus on the complexities about truth reviewed in Chapter 6, on renunciation of the foundationalist conception of justification, and especially on repudiation of the traditional idea that content and mode of presentation are separable (Taylor 1984; de Man 1986; Bové 1988). As yet I do not consider this extensive debate to resolve the cogency question, but I can attempt to briefly clarify Foucault's own position on the issue. Foucault clearly thinks that the cogency of his proffered novel construals lies, not in some putative ultimate truth that was previously missed or distorted and that they reveal, but in the potency of genealogy's "gray, meticulous, and patiently documentary" reweaving of the myriad details of a given history; in how archaeological holistic reconstructions facilitate understanding of alien or antecedent conceptual frameworks; and in how reconsideration of temporally distant techniques of the self enables productive new contemporary practices (Foucault 1977:76). But his view seems to beg the cogency question. The question is precisely what there is about these construals or reconstruals that prompts rethinking anything at all. If Foucault offers not so many *corrections* to our way of thinking but only alternative construals, why should we not treat his construals as interesting fictions or simply pay them no attention? If we must forgo objective truth, are we not better off taking our cue from the Stoics and accepting what passes for true in our society and culture for the sake of *ataraxia* or *nichtzerstoerbarkeit* or "unstirredupness" of the soul? (Matson 1987:160).

Looking at the matter in this way, the cogency question becomes, at base, a question about the point of Foucauldian problematizing philosophy; when this is realized, we begin to see the answer. If in attempting to understand the point of his work we seek out Foucault's reasons for offering his various construals, we find that almost everything he says about the aims of his projects (and he says a good deal) is specific to one or another particular project. This is so whether we look in the various works themselves or at his answers to interviewers' or interlocutors' questions (see, e.g., Foucault 1973:ix–xiv; 1979:23–24; 1980a:7–9; 1980b:95–96; 1989; compare Gutting 1994:2). We see that Foucault sketches or details a particular question or a number of questions that arise for him, or describes a particular problem that he finds or that he sets himself. But interesting as these remarks may be, our question about the overall point of Foucault's problematizing philosophy calls for something much more general. When we look for remarks of a higher level of generality we find reflections (some are quoted above) on the role of the intellectual and on the aim of philosophy as having to do with prompting intellectual change and enabling novelty of thought. We seem, then, to go in a circle, since the answer to the question about the point of problematizing philosophy is that the point of philosophizing is to problematize established truths and knowledges. It looks as if the value of novel construals is novelty for its own sake, and many will find that quite unsatisfactory in a philosophical context.

But if we probe a little more deeply, what begins to emerge makes the circle less than vicious and puts the cogency question in a new light. We begin to see that the cardinal point has nothing to do with the novel construals themselves but with what those construals forestall or prevent. The revealing perception is: The aim of problematizing established truths and knowledges is not to argumentatively compel anyone to adopt proffered alternatives. Recall the point made in Chapter 3, that there is "something ludicrous" about philosophy when it presumes "to dictate to others, to tell them where their truth is and how to find it" (Foucault 1986:8–9). Foucault tells us that the role of the intellectual "is not to tell others what they have to do" and (by implication) what they have to believe; he asks, "by what right would he do so?" (Foucault 1988b:265). Certainly it is not by right of discovering truths behind appearances. Rather than purveying new construals that are compelling by meeting or exceeding the measures of confirmation we think we have for our current truths and knowledges, Foucault sees that the job of the creative philosopher is "to question over and over again what is postulated as self-evident, to disturb people's mental habits, the way they do and think things, to dissipate what is familiar and accepted, to reexamine rules and institutions" (Foucault 1988b:265).

The point of this ceaseless problematization of established truths and knowledges is to enable us to resist being wholly determined by power-relations. If power's grip on who we are and what we think inevitably tightens, if institutions and practices inexorably grow more rigid and stultifying through refinement of management techniques and our own complicity, the only way that resistance can be enabled, sustained, and strengthened is to constantly "promote new forms of subjectivity" (Foucault 1983a:216). That can be accomplished only by changing the truths, knowledges, and discourses within which we are defined and in terms of which we define ourselves. A novel Foucauldian construal is not a thesis to be assessed for truth; it is an opportunity, a perspective-shifting idea that, like a concept as understood by Canguilhem, admits of quite diverse development. The construal's cogency, then, is not a function of its initial content, but of how it is taken up.

Rorty is again clearer in explaining how a novel construal is an occasion for perspectival or intellectual change. When Foucault writes *Discipline and Punish* or *The History of Sexuality* he provides not truths "found in a series of historically verifiable proofs" but rather certain experiences that each book "permits us to have" (Foucault 1991a:36). In Rorty's somewhat more familiar terms, a new metaphor is provided that enables new ways of thinking and speaking about accepted truths and knowledges, about established institutions and practices, and about our very selves (Rorty 1991c:3; compare Frye 1983). It is through new metaphors that an individual "escapes from inherited descriptions of the contingencies of ... existence and finds new descriptions" that enable her or him to "make a self" or redefine herself or himself "in terms which are, if only marginally, [one's] own" (Rorty 1989:29,43). New metaphors may "initially sound crazy"; their cogency is not in their original appearance but in how they are understood, appropriated, and used (Rorty 1991c:3). The cogency of Foucauldian alternative construals of established truths, institutions, or practices does not have to do with their content considered in isolation, but with how enabling or empowering those construals prove to be in the interactive process of interpretive appropriation. That is how "the effort to think one's own history can free thought ... and so enable it to think differently" (Foucault 1986:9).

Bibliography

Foucault's works are listed with the publication dates of the English translations and not of the French originals. For that reason there are some apparent anomalies, as in the case of *The Archaeology of Knowledge* seeming to antedate *The Order of Things*.

Allen, Barry (1991). "Government in Foucault." *Canadian Journal of Philosophy*, 21(4):421–40.
_____ (1993). *Truth in Philosophy.* Cambridge, Mass.: Harvard University Press.
Arac, Jonathan (ed.) (1991). *After Foucault.* New Brunswick, N.J.: Rutgers University Press.
Armstrong, Timothy (ed.) (1992). *Michel Foucault: Philosopher.* New York: Routledge.
Bartky, Sandra (1990). *Femininity and Domination.* New York: Routledge.
Baynes, Kenneth, James Bohman, and Thomas McCarthy (eds.) (1987). *After Philosophy.* Cambridge, Mass.: MIT Press.
Bell, Daniel (1992). "The Cultural Wars." *Wilson Quarterly*, Summer 1992, pp. 74–107.
Bernauer, James W. (1993). *Michel Foucault's Force of Flight: Toward an Ethics for Thought.* Atlantic Highlands, New Jersey and London: Humanities Press International.
Bernauer, James W., and David Rasmussen (eds.) (1988). *The Final Foucault.* Cambridge, Mass.: MIT Press.
Bernauer, S. J. (1987). "The Prisons of Man." *International Philosophical Quarterly*, December 1987, 27(4):365–80.
Bernstein, Richard (1983). *Beyond Objectivism and Relativism.* Philadelphia: University of Pennsylvania Press.
_____ (1992). *The New Constellation.* Cambridge, Mass.: MIT Press.
Bloom, Harold (1973). *The Anxiety of Influence.* Oxford: Oxford University Press.
Borradori, Giovanna (1994). *The American Philosopher.* Chicago: University of Chicago Press.
Bouchard, Donald (ed.) (1977). Michel Foucault, *Language, Counter-Memory, Practice: Selected Essays and Interviews.* Trns. Donald Bouchard and Sherry Simon. Ithaca: Cornell University Press.
Bové, Paul (1988). "The Foucault Phenomenon: The Problematics of Style." Foreword to Deleuze 1988.
Boyne, Roy (1990). *Foucault and Derrida: The Other Side of Reason.* London: Unwin Hyman.

Burrell, G. (1988). "Modernism, Post Modernism and the Organizational Analysis 2: The Contribution of Michel Foucault." *Organization Studies*, 9(2):221–235.

Caputo, John (1983). "The Thought of Being and the Conversation of Mankind: The Case of Heidegger and Rorty." *The Review of Metaphysics*, 36 (1983):661–85.

Carnap, Rudolf (1931). "Überwindung der Metaphysik durch Logische Analyse der Sprache." *Erkenntnis* (1931) 2. Reprinted in part in Murray 1978:23–34.

Cervantes, Miguel de (1963). *Don Quixote*. Baltimore: Penguin.

Code, Lorraine (1987). *Epistemic Responsibility*. Hanover, N. H.: Brown University Press (University Presses of New England).

_____ (1991). *What Can She Know? Feminist Theory and the Construction of Knowledge*. Ithaca: Cornell University Press.

Cowley, Fraser (1968). *A Critique of British Empiricism*. London: Macmillan.

Davidson, Arnold (1986). "Archaeology, Genealogy, Ethics." In Hoy 1986:221–33.

Davidson, Donald (1973/1974). "On the Very Idea of a Conceptual Scheme." *Proceedings and Addresses of the American Philosophical Association*, 47(1973–74):5–20.

_____ (1984). *Inquiries into Truth and Interpretation*. Oxford: Clarendon Press.

_____ (1986). "A Coherence Theory of Truth and Knowledge." In Ernest LePore (ed.) (1986). *Truth and Interpretation: Perspectives on the Philosophy of Donald Davidson*. New York: Blackwell, pp. 307–19.

_____ (1989). "The Myth of the Subjective." In Krausz 1989:159–72.

Dawkins, Richard (1976). *The Selfish Gene*. Oxford: Oxford University Press.

Deleuze, Gilles (1984). "Nomad Thought." In D. Allison (ed.) (1984). *The New Nietzsche*. Cambridge, Mass.: MIT Press, pp. 141–49.

_____ (1988). *Foucault*. Minneapolis: University of Minnesota Press.

_____ (1993). *The Fold: Leibniz and the Baroque*. Minneapolis: University of Minnesota Press.

de Man, Paul (1986). *The Resistance to Theory*. Minneapolis: University of Minnesota Press.

Dennett, Daniel (1991). *Consciousness Explained*. New York: Little, Brown.

Dewey, John (1938). *Logic: The Theory of Inquiry*. New York: Henry Holt.

Diamond, Irene, and Lee Quinby (eds.) (1988). *Feminism and Foucault: Reflections on Resistance*. Boston: Northeastern University Press.

Dreyfus, Hubert, and Paul Rabinow (1983). *Michel Foucault: Beyond Structuralism and Hermeneutics*. With an Afterword by Michel Foucault. Brighton, Sussex: The Harvester Press.

Edel, Abraham (1985). John McDermott, R. W. Sleeper, Abraham Edel, and Richard Rorty, "Symposium on Rorty's *Consequences of Pragmatism*." *Transactions of the Charles S. Peirce Society*, 21(1985):1–48.

Ehrenreich, Barbara, and Deirdre English (1973). *Complaints and Disorders: The Sexual Politics of Sickness*. New York: The Feminist Press, City University of New York.

Eribon, Didier (1991). *Michel Foucault*. Trns. Betsy Wing. Cambridge, Mass.: Harvard University Press.

Feyerabend, Paul (1978). *Against Method.* New York: Verso.

Fink-Eitel, Hinrich (1992). *Foucault: An Introduction.* Trns. Edward Dixon. Philadelphia: Pennbridge Books.

Flynn, Thomas (1989). "Foucault and Truth." *The Journal of Philosophy,* November 1989, 86(11):531–40.

_____ (1994). "Foucault's Mapping of History." In Gutting 1994:28–46.

Fodor, Jerry (1987). *Psychosemantics.* Cambridge, Mass.: MIT Press.

Foucault, Michel (1965). *Madness and Civilization: A History of Insanity in the Age of Reason.* Trns. Richard Howard. New York: Random House.

_____ (1971). "Nietzsche, Genealogy, History." In Rabinow 1984:76–100. Also in Foucault 1977. *Language, Counter-memory, Practice.* Ithaca: Cornell University Press, pp.139–64.

_____ (1972). *The Archaeology of Knowledge* (including *The Discourse on Language*). Trns. A.M. Sheridan-Smith. New York: Harper and Row.

_____ (1973). *The Order of Things.* New York: Vintage.

_____ (1974). "La maison de la folie." In Franco Basaglia and Franca Basaglia-Ongaro (eds.) (1980). *Les Criminels de paix: Recherches sur les intellectuels et leurs techniques comme préposé a l'oppression.* Paris: Presses Universitaires de France, pp. 145–60. (French translation of text published in Italian, in 1975, as "La casa della follia.") Quoted in Miller 1993:270–71.

_____ (1975). *The Birth of the Clinic: An Archaeology of Medical Perception.* New York: Vintage.

_____ (1976). "Two Lectures." In Foucault 1980b:78–108.

_____ (1977). *Language, Counter-Memory, Practice: Selected Essays and Interviews.* See Bouchard 1977.

_____ (1979). *Discipline and Punish.* Trns. Alan Sheridan. New York: Pantheon.

_____ (1980a). *The History of Sexuality* (Volume One). Trns. Robert Hurley. New York: Vintage.

_____ (1980b). *Power/Knowledge: Selected Interviews and Other Writings.* Colin Gordon (ed.) (1980). New York: Pantheon.

_____ (1983a). "The Subject and Power." Afterword to Dreyfus and Rabinow 1983:208–226.

_____ (1983b). "On the Genealogy of Ethics: An Overview of Work in Progress." In Dreyfus and Rabinow 1983:229–52.

_____ (1984a). "What is Enlightenment?" In Rabinow 1984.

_____ (1984b). "The Ethics of Care for the Self as a Practice of Freedom." In Bernauer and Rasmussen 1988:1–20.

_____ (1986). *The Use of Pleasure.* Trns. Robert Hurley. New York: Vintage.

_____ (1988a). *The Care of the Self.* Trns. Robert Hurley. New York: Vintage.

_____ (1988b). *Michel Foucault: Politics, Philosophy, Culture: Interviews and Other Writings 1977–1984.* Lawrence D. Kritzman (ed.) (1988). Oxford: Blackwell.

_____ (1988c). *Technologies of the Self: A Seminar with Michel Foucault.* L. H. Martin, et al. (eds.). Amherst: University of Massachusetts Press.

_____ (1989). *Foucault Live.* Trns. John Johnston, Sylvre Lotringer (eds.) (1989). New York: Semiotext(e).

———— (1991a). *Remarks on Marx: Conversations with Duccio Trombadori.* Trns. James Goldstein, James Cascaito. New York: Semiotext(e).

———— (1991b). "Questions of Method: An Interview with Michel Foucault." In Graham Burchell, Colin Gordon, and Peter Miller (eds.) (1991) *The Foucault Effect: Studies in Governmentality.* Chicago: University of Chicago Press. Also in Baynes 1987.

Fox-Keller, Evelyn (1985). *Reflections on Gender and Science.* New Haven: Yale University Press.

Franklin, Ursula (1990). *The Real World of Technology.* Canadian Broadcasting Co., Massey Lectures. Toronto: CBC Enterprises.

Frye, Marilyn (1983). *The Politics of Reality: Essays in Feminist Theory.* Freedom, Calif.: The Crossings Press.

Gadamer, Hans-Georg (1975). *Truth and Method.* New York: Seabury Press.

———— (1976). *Philosophical Hermeneutics.* Trns. David Linge. Berkeley: University of California Press.

———— (1984). Comment made in discussion following presentation of his "The Possibility of Practical Philosophy Today," the John Milton Scott lecture at Queen's University, Kingston, Ontario, November 21, 1984.

Gane, Mike (ed.) (1985). *Towards a Critique of Foucault.* London: Routledge and Kegan Paul.

Garver, Newton (ed.) (1973). *Speech and Phenomena: And Other Essays on Husserl's Theory of Signs.* (Translation of Derrida's *La Voix et le Phenomene* by David Allison.) Evanston: University of Illinois Press.

Grene, Marjorie (1976). "Life, Death and Language: Some Thoughts on Wittgenstein and Derrida." In *Philosophy In and Out of Europe.* Berkeley: University of California Press, pp. 142–54.

Gutting, Gary (ed.) (1994). *The Cambridge Companion to Foucault.* Cambridge and New York: Cambridge University Press.

Habermas, Jürgen (1987a). "Philosophy as Stand-In and Interpreter." In Baynes 1987:296–315.

———— (1987b). *The Philosophical Discourse of Modernity: Twelve Lectures.* Trns. Frederick Lawrence. Cambridge, Mass.: MIT Press.

Hacking, Ian (1981). "The Archaeology of Foucault," *The New York Review of Books.* Reprinted in Hoy 1986:27–40.

Harding, Sandra, and Merrill Hintikka (eds.) (1983). *Discovering Reality: Feminist Perspectives on Epistemology, Metaphysics, Methodology, and Philosophy of Science.* Dordrecht, Holland: Reidel.

Hartsock, Nancy (1990). "Foucault on Power: A Theory for Women?" In Nicholson 1990.

Harvey, David (1990). *The Condition of Modernity.* Oxford: Blackwell's.

Hekman, Susan (1990). *Gender and Knowledge: Elements of a Postmodern Feminism.* Boston: Northeastern University Press.

Hooper, Keith, and Michael Pratt (1993). "The Growth of Agricultural Capitalism and the Power of Accounting: A New Zealand Study." *Critical Perspectives on Accounting,* 4:247–74.

Hoy, David Couzens (ed.) (1986). *Foucault: a Critical Reader.* New York: Basil Blackwell.

Ingram, David (1994). "Foucault and Habermas on the Subject of Reason." In Gutting 1994:215–61.

James, William (1978). *Pragmatism and the Meaning of Truth.* Cambridge, Mass.: Harvard University Press.

_____ (1907). "Pragmatism's Conception of Truth." In Thayer 1982:209–26.

Jones, W. T. (1969). *A History of Philosophical: Kant to Wittgenstein and Sartre, Volume 4;* 2nd ed. New York: Harcourt, Brace and World.

Kempis, Thomas à (1894). *The Imitation of Christ.* London: James Parker and Co. (Original translator believed to be Lady Margaret, mother of Henry VII; no later translator given.)

Kiernan, Thomas (ed.) (1962). *Aristotle Dictionary.* New York: Philosophical Library.

Kinsey, Alfred C. (1948) *Sexual Behavior in the Human Male.* Philadelphia: Saunders.

_____ (1953). *Sexual Behavior in the Human Female.* Philadelphia: Saunders.

Krausz, Michael (ed.) 1989. *Relativism: Interpretation and Confrontation.* Notre Dame: University of Notre Dame Press.

Kritzman, Lawrence D. (ed.) (1988). *Michel Foucault: Politics, Philosophy, Culture: Interviews and Other Writings 1977–1984.* Oxford: Blackwell. Introduction, ix–xxv.

Kuhn, Thomas (1970). *The Structure of Scientific Revolutions.* Chicago: University of Chicago Press.

Kulp, Christopher (1992). *The End of Epistemology: Dewey and His Current Allies on the Spectator Theory of Knowledge.* Westport: Greenwood Press.

Latour, Bruno (1993). *We Have Never Been Modern.* Cambridge, Mass.: Harvard University Press.

Lawson, Hilary (1985). *Reflexivity: The Postmodern Predicament.* London: Hutchinson.

Lyotard, Jean-François (1992). *The Postmodern Explained.* Minneapolis: University of Minnesota Press.

Macey, David (1993). *The Lives of Michel Foucault.* London: Hutchinson.

Machado, Roberto (1992). "Archaeology and Epistemology." In Armstrong 1992:3–19.

MacIntyre, Alisdair (1977). "Epistemological Crises, Dramatic Narrative and the Philosophy of Science." *The Monist*, 60(4):453–72.

_____ (1981). *After Virtue.* Notre Dame: Notre Dame University Press.

_____ (1988). *Whose Justice? Which Rationality?* Notre Dame: University of Notre Dame Press.

Mackie, Marlene (1990). "Who Is Laughing Now? The Role of Humor in the Social Construction of Gender." *Atlantis*, 15(2):11–26.

Mahon, Michael (1992). *Foucault's Nietzschean Genealogy: Truth, Power and the Subject.* Albany: State University of New York Press.

Malpas, Jeffrey (1992). "Truth in the World." In *Donald Davidson and the Mirror of Meaning.* Cambridge: Cambridge University Press.

Marshall, Brenda (1992). *Teaching the Postmodern: Theory and Fiction.* New York: Routledge.

Martin, L. H., Huck Gutman, and Patrick Hutton (eds.) (1988). *Technologies of the Self: A Seminar with Michel Foucault.* Amherst: University of Massachusetts Press.

Matson, Wallace I. (1987). *A New History of Philosophy.* New York: Harcourt Brace Jovanovich.

May, Todd (1993). *Between Genealogy and Epistemology: Psychology, Politics, and Knowledge in the Thought of Michel Foucault.* University Park, Penn.: Pennsylvania State University Press.

Merquior, J. G. (1985). *Foucault.* Berkeley: University of California Press.

Miller, James (1993). *The Passion of Michel Foucault.* New York: Simon and Schuster.

Moulton, Janice (1983). "A Paradigm of Philosophy: The Adversary Method." In Harding and Hintikka 1983:149–64.

Murray, Michael (1978). *Heidegger and Modern Philosophy.* New Haven: Yale University Press.

Nehamas, Alexander (1985). *Nietzsche: Life as Literature.* Cambridge, Mass.: Harvard University Press.

Nicholson, Linda (ed.) 1990. *Feminism/Postmodernism.* New York: Routledge.

Nielsen, Kai. (1989). *After the Demise of the Tradition.* Boulder: Westview Press.

Nielsen, Kai, and Hendrick Hart. (1990). *In Search of Community in a Withering Tradition.* New York: University Press of America.

Nietzsche, Friedrich Wilhelm (1968a). *The Will to Power.* Walter Kaufman (ed.) (1967). Trns. Kaufman and R. J. Hollingdale. New York: Vintage Books.

———— (1968b). *Thus Spoke Zarathustra.* In Walter Kaufman (ed. and trns.) (1968). *The Portable Nietzsche.* New York: Penguin.

———— (1982). *Daybreak.* R. J. Hollingdale (trns.) (1982). Cambridge: Cambridge University Press.

Nola, Robert (1994). "Post-Modernism, A French Cultural Chernobyl: Foucault on Power/Knowledge." *Inquiry,* 37(1):3–43.

Norris, Christopher (1994). " 'What is enlightenment?': Kant and Foucault." In Gutting 1994:159–96.

O'Farrell, Clare (1989). *Foucault: Historian or Philosopher?* Houndmills, U.K.: Macmillan.

O'Hara, Daniel (1986). "What Was Foucault?" In Arac 1991:71–96.

Overstreet, Harry (1931). *The Enduring Quest.* New York: Norton.

Parfit, Derek (1984). *Reasons and Persons.* Oxford: Oxford University Press. See Chapters 14 and 15.

Peirce, Charles Sanders (1931). *The Collected Papers of Charles Sanders Peirce,* Charles Hartshorne and Paul Weiss (1931) (eds.). Cambridge, Mass.: Harvard University Press.

Polan, Dana (1982). "Fables of Transgression: The Reading of Politics and the Politics of Reading in Foucauldian Discourse." *boundary 2,* 10(3):361–82.

Prado, C. G. (1984). *Making Believe: Philosophical Reflections on Fiction.* Westport: Greenwood Press.

———— (1987). *The Limits of Pragmatism.* Atlantic Highlands: Humanities Press.

———— (1988) "Imagination and Justification," *The Monist,* 71(3):377–88.

_____ (1992). *Descartes and Foucault: A Contrastive Introduction.* Ottawa: Ottawa University Press.

Putnam, Hilary (1978). *Meaning and the Moral Sciences.* London and Boston: Routledge and Kegan Paul.

_____ (1987). "Why Reason Can't Be Naturalized." In Baynes 1987:22–44.

_____ (1988). *Representation and Reality.* Cambridge, Mass.:Bradford Books, MIT Press.

Rabinow, Paul (1984). *The Foucault Reader.* New York: Pantheon.

Rajchman, John (1985). *Michel Foucault: The Freedom of Philosophy.* New York: Columbia University Press.

Ramazanoglu, Caroline (ed.) (1993). *Up Against Foucault: Explorations of Some Tensions Between Foucault and Feminism.* New York: Routledge.

Ramberg, Bjorn (1989). *Donald Davidson's Philosophy of Language: An Introduction.* Oxford: Blackwell's.

Rée, Jonathan (1992). "Massacre of the Innocents." *Radical Philosophy* 62(Autumn):61–62.

Ricoeur, Paul (1992). *Oneself as Another.* Chicago: University of Chicago Press.

Rorty, Richard (1979a). *Philosophy and the Mirror of Nature.* Princeton: Princeton University Press.

_____ (1979b). "Transcendental Argument, Self-reference, and Pragmatism." In P. Bieri, et al. (eds.) (1979). *Transcendental Arguments and Science.* Dordrecht: Reidel.

_____ (1982). *The Consequences of Pragmatism.* Minneapolis: University of Minnesota Press.

_____ (1984). "Heidegger Wider den Pragmatisten." *Neue Hefte für Philosophie,* 22 (1984):1–22.

_____ (1986). "Foucault and Epistemology." In Hoy 1986:41–49.

_____ (1989). *Contingency, Irony, and Solidarity.* Cambridge: Cambridge University Press.

_____ (1991a). *Essays on Heidegger and Others: Philosophical Papers,* Volume 2. New York: Cambridge University Press.

_____ (1991b). "Moral Identity and Private Autonomy: the Case of Foucault." In Rorty 1991a:193–98. See also Rorty 1982:203–208.

_____ (1991c). "Feminism and Pragmatism." *Radical Philosophy,* Autumn 1991, 59:3–12.

_____ (1991d). *Objectivity, Relativism, and Truth: Philosophical Papers, Volume 1.* New York: Cambridge University Press.

_____ (1992). "Cosmopolitanism Without Emancipation: A Response to Lyotard." In Lash, Scott, and Jonathan Friedman (1992) (eds.) *Modernity and Identity.* Oxford: Blackwell's.

Russell, Bertrand (1945). *A History of Western Philosophy.* New York: Simon and Schuster.

Ryan, Alan (1993). "Foucault's Life and Hard Times." *The New York Review of Books,* 40(7):12–17.

Ryle, Gilbert (1929). "Sein und Zeit." *Mind,* 38:355–70.

Sawicki, Jana (1991). *Disciplining Foucault.* London: Routledge.

Schurmann, Reiner (1989). "Power and Truth in Foucault's Philosophy." *The Journal of Philosophy,* November 1989, 86(11):540–47.

Searle, John (1983). "The World Turned Upside Down." *The New York Review of Books,* October 27, 1983:74–79.

Seigel, J. (1990). "Avoiding the Subject: A Foucauldian Itinerary." *The Journal of the History of Ideas,* April 1990, 51(2):273–99.

Sellars, Wilfrid (1968). *Science and Metaphysics.* New York:Humanities Press.

Sheridan, Alan (1980). *Michel Foucault: The Will to Truth.* London: Tavistock Press.

Shumway, David (1992). *Michel Foucault.* Charlottesville: University of Virginia Press.

Staten, Henry (1984). *Wittgenstein and Derrida.* Lincoln: University of Nebraska Press.

Szeman, Imre (1993). "Foucault, Genealogy, History." *Problematique,* 3(Fall):49–73.

Taylor, Charles (1984). "Foucault on Freedom and Truth." In Hoy 1986:69–102.

_____ (1987). "Overcoming Epistemology." In Baynes et al. 1987:464–85.

_____ (1989). *Sources of the Self.* Cambridge, Mass.: Harvard University Press.

Thayer, H. S. (ed.) (1982). *Pragmatism: The Classic Writings.* Indianapolis: Hackett Publishing.

White, Alan (1970). *Truth.* Garden City: Anchor.

Williams, Bernard (1983). "Auto-da-Fe." *The New York Review of Books,* April 28, 1983.

Wisdom, John (1955). "Gods." In Antony Flew (ed.) 1955. *Logic and Language* (First Series). Oxford: Blackwell's, pp. 187–206.

Wittgenstein, Ludwig (1980). *Culture and Value.* G. H. Von Wright (ed.) Trns. Peter Winch. Chicago: University of Chicago Press.

About the Book and Author

Michel Foucault had a great influence upon a wide range of scholars, but it is often difficult for beginners to find their way into the complexities of his thought. This difficulty arises from a number of historical and substantive reasons that are especially germane if the reader comes to Foucault without prior acquaintance with Continental philosophy. C. G. Prado argues in this new introduction that the time is ripe for Anglo-American philosophy, in particular, to come to terms with Foucault.

In this clear, straightfoward introduction to Foucault's thought, Prado focuses on Foucault's "middle" work, *Discipline and Punish* and the first volume of *The History of Sexuality,* in which Foucault most clearly comes to grips with the historicization of truth and knowledge and the formation of subjectivity.

Understanding Foucault's thought on these difficult subjects requires working through much complexity and ambiguity, and Prado's direct and accessible introduction is the ideal place to start.

C. G. Prado is professor of philosophy at Queen's University in Kingston, Ontario. He is the author of several articles and books on contemporary trends in philosophy, including *Descartes and Foucault: A Contrastive Introduction* and *The Limits of Pragmatism.*

Index

Soul
  and judgment, 57
  penal system and introduction of,
    54–55, 59–60, 66
Structuralism, 21, 28, 70, 159
"Subject and Power, The" (Foucault),
  14
Subject/subjectivity
  and appropriating discourse as
    truth, 125, 134. *See also* Belief
  and change in penality, 51, 53–56,
    59–60, 61, 63–66
  experiential truth in reshaping, 136,
    138
  and genealogical analysis, 36, 42–43
  importance of Foucault's ideas on,
    11–12, 14, 110
  and importance of struggle for
    alternity, 163
  and intellectual inquiry, 80–81
  and power in genealogy of
    sexuality, 88–89, 104–105, 116–117
  and power-relations, 22, 68–69, 73,
    75–76, 85
  See also Self
Surveillance
  as disciplinary technique, 61
  and police, 60, 64
  regulation and self-, 100, 101
  sexuality and self-, 91, 97–98

Taylor, Charles, 8, 12, 73, 161

Truth, 4, 119–150
  constructivist notion of, 121–126
  experiential notion of, 134–138
  genealogy in problematizing, 152
  and genealogy of sexuality, 87, 93,
    94, 97–99
  historicist view of, 10, 43–44, 46–48,
    110–117
  importance of Foucault's ideas on,
    119–120, 145–150, 161–164
  and knowledge systems, 25
  as liberating, 103–104
  and Nietzsche, 22–23
  penality and new system of, 57, 64–
    65
  perspectivist notion of, 126–134
  in philosophical inquiry, 9–10, 151
  relativist notion of, 120–121
  semi-objectivist notion of, 138–145
  value of, 23, 128–129, 146, 148–149
"Two Lectures" (Foucault), 14, 44, 111

Universals. *See* Absolute(s)
Use of Pleasure, The (Foucault), 4, 159

Values, 37, 38. *See also* Belief; Societal
  norms
Victorian Age, 89

Wisdom, John, 135, 137, 145
Wittgenstein, Ludwig, 10, 123, 151,
  154
Women, 108
World War II, 7

BELMONT UNIVERSITY LIBRARY

23317869 2